LEISURE ARTS PRESENTS

THE SPIRIT OF CHRISTMAS

CREATIVE HOLIDAY IDEAS
BOOK NINE

Christmas is but one day out of the year, yet it's a time that inspires our most cherished memories. Whether it's recollections stirred by the fresh scent of pine or the gathering of family around the twinkling Christmas tree, the holiday season is a reminder of the things we hold closest to our hearts. Those endearing moments shared with loved ones and friends, like nibbling on home-baked treats while exchanging presents, will be treasured for years to come. To help you create the most memorable Yuletide yet, we present this book of great handmade gifts, home decorating projects, and delicious recipes. May the true spirit of Christmas — peace, hope, and love — be yours, and the joy you spread return manyfold!

LEISURE ARTS, INC.
Little Rock, Arkansas

THE SPIRIT OF CHRISTMAS

BOOK NINE

*"... and it was always said of him, that he knew how
to keep Christmas well, if any man alive possessed the
knowledge. May that be truly said of us, and all of us!"*

— From *A Christmas Carol* by Charles Dickens

EDITORIAL STAFF

Vice President and Editor-in-Chief: Anne Van Wagner Childs
Executive Director: Sandra Graham Case
Executive Editor: Susan Frantz Wiles
Publications Director: Carla Bentley
Creative Art Director: Gloria Bearden
Production Art Director: Melinda Stout

PRODUCTION
DESIGN
Design Director: Patricia Wallenfang Sowers
Senior Designer: Janice M. Adams
Designers: Sharon Heckel Gillam, Barbara Bryant Scott,
Diana Heien Suttle, Linda Diehl Tiano, Rebecca Sunwall
Werle, Donna Waldrip Pittard, and Patricia Ryan Wiest
Design Assistants: Kathy Womack Jones and Karen Story Tyler

FOODS
Foods Editor: Celia Fahr Harkey, R.D.
Assistant Foods Editor: Jane Kenner Prather
Test Kitchen Assistants: Nora Faye Spencer Clift and
Leslie Belote Dunn

TECHNICAL
Managing Editor: Kathy Rose Bradley
Technical Editor: Leslie Schick Gorrell
Senior Technical Writers: Ann Brawner Turner and
Briget Julia Laskowski
Technical Writers: Patricia Ann Miller, Chanda English Adams,
Emily Jane Barefoot, Candice Treat Murphy, and
Kimberly J. Smith

EDITORIAL
Associate Editor: Linda L. Trimble
Senior Editorial Writer: Robyn Sheffield-Edwards
Editorial Associates: Tammi Williamson Bradley and
Terri Leming Davidson
Copy Editor: Laura Lee Weland

ART
Book/Magazine Art Director: Diane M. Ghegan
Senior Production Artist: Michael A. Spigner
Photography Stylists: Sondra Daniel, Karen Smart Hall,
Aurora Huston, Emily Minnick, and Christina Tiano Myers

ADVERTISING AND DIRECT MAIL
Senior Editor: Tena Kelley Vaughn
Copywriters: Steven M. Cooper and Marla Shivers
Designer: Rhonda H. Hestir
Art Director: Jeff Curtis
Production Artist: Linda Lovette Smart
Publishing Systems Administrator: Cindy Lumpkin
Publishing Systems Assistant: Larry Flaxman

BUSINESS STAFF

Publisher: Bruce Akin
Vice President, Finance: Tom Siebenmorgen
Vice President, Retail Sales: Thomas L. Carlisle
Retail Sales Director: Richard Tignor
Vice President, Retail Marketing: Pam Stebbins
Retail Customer Services Director: Margaret Sweetin

Marketing Manager: Russ Barnett
Executive Director of Marketing and Circulation:
Guy A. Crossley
Circulation Manager: Byron L. Taylor
Print Production Manager: Laura Lockhart
Print Production Coordinator: Nancy Reddick Lister

Library of Congress Catalog Card Number 94-74356
International Standard Book Number 0-942237-65-X

TABLE OF CONTENTS

THE SIGHTS OF CHRISTMAS

Page 6

TABLE OF CONTENTS
(Continued)

THE SIGHTS OF CHRISTMAS

The decorations we display at Christmastime are more than just pretty baubles — they're expressions of our mood and spirit. Twinkling lights, welcoming wreaths, merry stockings, and the family tree — these are all the wonderful sights of Christmas! From the folksy appeal of a country celebration to the elegance of the Victorian Era, you'll find many wonderful embellishments for your evergreen, as well as the rest of your home, in our delightful decorating collections. Whichever festive trims you choose to deck your halls, may the magic they bring be enjoyed by all this Yuletide season!

ROLY-POLY PALS

This year, celebrate with an old-fashioned collection of the most beloved Christmas characters of all! You'll find a fond place in your heart for this band of merrymakers led by the jolly old gentleman himself. His frosty friend ushers in the wonders of winter, while a lovable bear reminds us of our very first teddy discovered on Christmas morning. Of course, we couldn't forget Santa's trusty reindeer, whose magical flight helps him deliver holiday cheer. And the story of why we celebrate this special day is best told through the glad tidings of a sweet angel. Easier to make than you might think, our roly-poly pals also frolic among the branches of our enchanting evergreen, which is decorated with wooden bead garlands, papier-mâché stars, pomegranates, simple ribbon-tied packages, and giant jingle bells. You'll also find a matching garland and gift box to deck the halls in coordinating fun. Instructions for the projects shown here and on the following pages begin on page 12.

As a charming focal point for the foyer or any room in your house, the **Roly-Poly Pals Tree** *(page 12)* is sure to delight your holiday guests, especially when topped with a multi-loop paper bow and trimmed with our papier-mâché **Roly-Poly Pals** *(page 12)*. Wooden beads and jute braid are strung along the boughs, and papier-mâché stars, artificial pomegranates, brass jingle bells, and ribbon-tied packages add an old-fashioned touch to the tree. To complete the look, a piece of checked homespun fabric is gathered beneath the tree.

To create a dazzling gift container, we painted a plain star-shaped papier-mâché box in holiday colors and topped it with a golden star ornament. The eye-catching **Star Box** *(page 13)* also makes a lovely tabletop accent when arranged with candles and one of our whimsical characters.

A cheery accent for the banister, a simple garland of greenery is embellished with our **Roly-Poly Pals** *(page 12)* and other tree trimmings. The snowman welcomes the holidays with outstretched arms, and our angel wears gold paper twist wings. A cute button-shaped nose makes you want to give teddy a big bear hug, and Santa's hat is festively trimmed with a tiny jingle bell. Twig antlers add woodsy appeal to our friendly reindeer.

11

ROLY-POLY PALS TREE (Shown on page 10)

Let there be no mistake — Santa's not the only one who loves Christmas! Made with papier-mâché and painted to resemble old-fashioned wooden toys, the charming Roly-Poly Pals (this page) on this 5¹/₂-foot-tall tree are all waiting for the big day.

Natural and red bead and braided jute garlands twine among the tree's boughs, setting a nostalgic mood. Papier-mâché stars and gift boxes tied up with red and cream ribbon add natural charm. The bow at the top is formed from 3"w natural paper

twist spritzed lightly with gold spray paint. Complementing the other elements on the tree, artificial pomegranates add burnished red hues, while giant 3" dia. brass jingle bells gleam and shine. A length of cozy plaid fabric makes a simple tree skirt.

ROLY-POLY PALS (Shown on pages 8 and 9)

For each ornament, you will need one 1³/₄" dia. and one 2³/₄" dia. plastic foam ball; instant papier-mâché; cream, red, green, dark brown, black, and gold acrylic paint; gesso; liner, medium round, and medium flat paintbrushes; foam brushes; matte clear acrylic spray; 2" bobby pin; floral pick and a piece of plastic foam for temporary stand for ornament; fine sandpaper; waxed paper; paper towels; soft cloth; toothpicks; hot glue gun; glue sticks; and jute twine.
For snowman ornament, you will **also** need orange acrylic paint, two 2¹/₂" long twigs, and a 1¹/₂" dia. mini wreath.
For Santa ornament, you will **also** need peach acrylic paint, 9mm jingle bell, and a craft knife.
For angel ornament, you will **also** need peach acrylic paint, 5" of 3"w natural paper twist (untwisted), and gold spray paint.
For bear ornament, you will **also** need tan and light tan acrylic paint and a craft knife.
For reindeer ornament, you will **also** need tan acrylic paint, two 2¹/₂" long twigs, and a craft knife.

SNOWMAN ORNAMENT

1. Press each foam ball against a flat surface to make an approx. 1¹/₄" dia. flattened area on ball. Glue flattened areas of foam balls together to form head and body of ornament. For hanger, push bobby pin into top of ornament, leaving ¹/₂" exposed. To make a temporary stand for ornament, insert 1 end of floral pick into

bottom of ornament and remaining end into foam piece.
2. (**Note:** Cover work surface with waxed paper. Keep fingers wet when working with papier-mâché. Use fingers to blend and smooth edges.) Follow manufacturer's instructions to mix papier-mâché. Spread a thin layer of papier-mâché evenly over ornament; allow to dry. Lightly sand ornament; use a damp paper towel to wipe off dust.
3. (**Note:** Refer to **Diagram** to shape features on ornament, using measurements given as general guidelines. Allow features to dry before applying gesso.) For base of hanger, press a ¹/₂" dia. papier-mâché ball over bobby pin at top of ornament; shape base and smooth edges, leaving approx. ¹/₄" of pin exposed.
4. For nose, roll a ³/₈" dia. papier-mâché ball into a carrot shape; press onto head. For buttons, press three ¹/₄" dia. papier-mâché balls onto body.
5. Use foam brush to apply 1 coat of gesso to ornament; allow to dry.
6. Referring to **Diagram**, use a pencil to draw lines for stripes on body.
7. (**Note:** For painting steps, use flat paintbrushes for basecoats and liner and round paintbrushes for outlines and details. Use the tip of a paintbrush handle to paint dots and a toothpick to paint small dots. Allow to dry after each paint color.) Paint stripes on body red, green, and cream.
8. Paint head cream and nose orange.
9. Paint base of hanger gold. Paint gold lines along edges of stripes on body as

desired. Paint gold dots approx. ⁵/₈" apart along desired stripes on body.
10. Paint a ¹/₄"w gold scalloped collar around neck of ornament.
11. Use black paint to paint dots for eyes and mouth. Paint buttons black. Dilute red paint with water and paint cheeks. Use undiluted red paint to paint a heart at each side of mouth. Paint cream highlights on cheeks and small cream dots for highlights in eyes.
12. Remove floral pick from ornament. Fill hole with papier-mâché, allow to dry, and apply gesso and paint to papier-mâché.
13. To antique ornament, dilute dark brown paint with water. Working on 1 small area at a time, use foam brush to apply diluted paint to ornament; wipe with soft cloth to remove excess paint.
14. Allowing to dry after each coat, apply 2 coats of acrylic spray to ornament.
15. Thread a length of twine through hanger; tie ends into a bow.
16. For arms, push twigs into body of snowman. Glue wreath to 1 arm.

SANTA ORNAMENT

1. Follow Steps 1 - 3 of Snowman Ornament instructions.
2. For hat, smooth a ¹/₂" x 1¹/₄" roll of papier-mâché across top and down 1 side of head onto body. For hat trim, press a ¹/₄" x 1¹/₄" roll of papier-mâché along bottom edge of hat and down and around side of head. For beard, smooth small pieces of papier-mâché onto face to form a 1³/₄"w x 1³/₈" long beard, leaving approx.

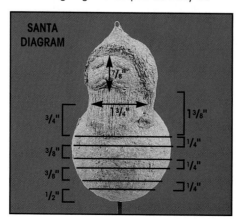

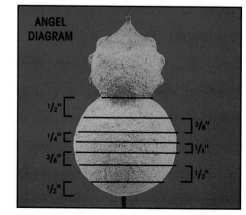

12

⁷/₈" below hat trim for face. For hair, smooth a ¹/₂" dia. ball of papier-mâché onto side of face opposite hat between beard and hat trim; smooth a ¹/₄" dia. ball of papier-mâché onto remaining side of face. Use small pieces of papier-mâché to form nose, mustache, and eyebrows; apply to face. Use long, straight strokes with craft knife to make texture in beard, hair, mustache, and eyebrows. Use up-and-down strokes with toothpick to make texture in hat trim.

3. Follow Steps 5 - 7 of Snowman Ornament instructions.

4. Paint face peach, hat red, and hat trim, hair, beard, mustache, and eyebrows cream.

5. Follow Step 9 of Snowman Ornament instructions. Dilute red paint with water and paint cheeks and mouth. Paint small cream dots on hat. Paint cream dots for eyes and cream highlights on cheeks. Paint small black dots for pupils in eyes. Paint black outlines along inner edges of eyes.

6. Follow Steps 12 - 15 of Snowman Ornament instructions.

7. Glue jingle bell to hat.

ANGEL ORNAMENT

1. Follow Steps 1 - 3 of Snowman Ornament instructions.

2. For hair, smooth three ¹/₄" dia. papier-mâché balls onto each side of head.

3. Follow Steps 5 - 7 of Snowman Ornament instructions.

4. Paint head peach and hair black.

5. Follow Steps 9 and 10 of Snowman Ornament instructions. Dilute red paint with water and paint cheeks. Paint cream dots for eyes and cream highlights on cheeks. Paint black oval for mouth and small black dots for pupils in eyes. Paint black outlines along inner edges of eyes.

6. Follow Steps 12 - 15 of Snowman Ornament instructions.

7. For wings, spray paint paper twist gold; allow to dry. Pinch paper twist together at center; glue center to back of angel's neck.

BEAR ORNAMENT

1. Follow Steps 1 - 3 of Snowman Ornament instructions.

2. For ears, flatten and indent centers of two ³/₄" dia. papier-mâché balls; press onto head. For muzzle, flatten and smooth a ⁵/₈" dia. papier-mâché ball onto center of face. For nose, press a ³/₁₆" dia. papier-mâché ball onto top of muzzle. Use craft knife to define mouth.

3. Follow Steps 5 - 7 of Snowman Ornament instructions.

4. Paint head tan and muzzle and inside of each ear light tan.

5. Follow Steps 9 and 10 of Snowman Ornament instructions. Dilute red paint with water and paint cheeks. Dilute dark brown paint with water and paint mouth. Paint nose black. Paint black dots for eyes and 3 small black dots on each side of muzzle. Paint black dashed lines on head to resemble stitching. Paint cream highlights on nose and cheeks and small cream dots for highlights in eyes.

6. Follow Steps 12 - 15 of Snowman Ornament instructions.

REINDEER ORNAMENT

1. Follow Steps 1 - 3 of Snowman Ornament instructions.

2. For ears, form 2 flattened, indented triangular shapes from ¹/₂" dia. papier-mâché balls; press onto head. For muzzle, flatten and smooth a 1" dia. papier-mâché ball onto center of face. For nose, press a ³/₁₆" dia. papier-mâché ball onto top of muzzle. Use craft knife to define mouth.

3. Follow Steps 5 - 7 of Snowman Ornament instructions.

4. For antlers, push twigs into top of head.

5. Paint head tan and antlers, top of head, and muzzle cream.

6. Follow Steps 9 and 10 of Snowman Ornament instructions. Dilute red paint with water and paint cheeks and insides of ears. Paint nose and mouth black. Paint black dots for eyes and 3 small black dots on each side of muzzle. Paint cream highlights on nose and cheeks and small cream dots for highlights in eyes.

7. Follow Steps 12 - 15 of Snowman Ornament instructions.

STAR BOX
(Shown on page 11)

You will need a 9³/₄"w x 4"h star-shaped papier-mâché box; a 3³/₄"w papier-mâché star with flat back; cream, red, green, dark brown, and gold acrylic paint; liner and small flat paintbrushes; foam brush; soft cloth; ¹/₂"w masking tape; hot glue gun; and glue sticks.

1. For border on lid, draw a line on top of lid ¹/₂" in from edges. For stripes on box, apply 4 lengths of masking tape to box between each pair of star points (**Fig. 1**).

Fig. 1

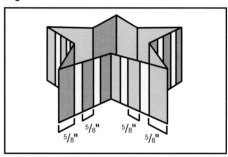

2. (**Note:** Allow to dry after each paint color.) Use flat paintbrush to paint top of lid inside drawn line cream; paint border and sides of lid red. Alternating colors between lengths of tape, paint green and red stripes on box. Remove masking tape. Paint unpainted areas of box cream.

3. Use liner paintbrush to paint gold lines along edges of cream area on top of lid and stripes on box. Spacing dots close together, use the tip of a paintbrush handle to paint gold dots along inner edge of gold line on lid. Spacing dots approx. ³/₄" apart, paint dots along centers of cream stripes on box.

4. To antique box, dilute dark brown paint with water. Working on 1 small area at a time, use foam brush to apply diluted paint to box and lid; wipe with soft cloth to remove excess paint.

5. Paint star gold; glue to lid.

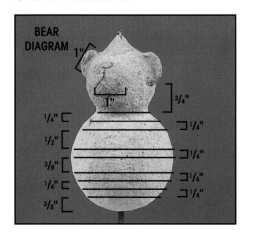

BEAR DIAGRAM

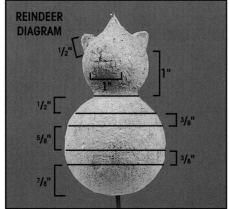

REINDEER DIAGRAM

TRADITIONAL ELEGANCE

Majestic in traditional red and green, this ensemble is steeped in Yuletide heritage. Sprigs of holly, treasured for its colorful berries, offer classic elegance to the tree, along with variegated ivy, which symbolizes love, and brilliant poinsettias. From shimmering filigree and jewel-encrusted glass balls to lush tassels and glistening ornament clusters, this grand array of decorations is enhanced with a "sash" of gilded red velvet ribbon and bows. Starry lamé fabric encircles the base of the tree for an opulent finish. Crafted from matching fabric, a mantel scarf is trimmed with golden tassels, and a simple wreath reflects the regal theme. A taffeta stocking topped with a woven ribbon cuff complements the collection. With their timeless appeal, these decorations will be enjoyed for many seasons to come. Instructions for the projects shown here and on the following pages begin on page 18.

A wreath of greenery is dressed up with a gilded red velvet bow, sprigs of ivy, and filigree-embellished balls to create our **Ornamental Wreath** *(page 18)*. Decked with an arrangement of candles and decorations from the tree, a shimmering **Multi-Panel Mantel Scarf** *(page 19)* makes a handsome display. Fashioned into dramatic points, the no-sew scarf is trimmed with gold braid and bejeweled tassels.

This beautiful **Ribbon-Cuffed Stocking** *(page 19)* of red moiré taffeta is topped with a striking band of woven holiday ribbons. Filled with small, delicately wrapped presents and grouped with other Christmas trims, it makes an eye-catching accent. *(Opposite)* **Elegant Ornaments** *(page 18)* featuring glittery filigree motifs, sponge-painting, and jewels adorn the **Traditional Elegance Tree** *(page 18)*. Draped with tiny white lights and red and gold bead garlands, the evergreen's natural beauty is enhanced with ivy, holly, magnolia leaves, and poinsettias. Completing the look of this regal tree are purchased tassels topped with gold medallion hangers, clusters of shiny red ornaments, and a cascade of red velvet bows touched with golden accents.

TRADITIONAL ELEGANCE TREE
(Shown on page 15)

This rich 7-foot-tall tree, layered with extra greenery and gleaming ornaments, provides a stunning backdrop for a lovely traditional Christmas.

A multitude of tiny white lights shimmers through the luxurious garlands on the tree — three of red and gold beads and a fourth formed from lush bows made of velvet ribbon touched with gold. The bow garland is made by wiring double-loop bows (formed from 2"w wired velvet ribbon) to another length of ribbon that gently winds from the top down to the lower branches of the tree.

Shiny red latex poinsettias, stems of silk holly and magnolia leaves, and lengths of silk variegated ivy are wired to the tree, filling it with the traditional colors of Christmas.

The Elegant Ornaments (this page) are made using three different painting techniques to enhance both shiny- and matte-finish glass ball ornaments. Some of the ornaments are tied to the tree with gold wire mesh ribbon. Purchased red ornament clusters are also hung from the branches of the tree for added color. More simple but elegant ornaments are made by hot gluing shiny gold medallions and hangers made from loops of 3/16" dia. gold cord to purchased tassels.

Festive gold fabric sprinkled with red stars skirts this brilliant tree.

ORNAMENTAL WREATH
(Shown on page 14)

The simplicity of the decorations on this 22" diameter artificial pine wreath is a reminder that elegance is often understated. The multi-loop bow made from 2"w wired red velvet ribbon is enhanced by stems of silk holly and plain and variegated ivy. To hang the trio of Filigree Ornaments (see Elegant Ornaments, this page) on the wreath, we removed the hangers from the tops of the ornaments and hot glued lengths of 3/16" dia. gold twisted cord into the openings.

ELEGANT ORNAMENTS (Shown on page 16)

FILIGREE ORNAMENTS
For each ornament, you will need a red matte-finish glass ball ornament large enough to accommodate a 2¼"w or a 3⅛"w design (we used 2⅝" dia. and 3¾" dia. ornaments), gold glitter acrylic paint, small round paintbrush, very fine gold glitter, artist's tracing paper, dressmaker's tracing paper, and removable tape.

1. Trace pattern for desired filigree motif onto artist's tracing paper; trim paper to ½" from design. Cut a piece of dressmaker's tracing paper same size as traced pattern.
2. Position dressmaker's tracing paper coated side down on ornament; tape in place. Position pattern on top of dressmaker's tracing paper; tape in place. Working from center of design outward, use a pencil to draw over lines of pattern to transfer pattern onto ornament.
3. (**Note:** Use a glass or cup with an opening slightly smaller than ornament to hold ornament while working.) Use gold glitter paint to paint motif on ornament. While paint is wet, sprinkle with glitter. Hang ornament to dry. Shake gently to remove excess glitter.
4. To store, loosely wrap individual ornaments in tissue paper.

SPONGE-PAINTED ORNAMENTS
For each ornament, you will need a glass ball ornament, gold spray paint, gold acrylic paint, very fine gold glitter, a small piece of natural sponge, and paper towels.

1. Spray paint ornament gold; allow to dry.
2. Dip dampened sponge piece in acrylic paint; do not saturate. Remove excess paint on a paper towel. Use a light stamping motion to sponge-paint ornament. While paint is wet, sprinkle with glitter. Hang ornament to dry. Shake gently to remove excess glitter.
3. To store, loosely wrap individual ornaments in tissue paper.

JEWELED ORNAMENTS
For each ornament, you will need a 3¼" dia. green shiny glass ball ornament, a 5" square of tagboard (manila folder), metallic gold dimensional paint in squeeze bottle, small round paintbrush, very fine gold glitter, 9 red 10mm round acrylic jewels, craft knife, cutting mat or thick layer of newspapers, tracing paper, graphite transfer paper, and a china marker.

1. To determine placement of painted points, trace point template pattern onto tracing paper. Use transfer paper to transfer pattern to center of tagboard. Use craft knife to cut circle from tagboard; discard circle.
2. (**Note:** Use a glass or cup with an opening slightly smaller than ornament to hold ornament while working. Use china marker to mark ornament.) To mark placement of points on ornament, center template on top of ornament and mark placement of dots on template on ornament (**Fig. 1**). Remove template from ornament. Centering second set of dots between and below first set of dots, mark a second set of dots on ornament; for points, connect dots (**Fig. 2**).

Fig. 1

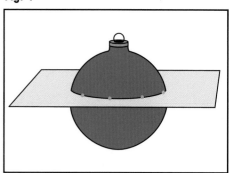

Fig. 2

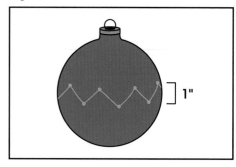

3. Use paintbrush to spread a thin layer of paint over top of ornament above marked lines. While paint is wet, sprinkle with glitter. Hang ornament to dry. Shake gently to remove excess glitter.
4. Using bottle tip, use paint to outline points. Make a dot of paint approx. same size as 1 jewel at bottom of each point. Holding jewel level, press 1 jewel firmly into each dot of paint (paint will cover edges of jewel). Hang ornament to dry.
5. To store, loosely wrap individual ornaments in tissue paper.

POINT TEMPLATE

18

RIBBON-CUFFED STOCKING (Shown on page 17)

You will need two 14" x 20" fabric pieces for stocking (we used red moiré taffeta), two 14" x 20" fabric pieces for stocking lining (we used red satin), a 6" x 16" piece of fusible woven interfacing for woven ribbon backing, a 5" x 15½" fabric piece for cuff lining (we used red moiré taffeta), 6" and 16" lengths of ribbon for cuff (our ribbons range in width from ⅛"w to 1⅜"w), 8" of ¼"w velvet ribbon for hanger, thread to match fabrics, pressing cloth, tracing paper, fabric marking pencil, and a permanent felt-tip pen with fine point.

1. For stocking pattern, match dotted lines and align arrows and trace top and bottom of stocking pattern, page 91, onto tracing paper; cut out.

2. Use stocking pattern and follow **Sewing Shapes**, page 158, to make stocking from stocking fabric pieces, leaving top edge of stocking open and trimming top edge of stocking along drawn line; do not turn right side out. Repeat to make stocking lining from lining fabric pieces; turn lining right side out.

3. Matching wrong sides, insert stocking into lining; pin top edges together.

4. For woven ribbon panel for cuff, use permanent pen to make marks at 1" intervals along all edges on fusible side of interfacing. With long edges at top and bottom and fusible side up, place interfacing on ironing board; pin corners to ironing board.

5. (**Note:** Test a small piece of each ribbon for the effects of ironing by ironing with pressing cloth before using. Do not use ribbons that shrink. For Steps 5 and 6, place ribbons right side up on interfacing, using marks along edges of interfacing as a guide for keeping ribbons straight.) For lengthwise ribbons, center one 16" ribbon lengthwise on interfacing; pin ends to ironing board. Placing ribbons side by side, pin remaining 16" ribbons to ironing board over interfacing.

6. For crosswise ribbons, lay 6" ribbons side by side in desired order across lengthwise ribbons; pin 1 end of each ribbon in place. One at a time, weave crosswise ribbons through lengthwise ribbons. Straighten ribbons, eliminating any gaps, and pin remaining ends in place.

7. (**Note:** Use pressing cloth for each pressing step.) Follow interfacing manufacturer's instructions to fuse ribbons to interfacing. Trim ribbon panel to 5" x 15½".

8. (**Note:** Except as noted, use a ¼" seam allowance for remaining sewing steps.) Place ribbon panel and cuff lining fabric piece right sides together. Sew 1 long edge (bottom edge) together; unfold and press seam allowance open. Matching right sides and short edges (side edges), fold ribbon panel and lining in half; sew short edges together to form a tube. Press seam allowance open. Turn tube right side out. Matching wrong sides and raw edges of ribbon panel and cuff lining, fold tube in half with lining facing out.

9. Matching raw edges of cuff and stocking, slip cuff over stocking. Center cuff seam (back of cuff) at center back of stocking (with front of cuff lining facing front, toe of stocking lining should point to right); pin raw edges together.

10. For hanger, fold ribbon in half. Matching ends of ribbon to raw edges of cuff and stocking, insert ribbon between cuff and stocking at heel-side seamline; pin in place. Using a ½" seam allowance, sew cuff and hanger to stocking. Turn stocking right side out; fold cuff down.

MULTI-PANEL MANTEL SCARF (Shown on page 14)

For each panel of scarf, you will need fabric, 1"w paper-backed fusible web tape, ¼"w gold trim, a 6½" long gold tassel, a ¾" x ⅞" oval jewel shank button, fabric marking pencil, 2 drapery weights, hot glue gun, and glue sticks.

1. (**Note:** Follow Step 1 to determine number of panels needed for scarf.) Measure front edge of mantel to determine desired finished width of scarf. Determine desired finished width of each panel (any number that divides evenly into finished scarf width will make a good panel width; our 62½"w scarf is made up of five 12½"w panels). Divide finished scarf width by finished panel width and round to the nearest whole number if necessary.

2. (**Note:** Follow Steps 2 - 8 to make each panel. If using a fabric with a repeated pattern, carefully match fabric pattern across panels.) To determine width of fabric piece for panel, add 4" to finished panel width. To determine length of fabric piece for panel, measure from back of mantel to desired finished drop length of panel (point of panel without tassel); add 2". Cut a piece of fabric the determined measurements.

3. For a 1" double hem along each long edge (side edge) of fabric piece, press edge of fabric 1" to wrong side. Follow manufacturer's instructions to fuse web tape along pressed edge. Do not remove paper backing. Press edge 1" to wrong side again. Unfold edge and remove paper backing. Refold edge and fuse in place. Repeat to hem 1 short edge (top edge) of fabric piece.

4. For point, press bottom corners of fabric piece diagonally to wrong side to form a point. Referring to **Fig. 1**, use fabric marking pencil to mark a dot at point and at top of each side edge of point. Unfold fabric.

Fig. 1

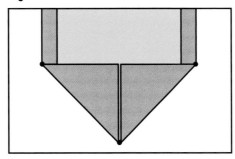

5. Fuse web tape along bottom edge of fabric piece and along each side edge from marked dot to first piece of web tape (**Fig. 2**).

Fig. 2

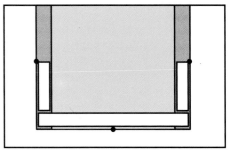

6. Remove paper backing. Fold bottom corners diagonally to wrong side again. Fuse in place.

7. Glue trim along edges on right side of panel, trimming to fit. Glue hanging loop of tassel to wrong side of panel at point. Glue button to point of panel above tassel.

8. Glue 1 drapery weight to each top corner on wrong side of panel.

9. With top edge of each panel along back edge of mantel, arrange panels on mantel.

Portraying a wondrous event that happened one starry night in Bethlehem, our Holy Family figures capture the true spirit of the season. A shimmering array of star cutouts and lustrous trimmings shower this enchanting set, which rests in a bed of spun gold on our glorious evergreen. A miniature stable also makes a sweet setting for the Nativity scene. Instructions for these heavenly projects begin on page 22.

At home in a little twig stable, our **Holy Family and Sheep** *(page 22)* are wonderful reminders of the meaning of Christmas. The charming figures are crafted from perforated plastic and cross stitched with embroidery floss. *(Opposite)* Our glorious tree features the same characters arranged among the boughs on a bed of golden angel hair. Embellished with dimensional paint and a crown of gold wired ribbon, a majestic star tops the evergreen, and a sprinkling of smaller stars and vertically draped gold bead garlands illuminate its branches. The tree is completed with an exquisite swaddling of cloth.

And, lo, the star, which they saw in the east, went before them, till it came and stood over where the young child was. When they saw the star, they rejoiced with exceeding great joy.

— MATTHEW 2:9-10

HOLY FAMILY AND SHEEP (Shown on pages 20 and 21)

X	DMC	B'ST	X	DMC	B'ST
◆	208		▨	895	
★	300		■	898	
△	301	/	⊕	987	
◇	310		=	989	
☆	322		⊠	3047	
▨	336		✧	3733	
-	353		✕	3755	
+	422		✳ *	/ *†	
▪	498		●	310	French Knot
■	550		●	498	French Knot
▫	646		● *		French Knot
◆	676		/	cutting line	
◇	680				
▨	712				
◉	754				
▪	844				
◉	869				

* Use 1 strand of Kreinik Balger®
Fine Braid (#8) 017HL gold.

† Work long stitches for halos and
trim on robes.

Leaving approx. 1" around design on all sides, work each
design on ivory perforated plastic (14 ct). Unless otherwise
noted, use 3 strands of floss for Cross Stitch and 1 strand for
Backstitch and French Knots. Follow blue cutting lines on
charts to cut out stitched pieces. For tabletop display, hot glue
1 or more 1¹/₂" wooden blocks to center on back of each
stitched piece with bottom block even with bottom edge.

46w x 113h

41w x 55h

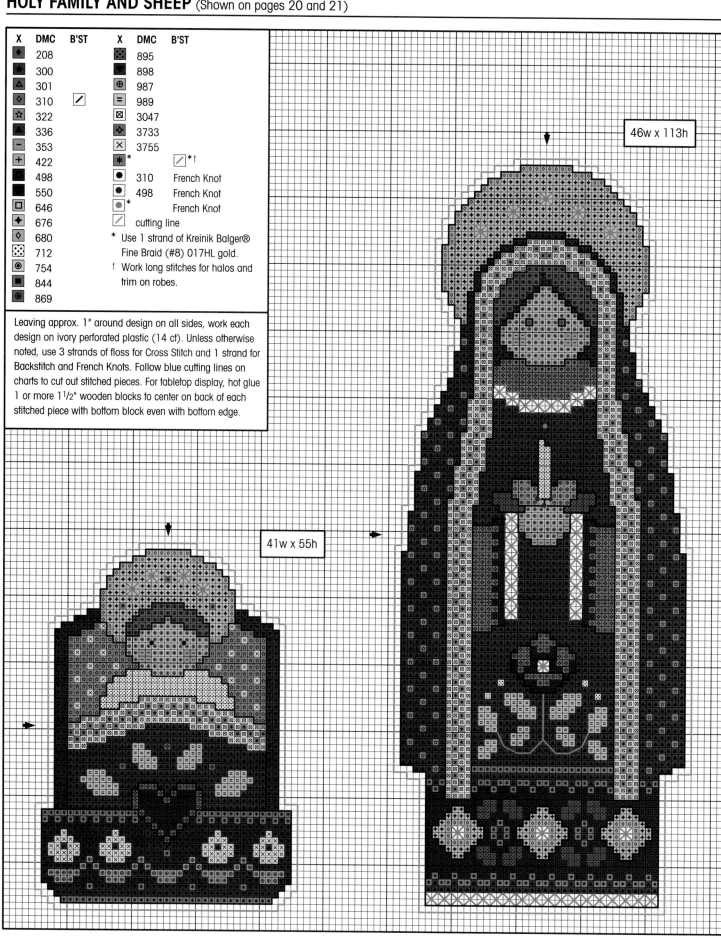

51w x 122h

41w x 43h

39w x 36h

48w x 46h

A FESTIVAL
OF TREES

Great gifts come in
small packages, and so do
our festive miniature trees!
Trimmed with novel accents,
these evergreens are tailor-
made for special people like a
brand-new baby or a favorite
teacher. You'll also be
enchanted by the golden
seashore theme and charmed
by a Yankee-Doodle-dandy
of a tree! These wonderful
tabletop accents are a fun
and easy way to spread
Yuletide cheer throughout
your home or office — or
to use as alternatives to the
traditional full-size Christmas
evergreen. The instructions
for these little treasures begin
on page 30.

Our **Quilter's Tree** *(page 33)*
offers six different miniature
quilt-block ornaments with
country appeal. The tree-
trimmers work up quickly and
inexpensively using 10 mesh
plastic canvas and embroidery
floss. This old-fashioned
feather tree also features
wooden spool candle ornaments
and tiny "sewing" baskets.

Decked with patriotic trims inspired by a favorite childhood tune, our **Yankee-Doodle Tree** *(page 34)* is a real dandy! Hobbyhorse ornaments, feathered paper hats, a colorful macaroni garland, and a spirited no-sew appliquéd tree skirt bring the song to life.

Mrs. Claus has sent Santa's suits and socks to be cleaned just in time for the holidays. Made by fusing flannel to cardboard cutouts, his duds are hung out to dry on a paper wire clothesline encircling our whimsical **North Pole Laundry Tree** *(page 32)*. Tiny washboards and washtubs filled with iridescent "bubbles" and fiberfill "suds" are scattered among its branches. Topped with a sign for the "North Pole Washateria" and displayed in a wicker laundry basket lined with cheery fabrics, the tree is sure to bring smiles to Yuletide guests!

(Opposite) Fun for the whole classroom, the **Teacher's Tree** *(page 31)* is laden with green paper twist gift bags, each bearing a student's name. The children will love going to the front of the room when school closes for the holidays to retrieve their sack filled with little treats! Purchased chalkboard ornaments, crayon "candles," and a ruler ribbon garland also decorate the tree, which is topped with a cluster of colorful crafting foam stars. Made of black crafting foam, the tree skirt is personalized with a white paint pen to complete this A$^+$ evergreen.

(*Opposite*) Welcome the family's newest arrival with the precious **Baby's First Christmas Tree** (*page 30*). This sweet holiday surprise is trimmed with delicate crocheted hearts, tiny nosegay-filled socks, baby shoes, pastel pacifiers, pretty bead garlands, and glass balls. A crocheted heart mounted on fabric-covered poster board makes a lovely tree topper, and the coordinating skirt is laced with the fanciful hearts, too. This tree will become a sentimental keepsake!

Adorned with treasures from the sea, this unique evergreen will make an enchanting centerpiece. The **Golden Seashore Tree** (*page 35*) is trimmed with glittering "sand castles" and draped with a garland of golden mesh ribbon and lavish beads. Burnished seashell clusters make stunning ornaments, along with golden "icicles" made by spray-painting spiral seashells. Miniature teal-blue lights glisten like the ocean waters, and a swath of elegant fabric wrapped around the tree's base lends added splendor.

BABY'S FIRST CHRISTMAS TREE (Shown on page 28)

When decorating for the holidays, help the newest member of the family celebrate with this sweet tree for the nursery. We decorated ours in pink for a little girl. Pastel egg and crystal cube garlands and pink glass ball ornaments complement the other trims made from baby's things. Shoes are tucked among the branches, tiny white socks are stuffed with small nosegays of silk and dried flowers, and pacifiers are hung with bows tied from narrow satin ribbon in soft pastels. The Crocheted Heart Ornaments complete the selection of pretties for the evergreen and are also used to create the Heart Tree Topper and the Heart-Trimmed Tree Skirt.

CROCHETED HEART ORNAMENTS
Finished Size: Approx. 3¼"w x 3"h

SUPPLIES
Bedspread Weight Cotton Thread
(size 10), approx. 13 yards
for **each** heart
Steel crochet hook, size 6 (1.80 mm)
or size needed for gauge
Nylon line for hangers

ABBREVIATIONS
ch(s)	chain(s)
dc	double crochet(s)
dtr	double treble crochet(s)
hdc	half double crochet(s)
mm	millimeters
Rnd(s)	Round(s)
sc	single crochet(s)
sp(s)	space(s)
st(s)	stitch(es)
tr	treble crochet(s)
tr tr	triple treble crochet(s)
YO	yarn over

★ — work instructions following ★ as many **more** times as indicated in addition to the first time.

( ) — work enclosed instructions **as many** times as specified by the number immediately following **or** work all enclosed instructions in the stitch or space indicated **or** contains explanatory remarks.

GAUGE: Rnds 1 and 2 = 1"
(DO NOT HESITATE TO CHANGE HOOK SIZE TO OBTAIN CORRECT GAUGE.)

HEART
Ch 5; join with slip st to form a ring.
Rnd 1 (Right side): Ch 1, 10 sc in ring; join with slip st to first sc.

Note #1: To work **Beginning Cluster**, ch 2, ★ YO, insert hook in st or sp indicated, YO and pull up a loop, YO and draw through 2 loops on hook; repeat from ★ once **more**, YO and draw through all 3 loops on hook.

Note #2: To work **Cluster**, ★ YO, insert hook in st or sp indicated, YO and pull up a loop, YO and draw through 2 loops on hook; repeat from ★ 2 times **more**, YO and draw through all 4 loops on hook.

Rnd 2: Work Beginning Cluster in same st, (ch 3, work Cluster in next sc) around, ch 1, hdc in top of Beginning Cluster to form last sp: 10 Clusters.

Rnd 3: Ch 1, sc in same sp, ch 5, (sc in next ch-3 sp, ch 5) around; join with slip st to first sc.

Rnd 4: Slip st in first ch-5 sp, work (Beginning Cluster, ch 3, Cluster) in same sp, (ch 3, work Cluster) twice in each ch-5 sp around, ch 1, hdc in top of Beginning Cluster to form last sp: 20 sps.

Note #3: To work **Treble Crochet (tr)**, YO twice, insert hook in sp indicated, YO and pull up a loop, (YO and draw through 2 loops on hook) 3 times.

Note #4: To work **Double Treble Crochet (dtr)**, YO 3 times, insert hook in sp indicated, YO and pull up a loop, (YO and draw through 2 loops on hook) 4 times.

Note #5: To work **Triple Treble Crochet (tr tr)**, YO 4 times, insert hook in sp indicated, YO and pull up a loop, (YO and draw through 2 loops on hook) 5 times.

Rnd 5: Ch 1, sc in same sp, (ch 5, dc) twice in next ch-3 sp, (ch 5, sc in next ch-3 sp) 3 times, ch 5, dc in next ch-3 sp, ch 5, tr in next ch-3 sp, ch 5, dtr in next ch-3 sp, ch 5, (tr tr, ch 5) 4 times in next ch-3 sp, tr in next ch-3 sp, ch 5, sc in next ch-3 sp, (ch 3, sc in next ch-3 sp) twice, ch 5, tr in next ch-3 sp, ch 5, (tr tr, ch 5) 4 times in next ch-3 sp, dtr in next ch-3 sp, ch 5, tr in next ch-3 sp, ch 5, dc in next ch-3 sp, (ch 5, sc in next ch-3 sp) twice, ch 2, dc in first sc to form last sp: 27 sps.

Rnd 6: Ch 1, sc in same sp, ch 3, dc in third ch from hook, (sc in next ch-5 sp, ch 3, dc in third ch from hook) 14 times, pull up a loop in next 2 ch-3 sps, YO and draw through all 3 loops on hook, ch 3, dc in third ch from hook, (sc in next ch-5 sp, ch 3, dc in third ch from hook) around; join with slip st to first sc, finish off.

For hanger, thread 5" of nylon line through top of ornament and knot ends together.

HEART TREE TOPPER
You will need one 7" square each of fabric for background, poster board, and paper-backed fusible web; 17" of ½"w pregathered lace trim; 1 Crocheted Heart Ornament without hanger (this page); 8" of florist wire; tracing paper; hot glue gun; and glue sticks.

1. Follow manufacturer's instructions to fuse web to wrong side of fabric square. Remove paper backing and fuse fabric square to poster board square.
2. Trace heart pattern onto tracing paper; cut out. Use pattern to cut heart from fabric-covered poster board.
3. Glue Crocheted Heart Ornament to fabric-covered heart.
4. Glue lace along edges on wrong side of fabric-covered heart, trimming to fit.
5. For hanger, glue center of wire to back of heart.

HEART-TRIMMED TREE SKIRT
You will need a 26" fabric square for skirt, 5¾" of ½"w single-fold bias tape to coordinate with fabric, thread to match fabric and bias tape, 13 Crocheted Heart Ornaments without hangers (this page), fabric marking pencil, thumbtack or pin, string, and fabric glue.

1. To mark outer cutting line, fold fabric square in half from top to bottom and again from left to right. Tie 1 end of string to fabric marking pencil. Insert thumbtack through string 12" from pencil. Insert thumbtack in fabric as shown in **Fig. 1** and mark ¼ of a circle. Repeat to mark inner cutting line, inserting thumbtack through string 1" from pencil.

Fig. 1

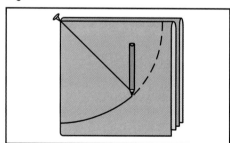

2. Cutting through all layers of fabric, cut out skirt along drawn lines. For opening at back of skirt, cut through 1 layer of fabric along 1 fold from outer edge to inner circle.
3. For hem, press outer edge of skirt ¼" to wrong side; press ¼" to wrong side again

BABY'S FIRST CHRISTMAS TREE (Continued)

and stitch in place. Repeat for each edge of skirt opening.

4. To bind inner edge of tree skirt, press each end of bias tape ¼" to wrong side. Matching wrong sides and long edges, press bias tape in half. Center raw edge of tree skirt in fold of binding; pin in place. Stitching from 1 end of binding to the other, stitch binding to tree skirt along inner edge of binding.

5. Beginning and ending approx. 7" from back opening and spacing hearts approx. 1¼" apart, glue hearts along outer edge of tree skirt, with each heart extending approx. 1" beyond edge of skirt.

TEACHER'S TREE (Shown on page 27)

Decorated with a tiny Treat Bag Ornament for every student in the classroom, this tree will make each child feel like a star — and what would Christmas be without stars? A great beginning for the decorations on this evergreen is a ⁵⁄₈"w yellow ruler ribbon garland. The Chalkboard Ornaments and crayon "candles" represent the teacher's tools of the trade. For the "candles," simply hot glue a crayon into a wooden bead and glue the "candle" to a branch. The Star Tree Topper displays the many colors of the holiday season, and at the base of the little pine is the Teacher's Tree Skirt. Made from sheets of black crafting foam, the skirt can be personalized for any classroom.

TREAT BAG ORNAMENTS

For each ornament, you will need 7" of 2³⁄₄"w paper twist (untwisted), ¹⁄₁₆" thick crafting foam, pinking shears, black felt-tip pen with fine point, tracing paper, hot glue gun, and glue sticks.

1. Matching short edges, fold paper twist in half. Glue side edges together to form bag. Use pinking shears to pink top edge of bag.
2. Trace desired small star pattern onto tracing paper; cut out. Use pattern to cut star from crafting foam. Use black pen to print student's name on star.
3. Glue star to bag.

CHALKBOARD ORNAMENTS

For each ornament, you will need a mini chalkboard ornament (ours are 3" x 2"), white colored pencil, ¹⁄₁₆" thick crafting foam in assorted colors, felt for backing, pinking shears, tracing paper, hot glue gun, and glue sticks.

1. Use white pencil to write message on chalkboard ornament.
2. Glue felt to back of ornament. Use pinking shears to trim felt to ¼" from ornament.
3. Trace desired small star pattern(s) onto tracing paper; cut out. Use pattern(s) to cut star(s) from crafting foam. Glue star(s) to frame of ornament.

STAR TREE TOPPER

You will need ¹⁄₁₆" thick crafting foam in assorted colors, felt for backing and hanger, pinking shears, tracing paper, hot glue gun, and glue sticks.

1. Trace star patterns onto tracing paper; cut out. Use patterns to cut 1 of each star from crafting foam. Glue small stars to large star.
2. Glue felt to back of large star. Use pinking shears to trim felt to ¼" from edges of star.
3. For hanger, cut a ³⁄₄" x 4" strip of felt. Position strip across center back of star. With center of strip raised to form a loop, glue ends of strip to star.

TEACHER'S TREE SKIRT

For an approx. 23½" dia. tree skirt, you will need four 12" x 18" sheets of black ¹⁄₁₆" thick crafting foam, thumbtack or pin, string, pinking shears, a white paint pen, hot glue gun, and glue sticks.

1. To mark outer cutting line on 1 sheet of crafting foam, tie 1 end of string to a pencil. Insert thumbtack through string 11³⁄₄" from pencil. Insert thumbtack in foam as shown in **Fig. 1** and mark ¼ of a circle. Repeat to mark inner cutting line, inserting thumbtack through string 1" from pencil. Use pinking shears to cut out foam piece along drawn lines. Use foam piece as a pattern to cut 3 more foam pieces for skirt.

Fig. 1

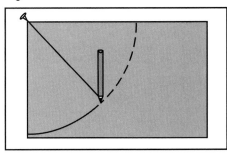

2. Matching straight edges, lay foam pieces on a flat surface to form a complete circle.
3. To join foam pieces, cut three 2" x 10³⁄₄" strips from foam scraps. Center and glue 1 foam strip over matched edges of 1 pair of foam pieces to join; repeat to join remaining foam pieces to form skirt. Turn skirt over.
4. Use paint pen to personalize tree skirt.

Duds and suds abound on wash day when Santa's clothes are laundered. From the washtubs to the washboards, this tree is reminiscent of laundry day years ago. The Santa's Laundry Ornaments, made from flannel fused to cardboard cutouts, are hung with mini clothespins on a paper wire clothesline. Doll socks complete Santa's wardrobe. We trimmed the miniature washboards by gluing a piece of fabric at the top and lengths of 1/16"w satin ribbon along the sides. The Washtub Ornaments hold iridescent ornament clusters that reflect the light like real bubbles! The Treetop Sign advertises St. Nick's favorite washateria, and a "laundry basket" filled with cheery red and white fabrics is a fitting holder for the tree.

SANTA'S LAUNDRY ORNAMENTS

For each set of clothing, you will need a 12" square of lightweight cardboard, two 12" squares of red flannel, an 8" square of cotton batting for trim, paper-backed fusible web, 7 1/4" of 3/8"w black satin ribbon, a 1/2" dia. white pom-pom, four approx. 3/8" dia. white buttons, 1/8" dia. white paper wire for clothesline, black felt-tip pen with fine point, pinking shears, fabric marking pencil, miniature clothespins, tracing paper, and craft glue.

1. Follow manufacturer's instructions to fuse web to 1 side of cardboard.
2. Use hat, coat, and pants patterns and follow **Tracing Patterns**, page 158. Use patterns to cut shapes from cardboard.
3. To cover front of each shape, remove paper backing from shapes and fuse shapes to 1 side of 1 flannel square, leaving approx. 1" between shapes. Cutting approx. 1/4" outside cardboard shapes, cut shapes from flannel. Clipping edges as necessary, glue edges of flannel to back of each shape.
4. To cover back of each shape, follow manufacturer's instructions to fuse web to 1 side of remaining flannel square. Use patterns to cut hat, coat, and pants from flannel. Fuse flannel shapes to backs of cardboard shapes.
5. For hat trim, use pinking shears to cut a 3/4" x 5" strip from batting. Overlapping ends at back, glue strip along bottom edge of hat. Glue pom-pom to top of hat.
6. For coat trim, use pinking shears to cut one 3/4" x 4" strip, three 3/4" x 3 1/2" strips, and one 3/4" x 7 1/4" strip from batting. Glue 4" long strip along center front of coat. Overlapping ends at back, glue one 3 1/2" long strip along bottom edge of each sleeve. Overlapping ends at center front, glue 7 1/4" long strip along bottom edge of coat; repeat to glue remaining 3 1/2" long strip along neck, easing at back to fit. For belt, glue black ribbon around coat, overlapping ends at back.
7. For pants trim, use pinking shears to cut two 3/4" x 3 1/4" strips from batting. Overlapping ends at back, glue 1 strip along bottom edge of each pants leg.
8. Trace coat pocket pattern onto tracing paper; cut out. Use fabric marking pencil to draw around pattern on each side of coat front. Use black pen to draw over pencil lines and to draw dashed lines to resemble stitching inside curved edge of each pocket. Draw a vertical line down center of pants and dashed lines to resemble stitching.

9. Glue 3 buttons to trim along front of coat. Glue 1 button to pants at waist.
10. For clothesline, wind paper wire around tree; secure ends with clothespins. Use clothespins to pin clothing to clothesline.

WASHTUB ORNAMENTS

For each ornament, you will need a miniature metal washtub (ours are 4" dia. x 2"h), polyester fiberfill, a clear iridescent ornament cluster with approx. 1" dia. ornaments (1 cluster may be used to make several ornaments), wire cutters, hot glue gun, and glue sticks.

1. Fill washtub with fiberfill; glue in place.
2. Use wire cutters to cut several ornaments from cluster. Arrange loose ornaments in fiberfill, pulling some fiberfill between ornaments to resemble soap suds; glue ornaments in place.

TREETOP SIGN

You will need white paper, red paper, black felt-tip pen with fine point, red felt-tip pen with medium point, tracing paper, graphite transfer paper, and spray adhesive.

1. Trace sign pattern onto tracing paper. Use transfer paper to transfer pattern to white paper. Cut out sign along outer lines.
2. Use black pen to draw over remaining transferred lines. Use red pen to color letters.
3. Use spray adhesive to glue sign to red paper. Cutting approx. 1/4" from sign, cut sign from red paper.

COAT

HAT

PANTS

COAT POCKET

THE North Pole WASHATERIA "WE SUDS SANTA'S DUDS"

Stitched on squares of plastic canvas, the patterns in the ornaments on this 20"-tall feather tree remind us of grandmother's quilts. Remember playing with the spools of thread she had in her sewing basket? We've inserted a candle in one end of a wooden spool to make each of our spool candles. Even the miniature baskets filled with tiny squares of fabric are reminiscent of the sewing baskets used long ago.

PLASTIC CANVAS QUILT-BLOCK ORNAMENTS

For each ornament, you will need 10 mesh plastic canvas, embroidery floss (see color key), and a #20 tapestry needle.

1. (Note: Follow all steps for each ornament.) To cut plastic canvas accurately, count threads (not holes) as shown in **Fig. 1**. Cut 2 squares of plastic canvas 14 x 14 threads each.

Fig. 1

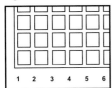

2. Using 12 strands of floss, follow charts and use Gobelin Stitch, Mosaic Stitch, and Scotch Stitch to work desired ornament design on each plastic canvas square.

3. With wrong sides together, use brown floss (DMC 433) and Overcast Stitch to join squares along unworked edges.
4. For hanger, thread a 6" length of floss through 1 corner of ornament. Knot ends together 2" from ornament and trim ends. For treetop ornament, thread a 6" length of floss through several threads on back of ornament and tie ornament to tree.

Gobelin Stitch: This basic straight stitch is worked over two or more intersections. The number of threads or intersections may vary according to the chart (**Fig. 2**).

Fig. 2

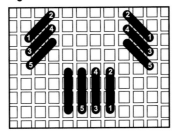

Mosaic Stitch: This three-stitch pattern forms small squares (**Fig. 3**).

Fig. 3

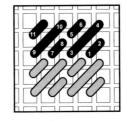

Scotch Stitch: This stitch forms a square. It may be worked over three or more horizontal threads by three or more vertical threads. **Fig. 4** shows it worked over three threads.

Fig. 4

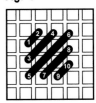

Overcast Stitch: This stitch covers the edge of the canvas and joins pieces of canvas (**Fig. 5**). It may be necessary to go through the same hole more than once to get an even coverage on the edge, especially at the corners.

Fig. 5

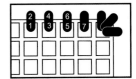

▨	DMC 433 (Overcast Stitch)
▨	DMC 543
▨	DMC 680
▨	DMC 816
▨	DMC 986

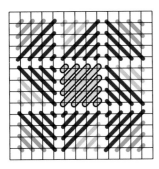

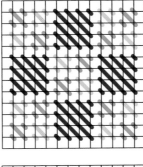

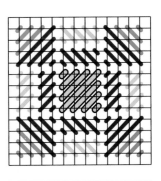

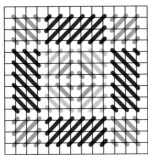

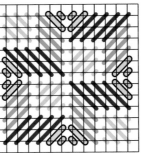

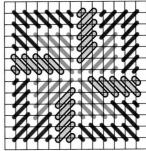

This dandy tree will spark your patriotic spirit with its gold star garland, 3/8"w red-and-white grosgrain ribbon garland, and noodle garland made from spray-painted red, white, and blue macaroni strung onto white string. Reined in place with satin ribbons are the easy-to-make Hobbyhorse Ornaments. The Paper Hat Ornaments adorned with feathers help carry out the "Yankee-Doodle" theme, and purchased 1 3/4"w gold wooden star ornaments add holiday sparkle to the tree. At the treetop, we've tied a neat bow of 1 1/2"w blue grosgrain ribbon. For the Yankee-Doodle Tree Skirt, appliqués cut from festive fabrics are fused to a muslin square for a big finale!

PAPER HAT ORNAMENTS

For each ornament, you will need a 5 1/2" square of newspaper, an approx. 5" long white feather, and craft glue.

1. Fold newspaper square in half from top to bottom.
2. Referring to **Fig. 1**, fold top corners of folded square diagonally toward bottom edges. Referring to **Fig. 2**, fold bottom edges up approx. 1/2" at front and back for brim.

Fig. 1

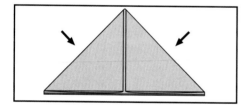

Fig. 2

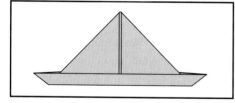

3. Secure center front of hat with a dot of glue behind brim.
4. Tuck feather under fold at center front of hat; glue to secure.

HOBBYHORSE ORNAMENTS

For each ornament, you will need two 6" x 8" fabric pieces, thread to match fabric, polyester fiberfill, two 1/4" dia. black pom-poms, 30" of 1/8"w satin ribbon, 8" of florist wire, 8 3/4" of 1/4" dia. wooden dowel, spray paint to coordinate with fabric, removable fabric marking pen, tracing paper, hot glue gun, and glue sticks.

1. Trace horse pattern onto tracing paper; cut out.
2. Matching wrong sides, pin fabric pieces together. Center pattern on fabric pieces. Use fabric marking pen to draw around pattern.
3. Using a short machine stitch and leaving bottom edge of horse shape open, sew fabric pieces together along drawn lines. Cutting along drawn line at bottom and approx. 3/4" from stitching line on remaining sides, cut out horse.
4. For mane, refer to ●'s on pattern and make cuts approx. 1/8" apart along edge of fabric to 1/8" from stitching line between ●'s. Referring to **Fig. 1**, trim remaining seam allowance to 1/8" from stitching.

Fig. 1

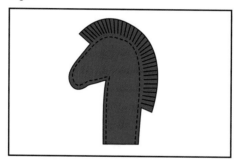

5. Spray paint dowel; allow to dry.
6. Stuff head only of horse with fiberfill. Insert dowel into neck of horse, leaving approx. 5" of dowel exposed. Continue stuffing horse shape to within 1/2" of bottom. Knot a length of thread around bottom of shape to secure.
7. For reins, drape center of ribbon over head above nose, using a dot of glue to secure ribbon to each side of head. Wrap ribbon ends around back of neck and tie; wrap ends once around neck and tie ends into a bow.
8. For eyes, refer to "X" on pattern for placement and glue 1 pom-pom to each side of head.
9. For hanger, thread wire under ribbon tied around neck.

YANKEE-DOODLE TREE SKIRT

You will need a 21 1/2" square of muslin, fabrics for appliqués, paper-backed fusible web, 1/4"w paper-backed fusible web tape, tracing paper, and a disappearing-ink fabric marking pen.

1. For skirt, fringe edges of muslin square 7/8".
2. Trace letter and star patterns, this page and page 35, onto tracing paper. For square pattern, draw a 3 1/2" square on tracing paper. Cut out patterns.
3. Follow manufacturer's instructions to fuse web to wrong sides of appliqué fabrics. Use patterns to cut 4 stars, 9 squares, and letters to spell out "Yankee Doodle went to town riding on a pony" from fabrics.
4. (**Note:** Refer to **Diagram**, page 35, for remaining steps.) Remove paper backing from shapes and letters and arrange on skirt; fuse in place.
5. For opening in skirt, use a ruler and fabric marking pen to draw a line from center of skirt to center back of skirt. Cut along drawn line. To hem each edge of opening, follow manufacturer's instructions to fuse web tape along edge on wrong side of skirt. Press edge to wrong side along inner edge of web tape, tapering hem as necessary at center of skirt. Unfold edge and remove paper backing; refold edge and fuse in place.

DIAGRAM

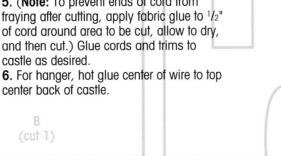

GOLDEN SEASHORE TREE (Shown on page 29)

Warm summers at the beach can be remembered even during winter's chill with this glittering tree. Perfect for a den or sunroom, it will please anyone who loves the beauty of the ocean. Among the golden elements on the tree, miniature teal blue lights sparkle like the waters of the sea. Lengths of 6"w gold mesh ribbons and strands of iridescent pearl, copper, gold, blue, and green beads are twisted together to form a garland. Clusters of seashells burnished with Rub 'n Buff® are glued to floral picks and tucked along the flowing garland. Have no fear, the Sand Castle Ornaments on this sparkling tree won't wash away with the tide. Made of foam core board and painted with Duncan Snow Accents™ for a sandy texture, they'll last throughout the holiday! The golden "icicles" are made from individual seashells that are spray painted gold, trimmed with ⅛" dia. gold twisted cord tied into a bow, and hung with a loop of cord. Highlighting the tree are small stems of gold curly ting-ting (available at craft stores or florist shops) tucked among the ornaments. A length of gold-striped fabric wraps the base of the tree like the golden sands on the shore.

SAND CASTLE ORNAMENTS

For each ornament, you will need a 9" square of ¼" thick white foam core board; desired metallic cords and trims (we used ⅛" dia. gold twisted cord, ½"w gimp, and ½"w loop fringe); Duncan Snow Accents™; metallic gold, peach, and iridescent glitter acrylic paint; medium flat paintbrushes; 8" of florist wire; tracing paper; craft knife; cutting mat or thick layer of newspapers; fabric glue; hot glue gun; and glue sticks.

1. Trace sand castle patterns onto tracing paper; cut out. Draw around patterns on foam core board for indicated numbers of shapes. Use craft knife to cut out shapes.

2. With bottom edges even, hot glue piece B to piece A, centering A between turrets on B. Centering top of C between turrets on B, glue C to B. Glue one D along each side of door on C. Glue E to top of C.

3. Paint castle with Duncan Snow Accents™; allow to dry.

4. (**Note:** Allow to dry after each paint color.) Paint castle peach. Paint castle with a light coat of iridescent glitter paint. Paint tops of turrets and tower (indicated by gold areas on patterns), door, and side edges of piece C around door gold.

5. (**Note:** To prevent ends of cord from fraying after cutting, apply fabric glue to ½" of cord around area to be cut, allow to dry, and then cut.) Glue cords and trims to castle as desired.

6. For hanger, hot glue center of wire to top center back of castle.

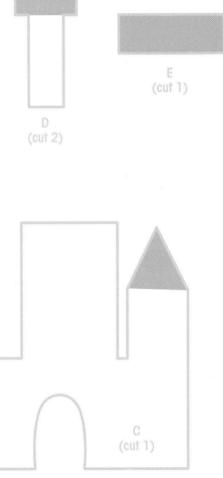

D
(cut 2)

E
(cut 1)

A
(cut 1)

B
(cut 1)

C
(cut 1)

VICTORIAN ROMANCE

aptivated by courtship and romance, the Victorians adored everything graceful and delicate. During this age of innocence, genteel ladies shared meaningful glances with suitors from behind the quick flutter of a fan, while gentlemen callers used the language of flowers to speak volumes without saying a word. A simple nosegay of roses was the most popular token to give as well as to receive, for it stood for true love. Needless to say, these elegant blooms were much in demand for decorating during Christmas. Featuring the splendor of that time, our collection is a pageant of floral forget-me-nots, gilded treasures, and fanciful keepsakes. Instructions for these sentimental projects begin on page 40.

Reminiscent of bygone greetings, our **Victorian Christmas Cards** *(page 40)* are easily crafted using photocopies of antique postcards and delicate charms. *(Opposite)* Laden with English garden blooms, our **Victorian Romance Tree** *(page 40)* is a cascade of silk pansies, hyacinths, and **Cabbage Rose Ornaments** *(page 41)*, which are made using wired ribbon and dried lemon leaves. Adorning the tree's branches are **Romantic Fan Ornaments** *(page 43)* embellished with silk ribbon embroidery and trims, miniature gilded frames with vintage art, pretty butterflies, delicate glass balls, and an opulent array of garlands. A lacy tablecloth is sweetly wrapped around the base.

Delicately embroidered with silk ribbon and trimmed with a pearl-topped bow, our **Victorian Stocking** *(page 42)* is made of linen and rich bengaline fabrics. Lace and other lovely trims complete this sentimental keepsake. *(Opposite)* A wire stand is transformed into our beautiful **Tabletop Tree** *(page 40)* covered in ivy garland and adorned with wired-ribbon roses, silk pansies and hyacinths, and butterflies. A coordinating bow of pretty ribbons with a gold charm accents the top. Capture the look of yesteryear with our **Old-fashioned Wrapping Paper** *(page 43)*. We photocopied a collage of antique postcards, then lightly sprayed the paper with wood tone spray to dress our packages in nostalgic charm.

VICTORIAN ROMANCE TREE
(Shown on page 37)

Lavishly embellished, our Victorian Romance Tree takes us back to a gentler time with flowers and fans, fine lace trims, silken ribbons, and gilded treasures.

Providing an intricate backdrop for the ornaments, cascades of garlands cover the tree. Lengths of lace trim, satin ribbons, and strings of dark iridescent and gold and pearl beads make easy garlands. Six-foot lengths of 1/2" dia. gold drapery cord with tasseled ends add richness. Laced along the boughs, lengths of wired organdy ribbon flecked with gold are anchored with brass charms hot glued at intervals along the ribbon lengths.

The Cabbage Rose Ornaments (page 41), made with wired silk ribbon and accented with dried lemon leaves, are arranged on the branches of the tree. To complete the floral array, silk hyacinths and pansies are intermingled with the roses. Purchased feather butterflies flit among the flowers.

Each Romantic Fan Ornament (page 43) is embroidered with silk ribbon, adorned with lace and a tassel, and suspended from the tree by a string of tiny pearls.

For the little framed portraits, we followed Steps 1, 2, and 4 of the Victorian Christmas Cards instructions (this page), trimming the illustrations to fit in the gilded frames.

To complement the nostalgic air of the tree, we added delicate glass ornaments. A lace tablecloth makes a pretty tree skirt.

TABLETOP TREE
(Shown on page 39)

This little tree is just right for an accent table or a buffet. To make the tree, we bent the top prongs of a 30" high wire tomato stand toward the center to form a point. Then we entwined the stand with ivy garland and decorated it with Cabbage Rose Ornaments (page 41), silk pansies and hyacinths, and feather butterflies. Bows tied from satin ribbons, sheer wired ribbon, and a drapery cord with tasseled ends are hot glued together at the top of the tree. A brass charm is glued to the center of the bows for a finishing touch.

VICTORIAN CHRISTMAS CARDS (Shown on page 36)

For each card, you will need a 6 1/4" x 9" piece of cream-colored heavy paper; a 6 1/2" x 4 3/4" envelope to match paper; an approx. 3 1/2" x 5" black-and-white illustration for card (we used the antique postcard designs on this page and page 41); white copier paper; Design Master® glossy wood tone spray (available at craft stores); colored pencils; a gold paint pen with extra-fine point; gold glitter paint; small round paintbrush; spray adhesive; and a brass charm, hot glue gun, and glue sticks (optional).

1. Make a photocopy of desired illustration.
2. (**Note:** Allow to dry after each paint step.) Lightly spray copied illustration with wood tone spray. Use colored pencils to color illustration. Cut out illustration.
3. For card, match short edges and fold cream-colored paper piece in half. Use spray adhesive to glue illustration to center front of card.
4. Use gold paint pen to highlight details on illustration.
5. Use paint pen and a ruler to draw a border along edges of illustration.
6. Use paintbrush to apply glitter paint to card as desired.
7. Open card and place on a protected surface. Lightly spray card with wood tone spray. Turn card over and repeat. Repeat for envelope if desired.
8. If desired, hot glue charm to front of card. If mailing card with charm, envelope should be marked "HAND CANCEL."

The postcard designs on this page and page 41 are copyright-free and may be photocopied for personal use.

CABBAGE ROSE ORNAMENTS (Shown on page 37)

For variety, we made ornaments with both individual roses and clusters of roses.

For each ornament, you will need 1³/₈"w wired ribbon for each rose (³/₄ yd for each small rose; 1¹/₂ yds for each large rose), dried lemon leaves, artificial flower stamens (optional), lightweight cardboard, a floral pick, low-temperature hot glue gun, low-temperature glue sticks, and tweezers.

1. (**Note:** Follow Steps 1 - 3 to make desired number of roses.) Gather 1 long edge (bottom edge) of ribbon by gently pulling wire from both ends with tweezers and pushing ribbon toward center.
2. (**Note:** For safety, a floral pick is used to hold rose until rose center is formed.) Wind wire pulled from 1 end of ribbon clockwise around 1 end of floral pick

(**Fig. 1**). To form center of rose, fold end of ribbon diagonally to meet bottom edge; if desired, glue stamens to ribbon next to folded end (**Fig. 2**). Roll folded end of ribbon tightly 2 to 3 times (**Fig. 3**), gluing bottom edge of ribbon to secure. Unwind wire to remove pick from rose center.

Fig. 1	Fig. 2	Fig. 3

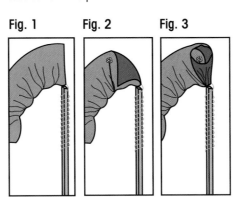

3. To form petals, continue to roll ribbon loosely around center with bottom edge winding slightly upward and gluing bottom edge in place as you go. At end of ribbon, fold end of ribbon diagonally to back of rose and glue in place. Clip ends of excess wire to approx. ¹/₂" from rose; bend each end to 1 side.
4. For backing, cut a piece of cardboard approx. same size as rose(s). Glue rose(s) to cardboard; glue leaves to cardboard around rose(s). Trim cardboard close to leaves and roses.

VICTORIAN STOCKING (Shown on page 38)

You will need two 14" x 20" fabric pieces for stocking front and back (we used cream bengaline), two 14" x 20" fabric pieces for stocking lining, one 4³/₄" x 15¹/₂" fabric piece each for cuff (we used cream linen) and cuff lining, one 4³/₄" x 15¹/₂" piece of lightweight fusible interfacing, 16" of 1"w beaded lace trim threaded with ribbon for trim on cuff, 1¹/₄ yds each of ³/₁₆" dia. twisted cord and ³/₈"w picot lace trim for trim on stocking, 7" of ³/₁₆" dia. cord for hanger, ¹/₂ yd of ³/₈"w double-face satin ribbon, thread to match fabrics, YLI 4mm silk ribbon and DMC embroidery floss (see key), chenille needles (size needed depends on density of cuff fabric), embroidery hoop, a 10mm x 15mm pearl cabochon, tracing paper, white tissue paper, tweezers (if needed), fabric marking pencil, hot glue gun, and glue sticks.

1. For stocking pattern, match dotted lines and align arrows and trace top and bottom of stocking pattern, page 91, onto tracing paper; cut out.
2. Use stocking pattern and follow **Sewing Shapes**, page 158, to make stocking from stocking fabric pieces, leaving top edge of stocking open and trimming top edge of stocking along drawn line; do not turn right side out. Repeat to make stocking lining from lining fabric pieces; turn lining right side out.
3. Matching wrong sides, insert stocking into lining; pin top edges together.
4. For cuff, use a pencil to trace embroidery pattern onto tissue paper. Cutting 1¹/₂" outside design, cut out pattern.
5. Follow manufacturer's instructions to fuse interfacing to wrong side of cuff fabric piece. Center pattern on right side of fabric piece with design 2" from top edge; pin or baste pattern securely in place.
6. (**Note:** Refer to stitch diagrams, page 43, to work embroidery stitches. Work design using 16" lengths of ribbon.) To thread needle with ribbon, thread 1 end of ribbon length through eye of needle. Pierce same end of ribbon ¹/₄" from end

with point of needle. Pull on remaining ribbon end, locking ribbon into eye of needle. Working over pattern, follow key to work design on fabric piece.
7. Using tweezers if necessary, carefully tear pattern away from stitched design.
8. (**Note:** Except as noted, use a ¹/₄" seam allowance for remaining sewing steps.) Place cuff and cuff lining fabric pieces right sides together. Sew pieces together along bottom edge of cuff; unfold and press seam allowance open. Matching right sides and short edges (side edges), fold cuff and lining in half; sew short edges together to form a tube. Press seam allowance open. Turn tube right side out. Matching wrong sides and raw edges of cuff and lining, fold tube in half with lining facing out.
9. Matching raw edges of cuff and stocking lining, slip cuff over stocking lining. Center cuff seam (back of cuff) at center back of stocking lining (with front of cuff lining facing front, toe of stocking should point to right); pin raw edges together.

10. For hanger, fold 7" cord length in half. Matching ends of cord to raw edges of cuff and stocking, insert cord between cuff and stocking at heel-side seamline; pin in place.
11. Using a ¹/₂" seam allowance, sew cuff and hanger to stocking. Turn stocking right side out.
12. For trim on cuff, press 1 end of beaded lace trim ¹/₂" to wrong side. Beginning with pressed end at back seam of cuff lining and matching right side of trim to lining, whipstitch top edge of trim along bottom edge of lining, overlapping ends.
13. For trim on stocking, begin at 1 top corner and whipstitch cord along side and bottom edges of stocking, trimming to fit. Pin picot lace trim along edges of stocking behind cord; whipstitch in place, trimming to fit. Fold cuff of stocking down.
14. Tie satin ribbon into a 3"w bow; trim streamers to 5" from bow. Arrange bow on stocking cuff and use small dots of glue to glue in place. Glue pearl cabochon to bow.

STITCH NAME	SYMBOL	YLI	DMC
Backstitch		033	—
Japanese Ribbon Stitch		033	—
		111	—
		113	—
French Knot		178	—
Spiderweb Rose		022	554
		084	327
		111	761
		113	223

STOCKING EMBROIDERY PATTERN

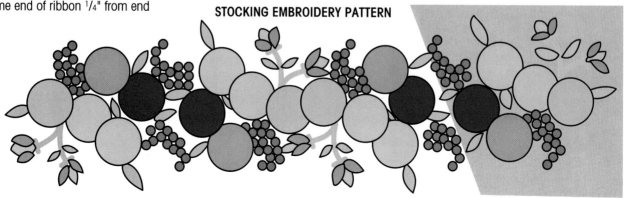

ORNAMENT EMBROIDERY PATTERN

VICTORIAN STOCKING (Continued)

STITCH DIAGRAMS

Backstitch: Following line to be stitched, come up at odd numbers and go down at even numbers (**Fig. 1**).

Fig. 1

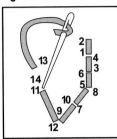

Japanese Ribbon Stitch: Come up at 1. Lay ribbon flat on fabric and go down at 2, piercing ribbon (**Fig. 2**). Gently pull needle through to back. Do not pull ribbon too tightly. Ribbon will curl at end of stitch as shown in **Fig. 3**.

Fig. 2

Fig. 3

French Knot: Come up at 1. Wrap ribbon twice around needle and insert needle at 2, holding end of ribbon with non-stitching fingers (**Fig. 4**). Tighten knot, then pull needle through fabric, holding ribbon until it must be released.

Fig. 4

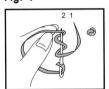

Spiderweb Rose: For anchor stitches, use 1 strand of floss to work 5 straight stitches from edge of circle to center, coming up at odd numbers and going down at even numbers (**Fig. 5**). For ribbon petals, bring needle up at center of anchor stitches; weave ribbon over and under anchor stitches (**Fig. 6**), keeping ribbon loose and allowing ribbon to twist. Continue to weave ribbon until anchor stitches are covered.

Fig. 5

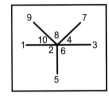

Fig. 6

ROMANTIC FAN ORNAMENTS (Shown on page 37)

For each ornament, you will need one 6" x 8" piece each of fabric for ornament front (we used bengaline), fabric for backing, lightweight fusible interfacing, batting, and lightweight cardboard; 12" of 3/8"w picot lace trim; 2/3 yd of 2mm pearl garland; 1/2 yd of 3/8"w double-face satin ribbon; thread to match ornament front fabric; YLI 4mm silk ribbon and DMC embroidery floss (see key, page 42); chenille needles (size needed depends on density of fabric); embroidery hoop; a 4 1/2" long tassel; a 10mm x 15mm pearl cabochon; white tissue paper; tracing paper; disappearing-ink fabric marking pen; tweezers (if needed); hot glue gun; and glue sticks.

1. Follow Steps 4 - 7 of Victorian Stocking instructions, page 42, to stitch ornament embroidery design (shown in grey area on stocking embroidery pattern, page 42) at center of ornament front fabric piece.
2. Trace pink lines of fan pattern onto tracing paper; cut out. Center pattern over embroidered design with top of pattern 1 1/4" above top of design; use fabric marking pen to draw around pattern. Cut out shape.

3. Trace grey lines of fan pattern onto tracing paper; cut out. Use pattern to cut 1 fan shape each from backing fabric, batting, and cardboard.
4. Glue batting piece to cardboard piece. Center cardboard piece batting side down on wrong side of embroidered fabric piece. At 1/4" intervals, clip fabric extending beyond cardboard to 1/16" from cardboard. Glue clipped edges to back of cardboard.
5. Glue straight edge of lace trim along scalloped edge on back of fan.
6. Matching edges, glue backing fabric piece to back of fan.
7. Beginning at bottom point of fan, whipstitch pearl garland along edges of fan, trimming to fit.
8. For hanger, fold a 5" length of pearl garland in half. Glue ends of garland to top center back of fan.
9. Tie satin ribbon into a 3"w bow; trim streamers to 5" from bow. Arrange bow on fan and use small dots of glue to glue in place. Glue hanging loop of tassel to bow so that top of tassel meets bottom of fan; trim excess from hanging loop if necessary. Glue pearl cabochon to bow.

OLD-FASHIONED WRAPPING PAPER
(Shown on page 39)

You will need desired black-and-white illustrations (we used the antique postcard illustrations on pages 40 and 41), 8 1/2" x 11" and 11" x 17" white copier paper, Design Master® glossy wood tone spray (available at craft stores), and craft glue stick.

1. Make several photocopies of desired illustrations on 8 1/2" x 11" paper; cut out.
2. Arrange cutouts randomly approx. 1/8" apart on one 11" x 17" paper piece. If necessary, trim some cutouts into smaller pieces to fill in any gaps. Glue cutouts in place.
3. Photocopy collage of cutouts as needed to make desired amount of wrapping paper.
4. Lightly spray copies with wood tone spray; allow to dry.

HANDMADE HOLIDAY

*I*nspired by the penny rugs of the early 1800's, our collection of handmade
holiday decorations will fill your abode with old-fashioned appeal. The original rugs,
rich in Colonial heritage, were a thrifty way to make use of fabric scraps, old clothing,
and worn-out blankets, as well as to brighten the home. Made by layering pieces of colorful
wool into different patterns, these primitive pretties were often decorated with appliqués
depicting themes from nature. This season, add a fresh folk-art look to your Christmas
decor using these crafting techniques from the past. Instructions begin on page 50.

Covered with rich wool fabric and topped with a heavenly messenger, our **Folk Angel Photo Album** *(page 55)* will
hold your cherished mementos of Christmases past! *(Opposite)* For homespun appeal, our **Handmade Holiday Tree**
(page 50) is decorated with **Folk-Art Appliquéd Ornaments** *(page 50)* and crowned with the **Folk Angel Tree Topper**
(page 50). You'll also find flowers blooming from fabric-covered wooden spools, gingham bows, and blackbird cutouts
perched among the branches. Garlands of wooden beads, pinked felt, and natural rope wrap the evergreen in charm.

A dramatic background of black wool provides a wonderful contrast for the vibrant appliqués embellishing these **Handmade Holiday Stockings** *(page 55)*. The quaint motifs are simply layered, glued together, and accented with decorative stitching. *(Shown on pages 46-47)* We combined penny rug and hooked rug crafting techniques to create our charming **Hooked Wall Hanging** *(page 52)*.

A plain black sweater is easily transformed into a beautiful **Handmade Holiday Tunic** *(page 54)* using several of our appliquéd ornament designs. Accenting the shirt's pockets and neckline, the woolen motifs are perfect for adding old-fashioned appeal to clothing. What a wonderful winter warmer!

Three quilt-block ornaments are set diagonally in the center of our room-brightening **Penny Table Rug** *(page 54)*. Surrounding the trio are stacks of "pennies," which are edged with blanket stitching and glued to a background of red woolen fabric. The bottom layers of the appliqués are cut with pinking shears for a delightful look.

HANDMADE HOLIDAY TREE
(Shown on Page 45)

What better time than Christmas to be surrounded by the warmth of crafting customs of times gone by! With their primitive appliqués of rustic wool fabrics, the ornaments on this seven-foot-tall tree rekindle the creative spirit of our Colonial ancestors.

To create the cozy feeling of this tree, we began with a home-crafted garland made by pinking the edges of 5/8"w wool strips (we used a rotary cutter with a pinking blade to cut ours). Lengths of rope and natural and dark blue wooden bead garlands add to the look.

The Folk-Art Appliquéd Ornaments and Folk Angel Tree Topper (this page) are made from scraps of wool fabrics in deep, rich colors, much like the penny rugs of bygone days (a penny table rug is included on page 54 of this section to enrich your holiday table).

Purchased wooden bird cutouts are painted black with dark yellow accents and blue eyes to resemble crows; a raffia loop is hot glued to the back of each for hanging. Silk flowers look fresh-picked from a country garden when glued into the tops of wooden spools that have been wrapped with strips of plaid wool. Cream and black gingham bows complete the homespun character of this tree.

FOLK ANGEL TREE TOPPER
(Shown on Page 45)

You will need 1 Angel Ornament (this page) with third background layer and hanger omitted, a 5 1/4" square of 100% wool fabric cut with pinking shears, an 8 1/4" square and a 6" square of 100% wool fabric for backing, a 6 1/4" square of lightweight cardboard, chenille stem for hanger, hot glue gun, and glue sticks.

1. For backing, glue cardboard square to center of 8 1/4" fabric square. Fold corners of fabric diagonally to back of cardboard and glue in place. Fold edges of fabric to back of cardboard and glue in place. Center 6" fabric square on back of covered cardboard and glue in place.
2. Glue 5 1/4" fabric square to center front of covered cardboard. Glue Angel Ornament to center of fabric square.
3. For hanger, glue center of chenille stem approx. 3" from top back corner of tree topper.

FOLK-ART APPLIQUÉD ORNAMENTS (Shown on Page 45)

You will need black and assorted colors of 100% wool fabrics (we used cream, dark yellow, dark peach, red, blue, green, light tan, dark tan, and brown), black and assorted colors of embroidery floss (we used cream, dark yellow, peach, red, blue, green, light rust, and tan), khaki wool fabric dye (optional; we used Cushing's Perfection Dyes™ Khaki Drab fabric dye), embroidery needle, tracing paper, fabric glue, and pinking shears.

ANGEL ORNAMENT
1. (**Note:** Follow Step 1 to felt fabrics. Felting wool fabric tightens the weave, thickens the fabric, and helps prevent fraying.) Machine wash fabrics in hot water, rinse in cold water, and dry in a hot dryer.
2. To subdue colors of fabrics, follow dye manufacturer's instructions to dye fabrics, if desired (we dyed our cream and dark yellow fabrics).
3. Trace angel ornament patterns separately onto tracing paper; cut out. Use green pattern to cut background piece from black fabric. Use blue patterns to cut appliqués from fabrics.
4. Use pinking shears and pattern shown in pink to cut remaining appliqué from fabric.
5. Overlapping appliqués as indicated on patterns, arrange appliqués on background piece. Use small dots of glue to secure appliqués. Allow to dry.
6. For second background layer, glue ornament to a larger piece of fabric. Allow to dry. Using pinking shears and cutting approx. 1/4" from first background piece, cut out ornament.
7. (**Note:** Refer to **Embroidery** instructions, page 158, and use 3 strands of floss for Step 7.) Work Blanket Stitch along edges of first background piece and all appliqués except halo. Work French Knots for eyes and two 1/8" long stitches side by side for mouth.
8. For third background layer, repeat Step 6.
9. For hanger, thread needle with a 5" length of black floss. Take a stitch through top of ornament. Unthread needle. Knot ends of floss together close to ornament and 1" from ends. Trim ends to 1/4" from second knot.

FLOWER ORNAMENT
1. To assemble ornament, use flower ornament patterns, page 51, and follow Steps 1 - 6 of Angel Ornament instructions.
2. (**Note:** Refer to **Embroidery** instructions, page 158, and use 3 strands of floss for Step 2.) Work Running Stitch approx. 1/4" from edges of largest oval on flower appliqué. Work Blanket Stitch along edges of remaining appliqués and first background piece.
3. To complete ornament, follow Steps 8 and 9 of Angel Ornament instructions.

QUILT-BLOCK ORNAMENT
1. To assemble ornament, use quilt-block ornament patterns, page 51, and follow Steps 1 - 6 (omitting Step 4) of Angel Ornament instructions.
2. Use 3 strands of floss and work Blanket Stitch, page 159, along edges of appliqués and first background piece.
3. To complete ornament, follow Steps 8 and 9 of Angel Ornament instructions.

BIRD ORNAMENT
1. To assemble ornament, use bird ornament patterns, page 51, and follow Steps 1 - 6 (omitting Step 4) of Angel Ornament instructions.
2. (**Note:** Refer to **Embroidery** instructions, page 158, and use 3 strands of floss for Step 2.) Work Blanket Stitch along edges of appliqués and first background piece. Referring to grey lines on pattern, work Stem Stitch for stems. Work French Knot for eye.
3. To complete ornament, follow Steps 8 and 9 of Angel Ornament instructions.

FLOWER BASKET ORNAMENT
1. To assemble ornament, use flower basket ornament patterns, page 51, and follow Steps 1 - 6 of Angel Ornament instructions.
2. (**Note:** Refer to **Embroidery** instructions, page 158, and use 3 strands of floss for Step 2.) Work Running Stitch approx. 1/8" from edges of pinked flower. Work Blanket Stitch along edges of remaining appliqués and first background piece. Work 1 French Knot at center of top flower and 3 French Knots at center of each remaining flower.
3. To complete ornament, follow Steps 8 and 9 of Angel Ornament instructions.

ANGEL
ORNAMENT

FLOWER
ORNAMENT

QUILT-BLOCK
ORNAMENT

BIRD
ORNAMENT

FLOWER BASKET
ORNAMENT

HOOKED WALL HANGING (Shown on Pages 46 - 47)

For an approx. 27½" x 16" wall hanging, you will need the following pieces of 100% wool fabric (see note below): assorted colors for hooked panels (see color key for colors we used), two 16" x 27½" pieces for wall hanging front and backing, two 3" x 16" strips and two 3" x 27½" strips cut with pinking shears for inner border, two 2⅝" x 16" strips and two 2⅝" x 27½" strips for middle border, two 4" x 19" strips and two 4" x 27½" strips for outer borders, two 8" squares and one 9" square for backgrounds of hooked panels, and a 3" x 24" piece for hanging sleeve; thread to match fabric for outer border; a 16" x 27½" piece of cotton batting; a piece of burlap at least 13" x 25" (burlap should be large enough to fit into hoop); tapestry yarn for details in hooked panels and assembly (we used dark yellow, dark brown, and black); khaki wool fabric dye (optional; we used Cushing's Perfection Dyes™ Khaki Drab fabric dye); either a rotary cutter with cutting mat and ruler or a strip-cutting machine (optional); embroidery or rug hoop; rug hook; tracing paper; Sulky™ transfer pen; tapestry needle; pinking shears; craft glue; and a 25" length of ½" dia. wooden dowel.

Note: We felted some of our fabrics to tighten the weave, thicken the fabric, and help prevent fraying. Because felting also shrinks fabric, fabrics should be felted before pieces are cut to size. To felt fabric, machine wash in hot water, rinse in cold water, and dry in a hot dryer.

COLOR KEY

COLOR (APPROX. # OF ¼" x 22" STRIPS)

- dyed cream (52)
- dark yellow (16)
- dyed dark yellow (2)
- peach (5)
- burgundy (12)
- blue green (3)
- dark green (7)
- light brown (2)
- brown plaid (10)

- dark brown yarn (Running Stitch)

HOOKED PANELS

1. To subdue colors of fabrics, follow dye manufacturer's instructions to dye fabrics, if desired (we dyed our cream fabric and some of our dark yellow fabric).
2. To prevent edges of burlap piece from fraying, machine stitch ½" inside edges.
3. Trace bird and star panel patterns, this page and page 53, onto tracing paper. Leaving at least 2" between designs, follow manufacturer's instructions and use transfer pen to transfer 1 star and 2 bird patterns (1 in reverse) to burlap piece.
4. Referring to color key for numbers of strips and cutting fabric along the grain, use scissors, a rotary cutter, or a strip-cutting machine to cut approx. ¼" x 22" strips of fabric for hooked panels (one strip will cover approx. 1 square inch of burlap.)
5. (**Note:** Follow Step 5 to hook each panel. We recommend practicing hooking technique on a scrap piece of burlap before hooking panels.) Center design in hoop. Work on 1 area of color at a time. Hook a row along outline of area first, then fill in

outlined area by working more rows. To hook rows, work from right to left, turning hoop as necessary. To begin, hold a strip of wool in left hand below burlap. With hook in right hand above burlap, push hook through burlap, catching strip with hook. Pull 1 end of strip through burlap to a height of approx. 1". Push hook through next hole and pull up a loop to a height of approx. ¼" (**Fig. 1, page 53**). Continue working from right to left, keeping loops even (**Fig. 2, page 53**). You may have to skip holes in burlap occasionally, depending on the thickness of your strips. The hooked loops should be touching but not packed too tightly. Turn hoop at end of row and continue. When end of strip is reached, pull it through to top side, leaving at least ¼" extending above loops. When beginning next strip, start in the same hole, leaving ending tail of first strip and beginning tail of second strip in same hole (**Fig. 3, page 53**); after hooking several more loops, trim ends of strips to same height as loops.

Fig. 1

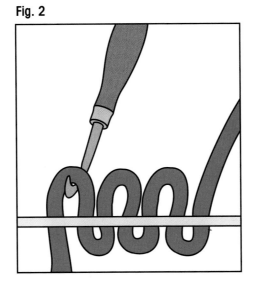

Fig. 2

Fig. 3

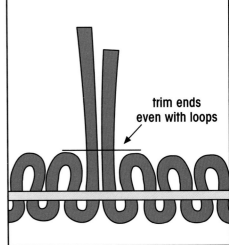

trim ends
even with loops

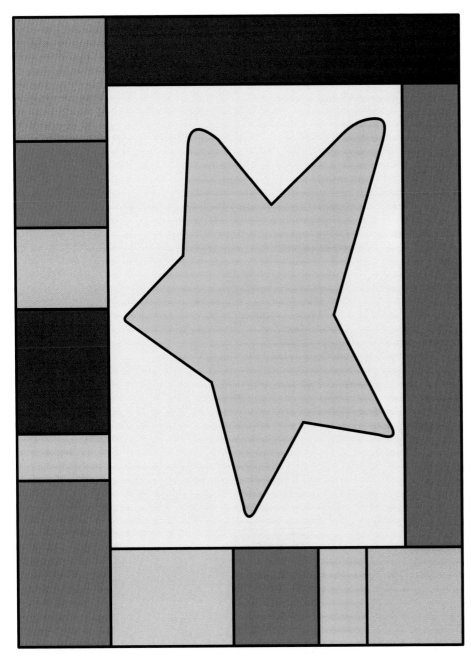

6. For details on bird panels, use 3 strands of tapestry yarn and a short Running Stitch, page 158, to work details indicated by brown lines on pattern.

7. After hooking is complete, place panels face down on a towel. Using a steam iron, press back of burlap to "set" hooked wool.

8. To prevent edges of panels from fraying after cutting, apply a line of craft glue along edges on back of each hooked design and rub glue into burlap (up to $1/2$" around each edge of hooked design); allow to dry.

9. Cutting through glue, cut out each panel along outer edges.

ASSEMBLING WALL HANGING

1. Layer backing fabric piece, batting, and front fabric piece together; pin layers together.

2. For inner border, place short fabric strips along side edges of wall hanging; place long strips along top and bottom edges of wall hanging. Baste in place.

3. For middle border, place long fabric strips along top and bottom edges of wall hanging; place short strips along side edges of wall hanging. Baste in place.

4. For outer border, place 1 long fabric strip along top edge of wall hanging, matching 1 long edge of strip to top edge of wall hanging. Use a $1 1/4$" seam allowance to sew matched edges together. Press strip to right side over seam. Repeat to sew remaining long strip to bottom edge and short strips to side edges of wall hanging.

5. Fold short edges of outer border to back of wall hanging; pin in place. Repeat with long edges. Whipstitch edges in place. Use

Continued on page 54

HOOKED WALL HANGING (Continued)

1 strand of yarn to work Running Stitch, page 158, approx. ¼" inside edge of middle border.

6. Glue star panel to center of 9" fabric square. Allow to dry. Use pinking shears to trim fabric to ½" from panel. Repeat for each bird panel, using 8" fabric squares.

HANDMADE HOLIDAY TUNIC
(Shown on Page 49)

You will need a tunic with 2 pockets, 100% wool fabrics and embroidery floss for appliqués (refer to Folk-Art Appliquéd Ornaments, page 50, for colors we used), khaki wool fabric dye (optional; we used Cushing's Perfection Dyes™ Khaki Drab fabric dye), tracing paper, fabric glue, and pinking shears.

1. (**Note:** Follow Step 1 to felt fabrics. Felting wool fabric tightens the weave, thickens the fabric, and helps prevent fraying.) Machine wash fabrics in hot water, rinse in cold water, and dry in a hot dryer.
2. To subdue colors of fabrics, follow dye manufacturer's instructions to dye fabrics, if desired (we dyed our dark yellow fabric).
3. For appliqués, trace appliqué patterns (shown in blue and pink) from Flower, Bird, and Quilt-Block Ornament patterns, page 51, separately onto tracing paper; cut out.
4. For flower appliqué, use blue patterns to cut appliqués from fabrics. Use pinking shears and pattern shown in pink to cut remaining flower appliqué from fabric. For bird and quilt-block appliqués, use blue patterns to cut 2 of each shape from fabrics.
5. Overlapping appliqués as indicated on patterns, arrange appliqués on tunic. Use small dots of glue to secure. Allow to dry.
6. (**Note:** Refer to **Embroidery** instructions, page 158, and use 3 strands of floss for Step 6.) Work Running Stitch approx. ¼" from edges of largest oval on flower appliqué. Work Blanket Stitch along edges of remaining appliqués. For stems and tendrils, work Stem Stitch and Running Stitch as desired. Work French Knots for eyes.

7. Arrange panels on wall hanging; pin in place. Use 1 strand of yarn to work Running Stitch, page 158, along center of fabric border around each panel, securing panels to wall hanging.
8. For hanging sleeve, press short edges, then long edges of fabric strip ½" to

(1 side) wrong side. Center sleeve on back of wall hanging approx. 1" from top edge; pin in place. Whipstitch long edges of sleeve to backing fabric.
9. Insert dowel into hanging sleeve.

PENNY TABLE RUG (Shown on Page 49)

You will need a 20" x 24" piece of 100% wool fabric for rug background, black and assorted colors of 100% wool fabric for "pennies" (we used 5 different colors), embroidery floss to coordinate with "penny" fabrics, 3 Quilt-Block Ornaments (page 50) with third background layer and hanger omitted, khaki wool fabric dye (optional; we used Cushing's Perfection Dyes™ Khaki Drab fabric dye), tracing paper, fabric glue, and pinking shears.

1. (**Note:** Follow Step 1 to felt "penny" fabrics. Felting wool fabric tightens the weave, thickens the fabric, and helps prevent fraying.) Machine wash fabrics in hot water, rinse in cold water, and dry in a hot dryer.
2. To subdue colors of fabrics, follow dye manufacturer's instructions to dye fabrics, if desired (we dyed our dark yellow fabric).

3. Trace circle patterns separately onto tracing paper; cut out.
4. Use small and medium circle patterns to cut 22 of each size circle from colored fabrics. Use large circle pattern and pinking shears to cut 22 large circles from black fabric.
5. To assemble "pennies," center medium, then small circles on large circles, using small dots of glue to secure; allow to dry. Use 3 strands of floss and work Blanket Stitch, page 159, along edges of small and medium circles on each "penny."
6. Referring to **Diagram**, arrange Quilt-Block Ornaments and "pennies" on background fabric and glue to secure. Allow to dry. Turn rug over and trim background fabric just inside edges of outer "pennies."

DIAGRAM

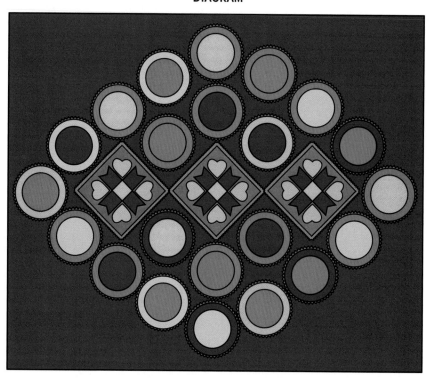

HANDMADE HOLIDAY STOCKINGS (Shown on Page 48)

For each stocking, you will need two 12" x 17" pieces of 100% wool fabric for stocking front and back, one 12" x 17" piece of black 100% wool fabric for appliqué background, 100% wool fabrics and embroidery floss for appliqués and hanger (refer to Folk-Art Appliquéd Ornaments, page 50, for colors we used for appliqués), thread to match stocking fabric, khaki wool fabric dye (optional; we used Cushing's Perfection Dyes™ Khaki Drab fabric dye), tracing paper, fabric marking pencil, fabric glue, and pinking shears.

FLOWER STOCKING

1. (**Note:** Follow Step 1 to felt appliqué fabrics. Felting wool fabric tightens the weave, thickens the fabric, and helps prevent fraying.) Machine wash fabrics in hot water, rinse in cold water, and dry in a hot dryer.
2. To subdue colors of fabrics, follow dye manufacturer's instructions to dye fabrics, if desired (we dyed our dark yellow fabric).
3. Matching dotted lines and aligning arrows, trace top and bottom of stocking pattern onto tracing paper; cut out.
4. Place stocking fabric pieces together. Center stocking pattern on fabric pieces and use fabric marking pencil to draw around pattern. Stitching directly on pencil lines and leaving top of stocking open, sew fabric pieces together. Cutting approx. 1/4" outside stitching line and drawn line at top of stocking, use pinking shears to cut out stocking.
5. Use stocking pattern to cut appliqué background from black fabric.
6. For appliqués, trace appliqué patterns (shown in blue and pink) from Flower Ornament pattern, page 51, separately onto tracing paper; cut out.
7. Use patterns shown in blue to cut 3 of each shape from fabrics. Use pinking shears and pattern shown in pink to cut 3 shapes from fabric.
8. Overlapping appliqués as indicated on patterns, arrange appliqués on appliqué

background. Use small dots of glue to secure appliqués. Allow to dry.
9. (**Note:** Refer to **Embroidery** instructions, page 158, and use 3 strands of floss for Steps 9 and 11.) Work Running Stitch approx. 1/4" from edges of largest oval on each flower appliqué. For tendrils, work Running Stitch as desired. Work Blanket Stitch along edges of remaining appliqués.
10. Center appliqué background on stocking front. Use small dots of glue to secure. Allow to dry.
11. Work Blanket Stitch along edges of appliqué background.
12. For hanger, use pinking shears to cut a 1⅝" x 7¼" fabric strip. Fold strip in half lengthwise; use a 1/4" seam allowance to sew long edges together. Matching ends, fold strip in half. Place ends of hanger 1½" inside stocking at heel-side seamline; make 1 large Cross Stitch, page 158, through front of stocking and ends of hanger to secure hanger to stocking.

BIRD STOCKING

1. For stocking, follow Steps 1 - 5 of Flower Stocking instructions.
2. For appliqués, trace appliqué patterns (shown in blue) from Bird Ornament pattern and heart only from Quilt-Block Ornament pattern, page 51, separately onto tracing paper; cut out.
3. Use patterns to cut 3 birds, 3 wings, 13 leaves, and 2 hearts from fabrics.
4. Overlapping bird appliqués as indicated on patterns, arrange appliqués on appliqué background as desired. Use small dots of glue to secure appliqués. Allow to dry.
5. (**Note:** Refer to **Embroidery** instructions, page 158, and use 3 strands of floss for Steps 5 and 6.) Work Blanket Stitch along edges of appliqués. For stems, work Stem Stitch as desired. Work French Knots for eyes.
6. To complete stocking, follow Steps 10 - 12 of Flower Stocking instructions.

FOLK ANGEL PHOTO ALBUM
(Shown on page 44)

You will need a 3-ring binder photo album, 100% wool fabric to cover album, a 5¼" square of 100% wool fabric cut with pinking shears, 1 Angel Ornament (page 50) with third background layer and hanger omitted, lightweight cardboard, hot glue gun, and glue sticks.

1. To cover outside of album, measure length (top to bottom) and width of open album. Cut a piece of fabric 2" larger on all sides than determined measurements.
2. Center open album on fabric piece. Fold corners of fabric diagonally over corners of album; glue in place. Fold short edges of fabric over side edges of album; glue in place. Fold long edges of fabric over top and bottom edges of album, trimming fabric to fit 1/4" under album hardware; glue in place.
3. To cover inside of album, cut two 2"w fabric strips 1" shorter than length (top to bottom) of album. Press ends of each strip 1/4" to wrong side. Center and glue 1 strip along each side of binding hardware with 1 long edge of each strip tucked approx. 1/4" under binding hardware.
4. Cut 2 pieces of cardboard 1/2" smaller on all sides than front of album. Cut 2 fabric pieces 1" larger on all sides than 1 cardboard piece.
5. Center 1 cardboard piece on 1 fabric piece. Fold corners of fabric diagonally over corners of cardboard piece; glue in place. Fold edges of fabric over edges of cardboard piece; glue in place. Repeat to cover remaining cardboard piece.
6. Center and glue covered cardboard pieces inside front and back of album.
7. Glue Angel Ornament to center of 5¼" fabric square. Glue square to center front of album.

STOCKING
TOP

STOCKING
BOTTOM

PEPPERMINT FUN

Rosy-cheeked reindeer, a jolly Santa, and giant peppermint sticks deliver holiday fun on these winsome Christmas decorations. Forming a candy-cane corral around the base of the tree, our festive fence is a charming way to keep your packages (and decorations) out of the reach of curious little hands. Santa and his high-flying friends also adorn our cheery Yuletide wreath to welcome holiday visitors in from the cold. Instructions begin on page 58.

Turn plain garden picket fencing into a playful **Peppermint Fun Tree Fence** *(page 58)* with these whimsical characters and candy-cane stripes. The **Peppermint Fun Tree** *(page 58)* is strung with iridescent beads and decked with glass balls, sprigs of holly and berries, and polka-dot bows made of wired ribbon. To complete the look, gifts are wrapped in red foil paper and topped with matching ribbon. *(Opposite)* Our **Peppermint Fun Wreath** *(page 58)* conveys warm greetings from Santa and his North Pole pals.

PEPPERMINT FUN TREE

(Shown on page 57)

A stick-thin Santa and two of his reindeer stand among bright candy canes at the foot of this cheery tree, which is decorated in festive red and white. Created from white wooden picket fencing (available at garden centers), the Peppermint Fun Tree Fence (this page) lends whimsical charm to our simply decorated tree, and it's ready to protect wrapped and tied treasures from curious gift-shakers or exploring pets.

To complement the fence, two garlands of red and iridescent white beads are draped among the tree's boughs. At the tips of the branches are bows tied from $2^1/2$"w wired white ribbon sprinkled with red dots. Stems of holly and $2^1/2$" dia. shiny red glass ball ornaments complete the decorations on the spirited tree, and a length of smart tartan plaid fabric is wrapped around its base.

PEPPERMINT FUN WREATH AND TREE FENCE

(Shown on pages 56 and 57)

For wreath or tree fence, you will need a $1/4$" x $2^1/2$" x $20^1/2$" wood piece for Santa; three $1/2$" dia. wooden plugs for noses; a 4" square of brown $1/16$" thick crafting foam for reindeer ears; four approx. 5" long twigs for antlers (we used birch); $1^1/3$ yds of $3/4$" dia. mini greenery garland and $3/4$ yd of $3/8$"w red velvet ribbon for Santa's wreath; white, peach, red, green, dark green, brown, and black acrylic paint; paintbrushes; black permanent felt-tip pens with fine and medium points; tracing paper; graphite transfer paper; matte clear acrylic spray; florists wire; wire cutters; sandpaper; tack cloth; ruler; hot glue gun; and glue sticks.

For wreath, you will **also** need a 9-picket length of white 18"h wooden picket fencing (available in 12-foot rolls at garden centers), a $1/4$" x $1^3/4$" x12" wood piece for "WELCOME" sign, five 1" x 9" strips of corrugated cardboard, and a 27" dia. wreath.

For tree fence, you will **also** need twice the length of white 18"h wooden picket fencing needed to fit around tree (available in 12-foot rolls at garden centers), and corrugated cardboard.

WREATH

1. Cut a 5-picket length from fencing; bend ends of wires on fencing length to 1 side. Remove 4 remaining pickets from fencing.

2. Sand loose pickets and wood pieces; wipe lightly with tack cloth to remove dust.

3. If necessary for consistent color, paint loose pickets and intact length of fencing white. Allow to dry.

4. To stabilize intact length of fencing, glue wires of fencing to pickets at front and back of each picket.

5. Paint $1/4$" x $2^1/2$" x $20^1/2$" wood piece white and $1/4$" x $1^3/4$" x 12" wood piece red; allow to dry.

6. Trace Santa, reindeer, and "WELCOME" patterns, page 59, onto tracing paper. With top of pattern even with 1 short edge (top) of wood piece, use transfer paper to transfer Santa pattern onto white wood piece. Use a pencil to draw a line $1^7/8$" from bottom edge of wood piece for pants cuffs. With top of pattern even with pointed end of each picket, transfer reindeer pattern onto 2 loose pickets. With pattern centered on wood piece, transfer "WELCOME" pattern to red wood piece.

7. (**Note:** For all painting steps, allow to dry after each paint color. If desired, extend painted areas onto sides of wood pieces and pickets.) For Santa, paint face peach. Paint mittens black. For toes of boots, paint two $1^1/4$" dia. black half circles along bottom edge of Santa. Use tip of paintbrush handle to paint eyes black. Paint mouth, hat, and suit red. Paint thin red stripes on hat trim and cuffs. Dilute red paint with water and paint cheeks. Referring to pattern if necessary, use fine-point black pen to draw over transferred lines on Santa.

8. (**Note:** Follow Steps 8 - 10 for each reindeer.) Paint reindeer brown. Paint mane on forehead peach. Paint hat red. Dilute red paint with water and paint cheeks. Paint bow tie green. Paint insides of bow tie loops dark green. For hooves, paint a $3/4$"w black stripe along bottom edge of reindeer. Use tip of paintbrush handle to paint eyes black. Paint thin white stripes on hat. Highlight cheeks with white paint. For plaid pattern on bow tie, paint very thin, wavy white horizontal and vertical lines. Referring to pattern if necessary, use medium-point black pen to draw over transferred lines on reindeer. Beginning at center bottom of reindeer, use pen and ruler to draw a $6^1/4$" long vertical line for legs.

9. For ears, trace pattern, page 59, onto tracing paper; cut out. Use a pencil to draw around pattern on crafting foam; cut out. Center ears on back of reindeer just below hat; glue in place.

10. For antlers, position twigs on back of reindeer behind hat; glue in place.

11. For noses, paint wooden plugs red; highlight with white. Glue noses to Santa and reindeer.

12. For pickets with candy cane stripes (remaining loose pickets), paint red stripes on pickets, alternating large stripes (approx. $1/2$"w) and small stripes (approx. $1/16$"w).

13. For "WELCOME" sign, paint letters white. For borders, paint $1/4$"w white stripes along top and bottom edges of wood piece. Alternating large stripes (approx. $1/4$"w) with small stripes (approx. $1/16$"w), paint red stripes along borders. Use fine-point black pen and ruler to draw a line along inside edge of each border.

14. Allowing to dry after each coat, apply 2 coats of acrylic spray to Santa, reindeer, candy cane pickets, and "WELCOME" sign.

15. Glue one 1" x 9" cardboard strip to center front of each picket in fencing length.

16. With bottom edges even, glue Santa wood piece to center fence picket, reindeer pickets to pickets on each side of Santa, and candy cane pickets to remaining fence pickets over cardboard pieces.

17. Glue "WELCOME" sign to pickets approx. $3^1/2$" from bottom edges of Santa and reindeer.

18. For Santa's wreath, wind greenery garland into a $4^1/2$" dia. circle; glue ends to secure. Make a multi-loop bow from ribbon; wrap bow with wire at center to secure. Trim ribbon ends. Glue bow to top of wreath. Glue wreath to Santa.

19. Wire decorated fencing to 27" dia. wreath.

TREE FENCE

1. Cut fencing length in half; bend ends of wires on half of fencing to 1 side. Count number of pickets in half of fencing. Cut the determined number of 1" x 9" strips from cardboard. Subtract 1 from determined number and remove that number of pickets from remaining length of fencing.

2. Follow Steps 2 - 5 of Wreath instructions to prepare loose pickets, intact length of fencing, and $1/4$" x $2^1/2$" x $20^1/2$" wood piece.

3. Follow Step 6 of Wreath instructions, tracing and transferring Santa and reindeer patterns only.

4. To complete Santa, reindeer, and candy cane pickets, follow Steps 7 - 12 of Wreath instructions.

5. Allowing to dry after each coat, apply 2 coats of acrylic spray to Santa, reindeer, and candy cane pickets.

6. To assemble fence, follow Steps 15 and 16 of Wreath instructions.

7. For Santa's wreath, follow Step 18 of Wreath instructions.

8. Position fence around tree as desired.

EARS

WELCOME

JOLLY OLD GENT

From his twinkling eyes to his beard as white as snow, St. Nick's magical charms are simply irresistible! He's the most generous fellow you'll ever know, fulfilling children's Christmas wishes everywhere he goes. Loaded down like the jolly old soul's sleigh, our tree is adorned with small wreaths featuring Santa's merry face, bundles of gifts, crêpe paper crackers, and tartan-wrapped balls and bows. The evergreen is sprinkled with teddy bears, trumpets, and other trims, too, and finished with a holly-embellished tree skirt. Santa, robed in velvet and fur, makes an enchanting centerpiece, and the benevolent gent is also found on a cozy cross-stitched afghan and a needlepoint pillow. There are two pretty photo frames, as well as an elegant tasseled chairback cover and coordinating table runner that are perfect for the dining room. Instructions for these projects begin on page 68.

With a basketful of gifts thrown over his shoulder, a kindly St. Nick inspects a cuddly teddy on our **Nostalgic Santa Pillow** (*page 71*). The needlepoint pillow, rich in detail and color, is stitched with Persian yarn.

Wrapped with glorious garlands and sprinkled with old-fashioned candlestick lights, our **Jolly Old Gent Tree** *(page 68)* is laden with treasures. Sweet teddies rest on patches of batting "snow" accented with glittery twigs and holly. Cute calendar ornaments, miniature trumpets, and glass balls also grace the tree's boughs. Our painted muslin **Santa's Sack Ornaments** *(page 68)*, packed with little gift-wrapped boxes, and **Merry Santa Wreaths** *(page 70)* add festive fun to the evergreen. Inspired by a favorite English party favor, Christmas crackers are easy to make. Handmade tartan ornaments and plaid taffeta bows lend a charming touch.

Christmas memories are sweetly displayed in our **Festive Frames** *(page 70)*. Made by gluing holiday fabrics and accents to precut mats and mat board, the frames make quick and inexpensive gifts, too!

To make this beautiful **Holly-Trimmed Tree Skirt** *(page 68)*, a red velvet circle is simply embellished with cheery plaid welting, gold trims, sprigs of silk holly, and merry bows.

Cross stitched using our needlepoint pillow design, this **Nostalgic Santa Afghan** *(page 71)* captures the jolly fellow spreading Christmas cheer. The cozy wrap is perfect for a long winter's nap. *(Opposite)* Cloaked in rich velvet and fur, our enchanting **Santa Centerpiece** *(page 69)* looks like the expensive collectible figures found in stores. This wonderful keepsake will be cherished for years to come.

Inspired by the splendor of the season, our **Tartan Chairback Cover** *(page 71)* features tassel ties so that the cover can be easily slipped on and off your chairs. *(Opposite)* Fashioned in the same style, a matching **Tartan Table Runner** *(page 71)* will add a touch of elegance to your holiday dining. Plaid and velvet fabrics and golden tassels and trims are a grand combination for both of these festive accessories.

JOLLY OLD GENT TREE
(Shown on page 61)

From its teddy bears with open arms to its festive shining "candles," this tree is a reminder that the Jolly Old Gent's arrival is drawing near.

To bring a touch of the "outdoors" to this seven-foot-tall tree and complement Santa's winter attire, we spray painted twigs white, decorated them with glitter, and grouped them with purchased sprigs of silk holly. We arranged torn pieces of batting sprinkled with artificial snow on some of the branches to resemble new-fallen snow. Adding sparkle are three purchased garlands of beads and stars.

Included among the handmade ornaments on the tree are the Merry Santa Wreaths (page 70). They are made by embellishing 8" dia. wreaths with ribbons and purchased porcelain Santa heads. The Santa's Sack Ornaments (this page), crafted from stiffened painted muslin, are filled with tiny, brightly wrapped packages that spill over onto the branches. A few other packages, too large for the sacks, are also tucked among the boughs.

Even the Jolly Old Gent himself would find our Christmas crackers full of fun. Each cracker is made by wrapping a length of cardboard tubing with crêpe paper and tying the ends with curling ribbon; for additional color, more ribbon lengths are glued around each one. Each cheery tartan ornament is made by stitching binding onto a circle of fabric, wrapping the fabric circle around a plastic foam ball, then tying it up with gold ribbon; a hanging loop of gold cord is glued at the top. Lengths of tartan fabric hemmed with fusible web tape are tied into bows to add a sweet old-fashioned feel to the tree.

Several purchased ornaments complete this resplendent tree. Cozy 6" jointed teddy bears are nestled among the greenery, and miniature wooden calendars that read "DEC 24th" remind us that Christmas is close at hand. Along with shimmering red matte and sparkling gold glass ornaments of varying sizes, miniature brass horns hang on the branches adding shiny notes.

The Holly-Trimmed Tree Skirt (this page), with its sprigs of silk holly and bright ribbon bows, brings an elegant touch to the base of the tree.

SANTA'S SACK ORNAMENTS
(Shown on page 62)

For each ornament, you will need a 6½" x 15" piece of muslin; thread to match muslin; liquid fabric stiffener; a large resealable plastic bag; Design Master® glossy wood tone spray; red spray paint; light red acrylic paint; small paintbrush; excelsior or tissue paper; ½ yd of jute twine; waxed paper; aluminum foil; hot glue gun; glue sticks; small boxes or pieces of plastic foam for gift packages; and wrapping paper, transparent tape, and curling ribbon to wrap packages.

1. Matching short edges, fold muslin in half; finger press folded edge (bottom of sack). Using a ¼" seam allowance, sew side edges of sack together. Match each side seam to fold line at bottom of sack; sew across each corner 1" from point (**Fig. 1**).

Fig. 1

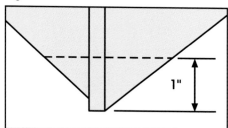

2. For casing, press top edge of sack ¾" to wrong side. Sew ½" from pressed edge. Turn sack right side out. Cut a small slit in casing on each side of 1 side seam. Thread twine through casing. Pull ends of twine, gathering top of sack slightly. Knot ends of twine together close to sack.
3. Cover work surface with waxed paper. Place sack in plastic bag and pour fabric stiffener into bag; work stiffener into sack to saturate. Remove sack from bag and wipe off excess stiffener. Stuff sack lightly with crumpled pieces of foil, shaping sack as desired. Allow sack to dry. Remove foil.
4. (**Note:** Allow to dry after each paint color.) Lightly spray sack with wood tone spray. Spray paint sack red. For highlights, use paintbrush and acrylic paint to paint prominent folds of sack.
5. Fill sack approx. ¾ full with excelsior or tissue paper.
6. For gift packages, wrap small boxes or plastic foam pieces with wrapping paper and tie with curling ribbon; curl ribbon ends. Place some packages in sack; glue 1 or more packages to side of sack.

HOLLY-TRIMMED TREE SKIRT
(Shown on page 63)

You will need one 54" fabric square each for tree skirt top and lining (pieced as necessary), a 5" x 4⅝ yd bias fabric strip (pieced as necessary) and 4⅝ yds of 1" dia. cotton cord for welting, thread to match fabrics, 4 yds of ⅝"w decorative ribbon for stripes, 4⅝ yds of ⅜"w decorative trim, 4 yds each of desired ribbons for bows (we used 1"w gold mesh and ⅞"w red satin), 6 silk holly sprays, hot glue gun, glue sticks, fabric marking pencil, yardstick, thumbtack or pin, and string.

1. Fold lining fabric in half from top to bottom and again from left to right.
2. To mark outer cutting line, tie 1 end of string to fabric marking pencil. Insert thumbtack through string 26" from pencil. Insert thumbtack in fabric as shown in **Fig. 1**, page 30, and mark ¼ of a circle. To mark inner cutting line, insert thumbtack through string 2" from pencil and repeat.
3. Cutting through all layers of fabric, cut out lining along marked lines. For opening at back of lining, cut through 1 layer of fabric along 1 fold from outer to inner edge.
4. Use lining as a pattern to cut skirt top from skirt top fabric.
5. For decorative ribbon stripes on skirt top, cut ⅝"w ribbon into six 24" lengths. Referring to **Fig. 1**, use yardstick and fabric marking pencil to draw 6 straight lines on skirt top from inner to outer edges, dividing skirt top into 7 equal sections (opening at back of skirt divides 2 sections). Center 1 ribbon length over each marked line and glue in place.

Fig. 1

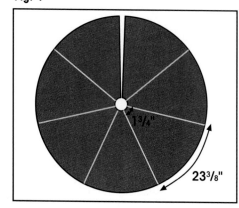

6. For welting, center cord lengthwise on wrong side of bias strip. Matching long edges, fold bias strip over cord. Using a zipper foot, machine baste along length of strip close to cord. Trim seam allowance to ½."

7. Matching raw edges, baste welting along outer edge on right side of skirt top, trimming welting to fit. At each end of welting, open fabric and trim 1" from cord; rebaste welting.

8. Pin skirt top and lining right sides together. Using zipper foot and stitching as close as possible to welting, sew outer curved edges together. Leaving an opening for turning, use a $1/2$" seam allowance to sew remaining edges of skirt top and lining together. Clip seam allowances at curves and corners, turn right side out, and press. Sew final closure by hand.

9. Beginning at 1 edge of skirt opening and folding $1/2$" at each end of trim to wrong side, glue decorative trim along outer edge of skirt close to welting, trimming to fit.

10. For each holly spray, cut one 24" length each from ribbons. Tie ribbons together into a bow and trim ends; glue bow to holly spray. Glue holly spray to skirt at end of 1 stripe.

SANTA CENTERPIECE (Shown on page 65)

For an approx. 14$1/2$"h Santa, you will need a 16"h x 5" dia. plastic foam cone, a 4$1/4$"h porcelain Santa head and 3$1/4$" long hands (available at craft stores), a 20" x 32" fabric piece for robe, a 17$1/2$" x 26" fabric piece for coat, an 11" fabric square for hat, one 10" x 16" and two 5" x 12" pieces of cotton batting, polyester fiberfill, white thread and thread to match fabrics, two 3$1/2$" lengths of $1/2$"w velvet ribbon to match robe fabric, white wool doll hair, white rabbit fur or artificial fur for trim, two 8" lengths of 18-gauge florist wire for arms, black fabric dye, liner paintbrush, lightweight cardboard, 9"h miniature artificial evergreen tree, miniature pipe (seasonally available at craft stores), 12mm jingle bell, artificial holly sprigs, artificial snow, removable fabric marking pen, low-temperature hot glue gun, low-temperature glue sticks, craft knife, cutting mat, drawing compass, tracing paper, and 1 Santa's Sack Ornament with extra gift packages (page 68).

1. Use craft knife to cut 4" from top of cone and discard. With 1 long edge of batting even with bottom edge of cone, wrap 10" x 16" batting piece around cone (leaving 2" at top of cone exposed); glue to secure. If necessary, use craft knife to trim top of cone to fit into saddle of head; glue Santa head to top of cone.

2. For each arm, center and glue 1 wire length along 1 short edge of one 5" x 12" batting piece; roll batting tightly around wire and glue to secure. Glue 1 hand to 1 end of wire. Insert remaining end of wire into side of cone approx. $1/2$" below top of saddle of head; glue to secure.

3. (**Note:** Refer to **Fig. 1** for Step 3.) For robe, match right sides and short edges and fold 20" x 32" fabric piece in half from top to bottom and again from left to right. For neck opening, use compass to draw $1/4$ of a circle with a 1$1/4$" radius on folded fabric. Cut a 4" x 11$1/2$" piece of tracing paper. Use fabric marking pen to draw around pattern on folded fabric.

Fig. 1

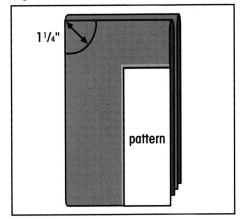

4. (**Note:** Use a $1/4$" seam allowance for sewing steps unless otherwise noted.) Cutting through all layers, cut out robe along marked lines. Unfold fabric once. Sew sleeve and side seams of robe. Clip seam allowances at corners, turn right side out, and press.

5. Baste $1/4$" from raw edges at neck and sleeves of robe. Place robe on Santa. Pull basting threads to gather robe at neck and sleeves; knot threads and trim ends. Arrange gathers evenly. Glue one 3$1/2$" ribbon length along edge of each sleeve, overlapping ends at seam and covering raw edge. Fold bottom raw edge of robe loosely to bottom of cone; glue to secure. Use compass to draw a 4$1/2$" dia. circle on cardboard; cut out circle. Glue circle to center bottom of cone.

6. For coat, use 17$1/2$" x 26" fabric piece and repeat Steps 3 and 4, using a 2$1/4$" x 8" piece of tracing paper for pattern. Use fabric marking pen and a ruler to mark cutting line at center front of coat. Cutting through 1 layer only, cut coat along marked line. To hem bottom edge of coat, press edge $1/4$" to right side and glue in place. Repeat for each opening edge at front of coat and each sleeve. Baste $1/4$" from raw edge at neckline.

7. For hat, use pattern and follow **Tracing Patterns**, page 158. Use pattern to cut hat from fabric. Matching right sides and straight edges, fold hat in half. Sew straight edges together. Clip seam allowance at point; turn right side out. To hem bottom edge of hat, press edge $1/4$" to right side and glue in place. Tack jingle bell to point of hat.

8. (**Note:** Use a pencil and ruler to mark cutting lines on wrong side of fur. When cutting fur, use a very sharp craft knife and cutting mat. Cut carefully through back of fur only, cutting with nap of fur.) For fur trim on coat, cut the following 1$1/2$"w strips from fur: two 12" strips for front opening edges, one 22$1/2$" strip for bottom edge, two 10" strips for sleeves, and one 7" strip for neckline. Fold long edges of each strip $1/4$" to wrong side and glue in place.

9. With nap of fur running downward, glue 12" strips along opening edges of coat. Glue 22$1/2$" strip along bottom edge of coat and 10" strips along edges of sleeves. Place coat on Santa and pull basting thread at neck, gathering coat around neck; knot thread and trim ends. Glue 7" fur strip along neckline of coat.

10. To paint fur to resemble ermine, use liner brush and fabric dye to lightly paint small sections of fur. Allow to dry.

11. For fur trim on hat, cut a 1" x 10" fur strip. Fold long edges of strip $1/4$" to wrong side and glue in place. Glue strip along bottom edge of hat.

12. For beard and hair, cut 3" to 6" lengths of doll hair. Fold 1 length in half and glue fold to face; repeat for remainder of beard and to cover back of head with hair. For mustache, cut a 3" length of hair; knot a length of white thread around center of hair length and trim ends. Glue mustache to face. Lightly brush and trim hair, beard, and mustache as desired.

13. Place hat on head; glue to secure. Glue pipe to mouth. Arrange arms; glue miniature tree to 1 hand and 1 gift package to remaining hand. Arrange Santa, Santa's Sack Ornament, extra gift packages, and holly sprigs on a layer of fiberfill sprinkled with artificial snow.

MERRY SANTA WREATHS

(Shown on page 62)

For each wreath, you will need an approx. 8" dia. grapevine wreath, a 4¼"h porcelain Santa head (available at craft stores), an 11" fabric square for hat, fabric for wreath background, assorted ribbons (we used ⅝"w gold mesh, ½"w plaid, and ¼"w satin), white thread and thread to match hat fabric, white wool doll hair, white rabbit fur or artificial fur for hat trim, 12mm jingle bell, tracing paper, lightweight cardboard, florist wire, wire cutters, low-temperature hot glue gun, and low-temperature glue sticks.

1. Beginning and ending at bottom of wreath, loosely wrap several ribbon lengths around wreath, trimming to fit; glue ends to wreath to secure. Tie two 24" ribbon lengths together into a bow; trim ends. Glue bow to bottom of wreath.
2. Use a pencil to draw around outside of wreath on cardboard. Cutting approx. ½" inside drawn line, cut out circle. Cut a circle from background fabric approx. ½" larger on all sides than cardboard circle. Center cardboard circle on wrong side of fabric circle. At ½" intervals, clip edges of fabric to ⅛" from edges of cardboard. Alternating sides and pulling fabric taut, glue clipped edges of fabric to wrong side of cardboard. If desired, glue a fabric circle slightly smaller than cardboard circle to back of cardboard circle. Glue right side of fabric-covered circle to back of wreath.
3. Wrap center of a 22" length of florist wire around neck of Santa head; twist ends tightly at back of neck.
4. For hat, follow Steps 7 and 11 of Santa Centerpiece instructions, page 69, using a ¼" seam allowance. For beard, hair, and mustache, follow Step 12 of Santa Centerpiece instructions.
5. To attach head to wreath, bend wire at back of neck up to center back of head and glue in place. Cut a small hole at center back of hat close to seam. Pull wire ends through hole; place hat on head and glue in place. Use wire ends to wire head to wreath.
6. For hanger, twist ends of a 5" length of florist wire together to form a loop. Glue loop to top back of wreath.

FESTIVE FRAMES (Shown on page 63)

For each frame, you will need a purchased precut mat for frame front (we used an 8" x 10" mat with a 4½" x 6½" opening and a 5" x 7" mat with a 3" x 4½" oval opening), mat board same size as purchased mat for frame back, mat board for frame stand (a 2" x 6" piece for 8" x 10" frame or a 1¼" x 4½" piece for 5" x 7" frame), fabric to cover frame, removable fabric marking pen, spray adhesive, hot glue gun, and glue sticks.
For gold-trimmed frame, you will **also** need decorative cord, ribbon, and trim.
For holly frame, you will **also** need miniature silk holly leaves and ¼" dia. decorative brass nailheads (available at craft stores).

GOLD-TRIMMED FRAME

1. To cover frame front, use fabric marking pen to draw around mat and mat opening on wrong side of fabric. Cutting 1" from drawn lines, cut out fabric shape. At corners of opening in fabric, clip fabric to ⅛" from drawn lines (**Fig. 1**).

Fig. 1

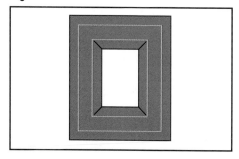

2. (**Note:** Unless otherwise noted, use hot glue for remaining steps.) Apply spray adhesive to frame front. Center frame front adhesive side down on wrong side of fabric; press in place. Fold fabric edges at opening of frame front to back; glue in place. Fold corners of fabric diagonally to back over corners of frame front; glue in place (**Fig. 2**). Fold remaining fabric edges to back of frame front; glue in place.

Fig. 2

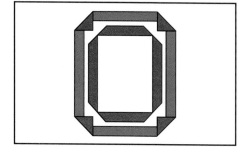

3. To cover frame back, measure width of mat board for frame back; add 2". Measure height of mat board; double measurement and add 2". Cut a fabric piece the determined measurements.
4. Apply spray adhesive to frame back. Place frame back adhesive side down at 1 end of fabric piece and press in place (**Fig. 3**). Fold side edges of fabric to wrong side along side edges of frame back; glue in place. Fold bottom edge of fabric over frame back; glue in place. Fold top edge of fabric 1" to wrong side; glue in place. Fold top half of fabric over frame back; glue in place.

Fig. 3

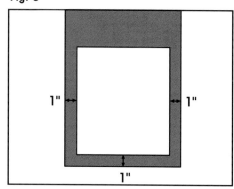

5. Glue side and bottom edges of frame back to frame front, leaving opening at top for inserting photo.
6. To cover frame stand, repeat Steps 3 and 4, using mat board piece for frame stand. Bend top 1½" of covered frame stand to right side. With frame stand centered on back of frame and bottom of frame stand even with bottom of frame, glue area of frame stand above bend to back of frame.
7. (**Note:** To prevent ends of cord from fraying after cutting, apply glue to ½" around area to be cut, then cut cord.) Beginning at center bottom of frame, glue cord along outer edges of frame, trimming to fit (leaving opening at top for inserting photo). Repeat to glue ribbon and trim around opening of frame, mitering ribbon and trim at corners.

HOLLY FRAME

1. Follow Step 1 of Gold-Trimmed Frame instructions, clipping fabric at opening at ½" intervals.
2. Follow Steps 2 - 6 of Gold-Trimmed Frame instructions.
3. Arrange holly leaves around frame opening; glue in place. Press decorative nailheads into frame to resemble berries; if necessary, glue in place.

TARTAN TABLE RUNNER AND CHAIRBACK COVER (Shown on pages 66 and 67)

For a 16$\frac{1}{2}$"w table runner or chairback cover, you will need fabrics for runner or cover, lining, and center panel; paper-backed fusible web; thread to match fabrics; $\frac{1}{4}$" dia. cording with $\frac{1}{4}$"w flange; $\frac{1}{2}$"w gimp trim; two 21" long drapery tiebacks with tassels; fabric marking pencil; hot glue gun; and glue sticks.
For each chairback cover, you will **also** need a third drapery tieback.

TABLE RUNNER
1. Determine desired finished length of runner; add $\frac{3}{4}$".
2. Cut 1 piece each from runner and lining fabrics 16$\frac{1}{2}$"w by the measurement determined in Step 1. For center panel, cut a 12"w fabric piece 7$\frac{3}{4}$" shorter than determined measurement.
3. Pin runner and lining fabric pieces right sides together. Referring to **Fig. 1**, use fabric marking pencil and a ruler to draw a point on wrong side of lining at each end. Cutting through both layers, cut along drawn lines. Repeat to cut a point at each end of center panel fabric piece, measuring 6" from each corner for each side of point.

Fig. 1

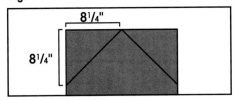

4. (**Note:** To prevent ends of cording from fraying after cutting, apply glue to $\frac{1}{2}$" of cording around area to be cut, then cut cording.) For cording, measure edges of runner fabric piece; add 1". Cut a length of cording the determined measurement. Beginning and ending at 1 point of runner fabric piece, match flange of cording to raw edge on right side of fabric piece and baste in place, trimming ends to fit.
5. Pin runner and lining fabric pieces right sides together. Stitching as close to cording as possible and leaving an opening for turning, use a zipper foot to sew runner and lining together. Clip corners, turn right side out, and press. Sew final closure by hand.
6. For center panel, follow manufacturer's instructions to fuse web to wrong side of center panel fabric piece. Remove paper backing. Center and fuse panel to runner. For trim, glue gimp trim along edges of panel, mitering trim at corners and trimming to fit.
7. Tie drapery tiebacks into bows. Glue bows to points of runner.

CHAIRBACK COVER
1. To determine length of cover, measure from top of chairback to desired finished length of point at back of cover; multiply by 2 and subtract 7$\frac{1}{4}$".
2. Follow Steps 2 - 6 of Table Runner instructions, cutting center panel 6$\frac{1}{2}$" shorter than determined measurement and cutting a point at 1 end only of each fabric piece.
3. Tie 1 tieback into a bow and glue to point of cover.
4. Fold cover and place on chairback with point at back. Determine desired placement of ties on cover (we positioned our ties approx. 11" from fold at top of cover); use pins to mark determined placement points at side edges on front and back of cover. Remove cover from chair.
5. Cut remaining tiebacks in half. At each side of cover, glue approx. $\frac{1}{2}$" of cut end of 1 tieback half to wrong side of cover at each determined placement point.
6. Place cover on chairback and tie ties into bows.

NOSTALGIC SANTA PILLOW AND AFGHAN (Shown on pages 60 and 64)

For an approx. 16" x 13$\frac{3}{4}$" needlepoint pillow, you will need a 22" x 20" piece of 10 mesh needlepoint canvas; a 16" x 18" fabric piece for pillow back; Paternayan Persian yarn (see color key, page 73); a 3" x 1$\frac{2}{3}$ yd bias fabric strip (pieced as necessary) and 1$\frac{2}{3}$ yds of $\frac{3}{8}$" dia. cotton cord for welting; thread to match fabrics; #22 tapestry needle; masking tape; polyester fiberfill; and blocking board, spray bottle filled with water, and T-pins (optional).
For an approx. 45" x 56" cross-stitched afghan, you will need 1$\frac{1}{4}$ yds of Royal Blue Anne Cloth (18 ct), DMC embroidery floss (see color key, page 73), and an embroidery hoop (optional).

PILLOW
1. Cover edges of canvas with masking tape. Work design, pages 72 and 73, on canvas using 2 strands of yarn. Work 1 Tent Stitch to correspond to each square in chart. Complete background of design as noted in color key. When working a single row of stitches, use the Continental method (**Fig. 1**). When working an area having several rows of stitches, use the Basketweave method (**Fig. 2**).

Fig. 1   **Fig. 2**

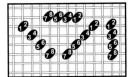

2. (**Note:** Either have an experienced dry cleaner clean and block stitched piece or follow Step 2.) Use spray bottle to lightly dampen stitched piece. Place stitched piece on blocking board and align canvas threads with horizontal and vertical lines on board. Use T-pins spaced approx. $\frac{1}{2}$" apart to pin stitched piece to board. Allow to dry.
3. For pillow front, trim canvas to $\frac{1}{2}$" from stitched design. Cut pillow back fabric piece same size as pillow front.
4. For welting, press 1 end of bias strip $\frac{1}{2}$" to wrong side. Center cord on wrong side of bias strip. Matching long edges, fold strip over cord. Using zipper foot, baste along length of strip close to cord; trim seam allowance to $\frac{5}{8}$". Beginning at center bottom of pillow front and matching raw edges, pin welting to right side of pillow front, clipping seam allowance at corners. Overlap ends of welting 1" and trim excess. Remove basting from 1" of finished end of welting and trim ends of cord to fit. Overlap pressed end of fabric over unfinished end of welting; baste ends in place.
5. Place pillow front and back right sides together. Stitching as close as possible to welting and leaving an opening for turning, use zipper foot to sew front and back together. Clip corners, turn right side out, and press. Stuff pillow with fiberfill. Sew final closure by hand.

AFGHAN
1. To fringe afghan, trim selvages from Anne Cloth. Measure 5$\frac{1}{2}$" from each raw edge of fabric and pull out 1 fabric thread. Fringe fabric up to missing threads. Tie an overhand knot at each corner with 4 horizontal and 4 vertical threads. Working from corners, use 8 fabric threads for each knot until all threads are knotted.
2. With design positioned approx. 3$\frac{3}{4}$" from fringe at bottom and right edges of afghan, work design, pages 72 and 73, over 2 fabric threads on afghan. Use 6 strands of floss for Cross Stitch. Count each stripe in fabric as 1 stitch wide, working stitch over all 4 threads.

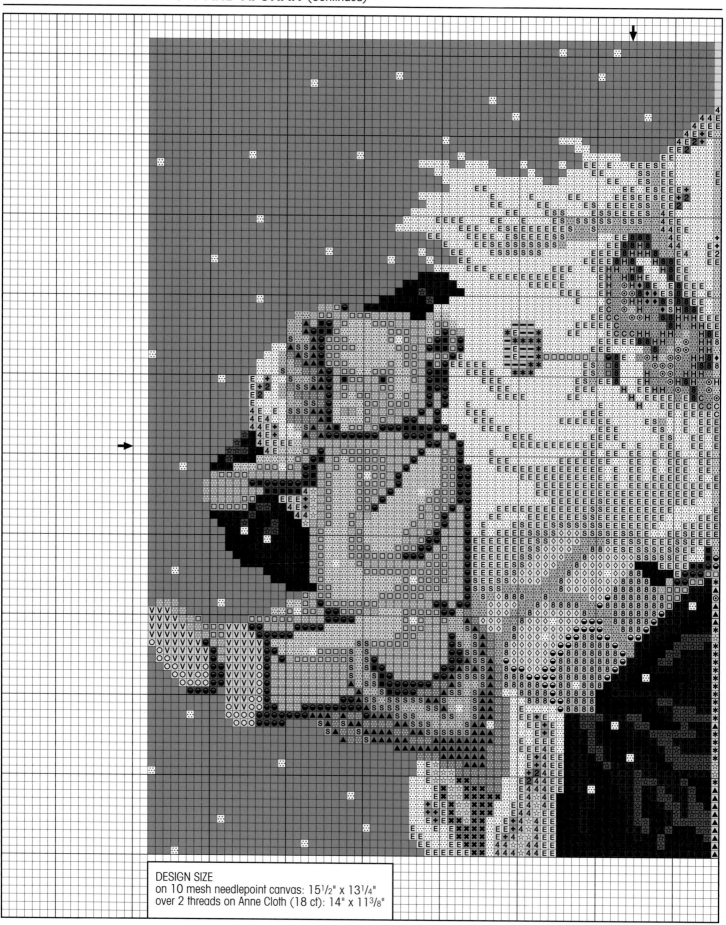

DESIGN SIZE
on 10 mesh needlepoint canvas: 15½" x 13¼"
over 2 threads on Anne Cloth (18 ct): 14" x 11³/₈"

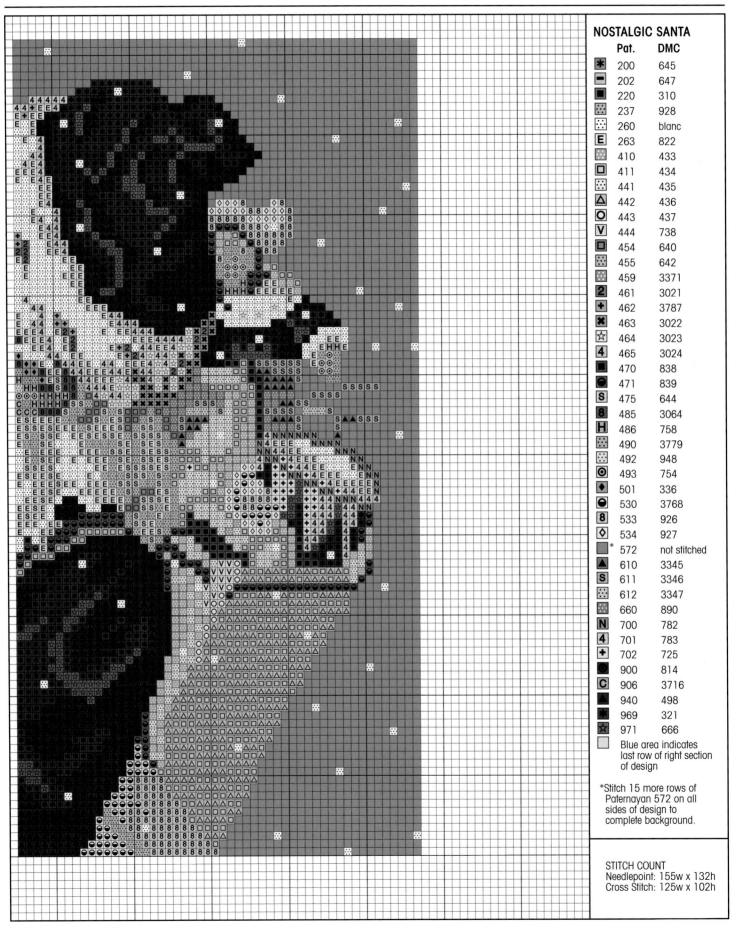

NOSTALGIC SANTA

	Pat.	DMC
✳	200	645
▬	202	647
■	220	310
⣿	237	928
⣀	260	blanc
E	263	822
⣿	410	433
▢	411	434
⣿	441	435
△	442	436
⦿	443	437
V	444	738
▢	454	640
⣿	455	642
⣿	459	3371
2	461	3021
✛	462	3787
✖	463	3022
☆	464	3023
4	465	3024
■	470	838
◕	471	839
S	475	644
8	485	3064
H	486	758
⣿	490	3779
⣿	492	948
◉	493	754
◆	501	336
◓	530	3768
8	533	926
◇	534	927
▨ *	572	not stitched
▲	610	3345
S	611	3346
⣿	612	3347
⣿	660	890
N	700	782
4	701	783
✛	702	725
◓	900	814
C	906	3716
◣	940	498
✳	969	321
☆	971	666
▢		Blue area indicates last row of right section of design

*Stitch 15 more rows of Paternayan 572 on all sides of design to complete background.

STITCH COUNT
Needlepoint: 155w x 132h
Cross Stitch: 125w x 102h

BIG TOP CHRISTMAS

For a show-stopping Christmas, decorate the playroom with our Big Top tree. Zany clowns with curly hair, big red noses, and funny hats parade across its branches, which are strung with yummy garlands of popcorn, gum balls, and circus peanuts. Peppermint sticks and candies, little flags, and miniature bags of fluffy white popcorn add lighthearted fun to the tree. Topped with a cheery banner, it's sure to delight young and old alike. There's even a colorful tent-style tree skirt! This holiday season, enjoy the "greatest show on earth" in your own home. Instructions begin on page 76.

The main attraction of our whimsical **Big Top Christmas Tree** *(page 76)*, our cute **Clown Ornaments** *(page 77)* are easily crafted from plain papier-mâché ornaments, crafting foam, paints, and other trims. **Popcorn Bags** *(page 76)* and **High-flying Flag Ornaments** *(page 79)* add fun to the crowd-pleasing evergreen. *(Opposite)* The tree is topped with our merry **Treetop Banner** *(page 78)* and finished with a brightly colored **Big Top Tree Skirt** *(page 76)* that resembles a circus tent.

BIG TOP CHRISTMAS TREE
(Shown on page 75)

Ladies and gentlemen! Children of all ages! Welcome to the Big Top Christmas! We decorated this seven-foot-tall flocked tree with lighthearted reminders of all the fun to be had when the circus comes to town.

Garlands of popcorn, gum balls, and circus peanuts start the show. Miniature Popcorn Bags (this page), which are simply tiny paper bags decorated with fabric and filled with popcorn, are also tucked among the branches. Real peppermint sticks are tied to the tree with ribbon, and red glass ball ornaments and sprays of purchased plastic "candies" complete the cheerful scene.

The merry Clown Ornaments (page 77), made from purchased papier-mâché shapes that are decorated with colorful crafting foam and curly doll hair, bring back memories of the comical antics of real-life clowns. The High-Flying Flag Ornaments (page 79), each a pair of painted canvas flags, wave among the branches, complementing the brightly painted canvas Treetop Banner (page 78), which entices everyone to come to the big top.

Reminiscent of a circus tent, the bright red and green Big Top Tree Skirt (this page) finishes the evergreen in playful fun.

POPCORN BAGS
(Shown on page 74)

For each bag, you will need a small paper bag (our brown paper bags are 3¹/₂" x 5¹/₂"), fabric piece same size as front of bag, white paper, red permanent felt-tip pen with medium point, pinking shears, and craft glue.

1. Glue fabric piece to front of bag; allow to dry. Use pinking shears to trim top edge of bag.
2. For label, lightly trace pattern onto white paper. Use red pen to draw over traced lines. Cut out label approx. ¹/₈" outside border. Glue label to bag; allow to dry.

BIG TOP TREE SKIRT (Shown on page 75)

You will need, 2 yds each of red and green fabric for skirt top and scallops (we used broadcloth), a 52" square of white fabric for lining (pieced as necessary), thread to match fabrics, yardstick, drawing compass, tracing paper, and transparent tape.

1. For tree skirt section pattern, tape tracing paper together to make a 25¹/₄" x 14¹/₂" rectangle. Referring to **Fig. 1**, use yardstick to draw a line diagonally across rectangle. Mark a dot on line 25¹/₄" from top end. Draw a second line from dot to top right corner of rectangle. Cut out pattern.

Fig. 1

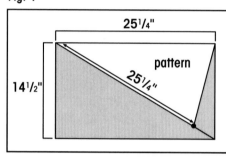

2. Use section pattern to cut 6 sections each from red and green fabrics for skirt top.
3. (**Note:** Use a ¹/₄" seam allowance for all sewing steps.) With right sides facing and matching long edges and points, sew sections together to form skirt top, alternating colors and leaving final seam unsewn for tree skirt opening (**Fig. 2**). Clip seam allowances at points; press seam allowances to 1 side.

Fig. 2

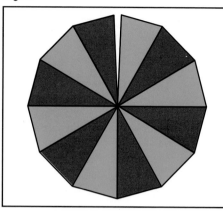

4. Use compass to draw a 1" dia. circle at center of skirt top. Cut circle from skirt top and discard.
5. Use skirt top as a pattern to cut lining from white fabric.
6. For scallop pattern, follow **Tracing Patterns**, page 158. Use pattern to cut 12 scallop pieces each from red and green fabrics.
7. Matching right sides and raw edges, place 1 red scallop piece and 1 green scallop piece together. Sew pieces together along curved edges. Clip seam allowance, turn right side out, and press. Repeat for remaining scallops.
8. Referring to **Fig. 3**, match raw edges and pin scallops along outer edge on right side of skirt top, alternating scallop colors so that lining side of each scallop matches the skirt section it is placed on. Baste scallops in place along raw edges.

Fig. 3

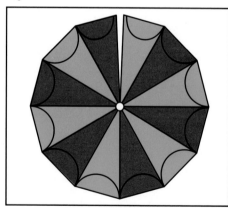

9. Place skirt top and lining right sides together (scallops will be between top and lining). Leaving an opening for turning along 1 edge of opening at back of skirt, sew lining to skirt top. Clip seam allowance at corners, turn right side out, and press. Hand sew opening closed.

SCALLOP

CLOWN ORNAMENTS (Shown on page 74)

For each ornament, you will need an approx. 2³/₄" dia. bulb-shaped papier-mâché ornament, white and red acrylic paint, paintbrushes, black paint pen with fine point, pink and red ¹/₁₆" thick crafting foam, hot glue gun, glue sticks, and tracing paper.

For each clown ornament with blue hair, you will **also** need assorted colors of ¹/₁₆" thick crafting foam for collar and tie, any color curly doll hair, blue and either yellow or orange spray paint, 2³/₄" dia. straw hat, small silk daisy, ⁵/₈" dia. wooden plug for nose, and straight pins with small heads.

For each clown ornament with red hair, you will **also** need assorted colors of ¹/₁₆" thick crafting foam for hat, red curly doll hair, ¹/₂" dia. wooden plug for nose, and a 20mm red wooden bead.

For each clown ornament with blond hair, you will **also** need ¹/₁₆" thick crafting foam for tie, blond curly doll hair, 2³/₄" dia. straw hat, small silk daisy, either yellow or orange spray paint, ⁵/₈" dia. wooden plug for nose, and a straight pin with a small head.

CLOWN ORNAMENT WITH BLUE HAIR
1. Allowing to dry after each coat, paint ornament white.
2. Use blue spray paint to paint a small amount of hair; allow to dry. Arrange hair on top of ornament; pull ornament hanger through hair. Glue hair in place.

3. Spray paint hat yellow or orange; allow to dry. For flower on hat, either remove stem from daisy and glue daisy to hat brim or insert end of stem through crown of hat and use glue to secure end of stem inside hat. Pull ornament hanger through top of hat; glue hat to top of ornament.
4. Trace patterns shown in blue onto tracing paper; cut out. Use patterns to cut indicated numbers of shapes from crafting foam.
5. For nose, paint wooden plug red. Use black paint pen to paint X's on ornament for eyes, to paint eyebrows on ornament, to paint center of mouth, and to paint 2 "stitches" at top of tie. Allow to dry.
6. Glue nose, cheeks, and mouth to face.
7. For tie, glue dots to tie. Glue top of tie to bottom of ornament. For collar, wrap collar around bottom of ornament and top of tie with ends at front. Use a pin to secure each top corner of collar to tie and ornament.

CLOWN ORNAMENT WITH RED HAIR
1. Allowing to dry after each coat, paint ornament white.
2. Arrange hair on top of ornament; pull ornament hanger through hair. Glue hair in place.
3. Trace patterns shown in red onto tracing paper; cut out. Use patterns to cut indicated numbers of shapes from crafting foam.

4. For nose, paint wooden plug red. Use black paint pen to paint X's on ornament for eyes, to paint eyebrows on ornament, and to paint line on mouth. Allow to dry.
5. Glue nose, cheeks, and mouth to face.
6. For hat, overlap straight edges of foam piece, forming a cone; glue to secure. Glue dots to hat. Pull ornament hanger through top of hat; glue hat to top of ornament. With end of hanger behind bead, glue bead to top of hat.

CLOWN ORNAMENT WITH BLOND HAIR
1. Allowing to dry after each coat, paint ornament white.
2. Arrange hair on top of ornament; pull ornament hanger through hair. Glue hair in place.
3. For hat, follow Step 3 of Clown Ornament with Blue Hair instructions.
4. Trace patterns shown in yellow onto tracing paper; cut out. Use patterns to cut indicated numbers of shapes from crafting foam.
5. For nose, paint wooden plug red. Use black paint pen to paint X's on ornament for eyes and to paint detail lines on bow tie. Allow to dry.
6. Glue nose, cheeks, and mouth to face.
7. Use a pin to pin bow tie to bottom of ornament.

TIE
(cut 1)

HAT
(cut 1)

COLLAR
(cut 1)

MOUTH
(cut 1 from red)

CHEEK
(cut 2 from pink)

MOUTH
(cut 1 from red)

CHEEK
(cut 2 from pink)

DOT
(cut 4)

CHEEK
(cut 2 from pink)

MOUTH
(cut 1 from red)

DOT
(cut 4)

BOW TIE
(cut 1)

TREETOP BANNER (Shown on page 75)

You will need a 7" x 18" piece of unprimed artist's canvas; two 8" lengths of 1/4" dia. wooden dowel; two 16mm wooden beads to fit dowel ends; white gesso; foam brush; yellow, red, and green acrylic paint; small round and medium flat paintbrushes; white paint pen with fine point; tracing paper; graphite transfer paper; hot glue gun; and glue sticks.

1. Use foam brush to apply gesso to 1 side of canvas; allow to dry. Repeat to apply gesso to remaining side of canvas.

2. Matching dotted lines and aligning arrows, trace right and left sides of banner pattern, this page and page 79, onto tracing paper. Use transfer paper to transfer banner design to canvas; cut banner from canvas.

3. (**Note:** Allow to dry after each paint color.) Paint banner background red, letters green, and borders yellow. Use white paint pen to outline letters.

4. Glue 1 bead to 1 end (top) of each dowel. Paint dowels and beads green; allow to dry.

5. Wrap 3/4" at 1 end of banner around top of 1 dowel just below bead; glue to secure. Repeat for remaining end of banner.

HIGH-FLYING FLAG ORNAMENTS

(Shown on page 74)

For each ornament, you will need a 6" x 8" piece of unprimed artist's canvas; one 5¹/₂" length and one 8¹/₂" length of ¹/₄" dia. wooden dowel; two 16mm wooden beads to fit dowel ends; white gesso; foam brush; yellow, orange, red, green, blue, and purple acrylic paint; small round and medium flat paintbrushes; tracing paper; graphite transfer paper; hot glue gun; and glue sticks.

1. Use foam brush to apply gesso to 1 side of canvas; allow to dry. Repeat to apply gesso to remaining side of canvas.
2. Trace flag pattern onto tracing paper. Use transfer paper to transfer 2 flags to canvas (if desired, turn pattern over to transfer flags in reverse); cut flags from canvas.
3. (**Note:** Allow to dry after each paint color.) Paint backgrounds, dots, and borders on flags as desired.
4. Glue 1 bead to 1 end (top) of each dowel. Paint dowels and beads as desired to coordinate with flags.
5. For creases in each flag, fold straight end of flag approx. 2¹/₄" to right side and pointed end of flag approx. 2¹/₄" to wrong side and finger press folds; unfold.
6. Wrap ³/₄" at straight end of each flag around top of 1 dowel just below bead; glue to secure.
7. Glue dowel of short flag to front of dowel of tall flag.

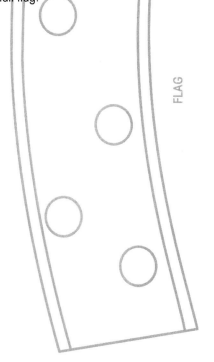

FLAG

PINES AND PLAIDS

Echoing the rustic charm of a North Woods Christmas, dried naturals and homey plaid fabrics create a cozy setting for the holiday season. You'll enjoy the warmth and rugged splendor our collection brings! In keeping with the spirit of the great outdoors, we dressed Santa up as a jolly lumberjack with a tiny evergreen tucked under his arm. Quilt-block and tree-shaped ornaments, baskets of pinecones, and other heartwarming trimmings complete the ensemble's woodsy look. Nestled in nooks and crannies, the handcrafted accents will convey a down-home feeling as inviting as a holiday greeting, a crackling fire, and the refreshing scent of evergreens. Instructions begin on page 86.

A natural beauty, our **Pinecone Wreath** (*page 90*) is a welcoming sight, especially when accented with pretty torn-fabric bows. It will add outdoor charm wherever it's hung!

For a long winter's nap, wrap yourself in cozy comfort with this enchanting **Christmas Tree Throw** *(page 89)* and snuggle up with the coordinating woodsy **Santa Pillow** *(page 86)*. *(Opposite)* Wooden star cutouts are sprinkled among the branches of the **Pines and Plaids Tree** *(page 86)* to "light" Santa's pathway while he's searching for the perfect Christmas evergreen. Toting a fresh-cut sapling, each of our cute **Santa Ornaments** *(page 87)* is dressed in logger apparel. As the jolly old gent travels home, he'll find quaint little baskets of pinecones and larger individual pinecones nestled among the tree's boughs, which are draped in wooden bead garlands. The **Christmas Tree Ornaments** *(page 86)* and **Patchwork Ornaments** *(page 87)* add country appeal. Alternating blocks of pine tree appliqués and plaid fabrics make the **Nine-Patch Tree Skirt** *(page 88)* the ideal finishing touch.

Charming accents for the mantel, these **Patchwork Stockings** *(page 90)* are made using cheery plaid fabrics in Christmasy colors. Each is embellished with one of our woodsy Yuletide ornaments. *(Opposite)* A purchased button-front shirt is crafted into this comfy country **Patchwork Dress** *(page 89)*. Plaid fabrics are sewn to the collar and cuffs and trees are machine appliquéd to the skirt. An easy-to-make dress clip allows you to adjust the fit by adding a gather at the back of the outfit. We made the eye-catching **Nine-Patch Table Topper** *(page 88)* using the tree skirt pattern.

PINES AND PLAIDS TREE
(Shown on page 81)

On this rustic 6½-foot-tall tree, our merry Santa Ornaments (page 87) wander among the pines to find the perfect tree for a North Pole hideaway.

Bright red and natural wood bead garlands, large pinecones, and baskets filled with small pinecones set the scene on this tree. Additional greenery is tucked among the tree's boughs, and the branch tips are brightened with wooden star ornaments. The Christmas Tree Ornaments (this page) give Santa a choice of shapes from which to choose, and both the Patchwork Ornaments (page 87) and the quilted Nine-Patch Tree Skirt (page 88) surround the tree in warm plaid comfort.

CHRISTMAS TREE ORNAMENTS
(Shown on page 82)

For each ornament, you will need two 5" x 6" pieces each of fabric and cotton batting for tree, a 6" fabric square for bag, thread to match fabrics, paper-backed fusible web, polyester fiberfill, an approx. ¼" dia. x 6" long twig for trunk, a 1" dia. plastic foam ball, 12" of cotton string, a 1"w wooden star cutout, 8" of florist wire for hanger, drawing compass, tracing paper, removable fabric marking pen, hot glue gun, and glue sticks.

1. Use desired tree pattern, page 88, and follow **Tracing Patterns**, page 158. For pattern for bag, use compass to draw a 5½" dia. circle on tracing paper; cut out.
2. Follow manufacturer's instructions to fuse web to wrong sides of fabric pieces for tree. Fuse fabric pieces to batting pieces. Matching wrong sides, pin fabric pieces together. Use fabric marking pen to draw around tree pattern on 1 fabric piece. Stitching through all layers and leaving a ½" opening at center bottom of tree for trunk, sew approx. ¼" inside drawn lines of tree. Cut out tree along drawn lines.
3. Use circle pattern to cut a circle from fabric for bag. Baste ⅜" from edges.
4. Insert 1 end of twig into opening at bottom of tree and remaining end ½" into foam ball; glue to secure. Wrap ball with fiberfill. Center ball on wrong side of fabric circle. Pull basting thread, gathering circle around ball; knot thread and trim ends. Tie string into a bow around gathers; trim ends. Glue star cutout to top of tree.
5. For hanger, glue center of wire to center back of tree.

SANTA PILLOW (Shown on page 83)

For an approx. 16" square pillow, you will need a 13" fabric square for pillow front; a 16½" fabric square for pillow back; fabrics for pieced borders (we used 8 different fabrics); fabrics for appliqués; 1⅞ yds of ¼" dia. cotton cord and a 2" x 1⅞ yd bias fabric strip for welting; paper-backed fusible web; tear-away stabilizer; thread to match fabrics; clear nylon thread for appliqué; two ¼" dia. buttons; polyester fiberfill; artificial red berry for nose; cosmetic blush; white wool doll hair; tracing paper; drawing compass; black permanent felt-tip pen with fine point; pinking shears; rotary cutter, cutting mat, and ruler (optional); hot glue gun; and glue sticks.

1. (**Note:** Unless otherwise noted, use a ¼" seam allowance for sewing steps. We recommend using a rotary cutter for cutting strips.) For pieced borders on pillow front, cut nine 2½" x 10" strips from fabrics. Matching right sides, sew strips together along long edges to form pieced panel. Press seam allowances to 1 side. Cut four 2¼"w strips from pieced panel (**Fig. 1**).

Fig. 1

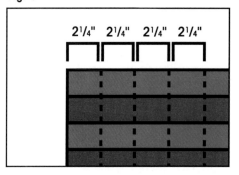

2. With right sides facing, center 1 pieced strip along top edge of pillow front fabric piece. Stitching along top edge of fabric piece, sew strip to fabric piece. Trim ends of strip even with edges of fabric piece. Press strip to right side and press seam allowance toward strip. Repeat to sew remaining strips to bottom edge, then side edges of pillow front.
3. Follow manufacturer's instructions to fuse web to wrong sides of fabrics for appliqués.
4. Trace all patterns except saw handle and saw blade, this page and page 87, separately onto tracing paper. For face pattern, use compass to draw a 2" dia. circle on tracing paper. Cut out patterns. For large tree patterns, use tree trunk pattern and desired tree pattern, page 88, and follow **Tracing Patterns**, page 158.

5. Use patterns to cut 1 face, 1 large tree, 1 large tree trunk and indicated numbers of remaining shapes from fabrics. Use pinking shears to cut 1 approx. ½" square and 1 approx. ⅝" square from fabrics for patches.
6. Remove paper backing from appliqués, arrange on pillow front, and fuse in place.
7. Cut a piece of stabilizer slightly larger than appliqué design. Baste stabilizer to wrong side of pillow front under design. Using nylon thread and a medium width zigzag stitch with a short stitch length, stitch over raw edges of all appliqués except patches. Remove stabilizer.
8. Sew buttons to suspenders.
9. For face, follow Step 7 of Santa Ornaments instructions, page 87.
10. For welting, press 1 end of bias strip ½" to wrong side. Center cord on wrong side of bias strip. Matching long edges, fold strip over cord. Using zipper foot, baste along length of strip close to cord; trim seam allowance to ½". Beginning at center bottom of pillow front and matching raw edges, pin welting to right side of pillow front, clipping seam allowance at corners. Overlap ends of welting 1" and trim excess. Remove basting from 1" of finished end of welting and trim ends of cord to fit. Overlap pressed end of fabric over unfinished end of welting. Baste ends in place.
11. Place pillow front and back right sides together. Stitching as close as possible to welting and leaving an opening for turning, use zipper foot to sew front and back together. Clip corners, turn right side out, and press. Stuff with fiberfill. Sew final closure by hand.

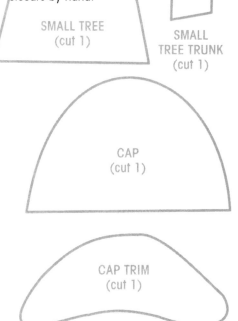

SMALL TREE
(cut 1)

SMALL TREE TRUNK
(cut 1)

CAP
(cut 1)

CAP TRIM
(cut 1)

SANTA ORNAMENTS (Shown on page 82)

For each ornament, you will need fabrics for Santa (we used felt for mittens and muslin for face), 5" of 3"w ribbing for cap, two 8" x 10" pieces and one 4" square of cotton batting, paper-backed fusible web, thread to match fabrics, a 1/2" white pom-pom, artificial red berry for nose, cosmetic blush, white wool doll hair, white poster board, a sprig of pine, 8" of florist wire, Design Master® glossy wood tone spray (available at craft stores), silver spray paint, black permanent felt-tip pen with fine point, tracing paper, drawing compass, pinking shears, hot glue gun, and glue sticks.

1. Follow manufacturer's instructions to fuse web to wrong sides of all fabrics except fabric for face.
2. Trace patterns separately onto tracing paper; cut out.
3. Use patterns to cut saw handle and blade from poster board. Cut indicated numbers of remaining shapes from fabrics. Cut an 8" x 10" fabric piece for ornament back. Use pinking shears to trim bottom edge of saw blade and to cut 3 approx. 1/2" fabric squares for patches. Remove paper backing from all fabric pieces.
4. For Santa front, arrange shirt and pants at center of one 8" x 10" batting piece; fuse in place. For Santa back, fuse ornament back fabric piece to remaining 8" x 10" batting piece. Pin front and back wrong sides together. Referring to grey lines on patterns and stitching through all layers, stitch approx. 1/8" inside edges of shirt and pants. Cut out Santa along outer edges of shirt and pants. Cut along sides of sleeves next to pants to separate sleeves from pants.
5. Arrange suspenders on Santa; fuse in place. For mittens, place 1 mitten shape on

front and matching mitten shape on back of Santa at bottom of each sleeve; fuse in place. Repeat to fuse boots to bottoms of pants, overlapping boots approx. 1" over bottoms of pant legs.
6. For head, use compass to draw a 2 1/8" dia. circle on poster board and batting square and a 3" dia. circle on fabric for face. Cut out circles. Center batting circle, then poster board circle on wrong side of fabric circle. Glue edges of fabric circle to back of poster board circle. Glue head to top of shirt.
7. Glue berry to center of face for nose. Use fingertip to apply a small amount of blush to face for cheeks. For eyes, use black pen to draw 2 dots approx. 1/4" above nose; draw an "X" through each dot. For beard, cut several 2 1/4" lengths from doll hair; glue 1 end of each length to face below nose.
8. For cap, match short edges and fold ribbing in half. Using a 1/4" seam allowance, sew short edges together to form a tube. Baste 1/4" from 1 end (top) of tube. Pull basting thread, drawing up gathers tightly; knot thread and trim ends. Turn cap right side out. Glue pom-pom to top of cap. Fold bottom of cap 1/2" to right side. Place cap on head; glue to secure.
9. Arrange patches on Santa as desired; fuse in place.
10. To complete saw, lightly spray saw handle with wood tone spray and spray paint saw blade silver; allow to dry. Referring to grey area on pattern, use black pen to draw "opening" in handle. Glue handle to blade.
11. Glue saw to Santa under 1 arm. Wrap free arm around sprig of pine; glue to secure.
12. For hanger, glue center of wire to center back of Santa.

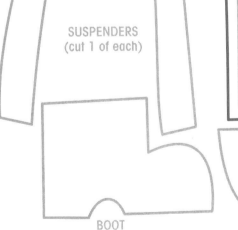

SUSPENDERS
(cut 1 of each)

BOOT
(for ornament, cut 4, 2 in reverse;
for pillow, cut 2, 1 in reverse)

RIGHT MITTEN

LEFT MITTEN

(for ornament,
cut 2 of each, 1 each in reverse;
for pillow, cut 1 of each)

PANTS
(cut 1)

SHIRT
(cut 1)

SAW HANDLE
(cut 1)

SAW BLADE
(cut 1)

PATCHWORK ORNAMENTS
(Shown on page 82)

For each ornament, you will need 3 fabrics for patchwork design, a 4" square of cotton batting, paper-backed fusible web, embroidery floss, a 5/8" dia. wooden button, 9" of jute twine, pinking shears, hot glue gun, and glue sticks.

1. Follow manufacturer's instructions to fuse web to wrong sides of fabrics. Cut a 3 1/2" square from 1 fabric, a 2" square from second fabric, and two 1" squares from remaining fabric.
2. Arrange fabric squares at center of batting square; fuse in place. Use pinking shears to trim batting to approx. 1/8" from edges of 3 1/2" fabric square.
3. Using 4 strands of floss, work a long Running Stitch, page 158, approx. 1/8" inside edges of 3 1/2" fabric square.
4. Glue button to 1 corner (top) of ornament.
5. For hanger, fold twine in half to form a loop; glue ends to top center back of ornament.

NINE-PATCH TABLE TOPPER AND TREE SKIRT (Shown on pages 82 and 84)

For an approx. 50$\frac{1}{2}$" square table topper or tree skirt, you will need the following 44/45"w fabrics: $\frac{7}{8}$ yd for tree blocks, $\frac{3}{4}$ yd total for tree appliqués, $\frac{3}{4}$ yd total of 1 color and $\frac{3}{4}$ yd total of a second color for nine-patch blocks (we used 6 different greens for color 1 and 3 different reds for color 2), $\frac{1}{4}$ yd for inner border, and 1$\frac{1}{2}$ yds for outer border and binding; a 12" fabric square for tree trunk appliqués; one 54" square each of fabric for backing (pieced as necessary) and polyester bonded batting; paper-backed fusible web; tear-away stabilizer; sewing and quilting thread to match fabrics; clear nylon thread for appliqué; rotary cutter and cutting mat (optional); silver pencil; ruler; quilting hoop; tracing paper; and a drawing compass (for tree skirt only).

Note: Before beginning project, wash, dry, and press all fabrics. We recommend using a rotary cutter for cutting squares and strips. For sewing steps, match right sides and raw edges and use a $\frac{1}{4}$" seam allowance unless otherwise noted. Press seam allowances toward darker fabric when possible.

TABLE TOPPER

1. For tree blocks cut twenty-four 6$\frac{1}{2}$" squares from tree block fabric.
2. For tree and tree trunk appliqués, follow manufacturer's instructions to fuse web to wrong sides of fabrics. Use patterns and follow **Tracing Patterns**, page 158. Use patterns to cut 8 of each tree shape and 24 tree trunks from fabrics. Remove paper backing. Overlapping trees over trunks, center and fuse 1 trunk and 1 tree to each tree block.
3. For each tree appliqué, cut a piece of stabilizer slightly larger than design. Baste stabilizer to wrong side of fabric under design. Using nylon thread and a medium width zigzag stitch with a short stitch length, stitch over raw edges of tree and trunk appliqués. Remove stabilizer.
4. For nine-patch blocks, cut fifteen 2$\frac{1}{2}$" x 24" strips from "color 1" fabrics and twelve 2$\frac{1}{2}$" x 24" strips from "color 2" fabrics. Alternating colors, sew strips together along long edges in sets of 3 to form 6 "color 1-color 2-color 1" pieced panels and 3 "color 2-color 1-color 2" pieced panels. Cut 2$\frac{1}{2}$"w strips from each panel (**Fig. 1**). For each block, sew 3 pieced strips together (**Fig. 2**); repeat for a total of 25 blocks (you will have 6 extra strips).

Fig. 1

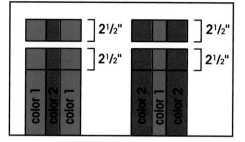

Fig 2

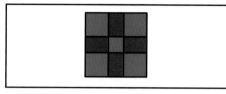

5. (**Note:** Refer to **Diagram** to assemble table topper.) For each row, sew 7 blocks together, alternating tree and nine-patch blocks. Sew rows together.
6. For inner border, cut two 1$\frac{1}{2}$" x 42$\frac{1}{2}$" and two 1$\frac{1}{2}$" x 44$\frac{1}{2}$" fabric strips. Sew shorter strips along side edges of topper and longer strips along top and bottom edges of topper. For outer border, repeat, using two 3$\frac{1}{2}$" x 44$\frac{1}{2}$" and two 3$\frac{1}{2}$" x 50$\frac{1}{2}$" fabric strips.
7. Referring to **Diagram**, use silver pencil and ruler to mark 2$\frac{1}{2}$"w zigzag quilting design on outer border (points of zigzag design are 4" apart).
8. Place backing fabric wrong side up. Place batting on backing fabric. Center pieced top right side up on batting. Placing pins approx. 4" apart, pin layers together. Basting from center outward, baste layers together from corner to corner; with basting lines 3" to 4" apart and outer basting lines approx. $\frac{1}{4}$" from edges of pieced top, baste from top to bottom and from side to side.
9. (**Note:** Secure table topper in hoop, making sure top and backing are smooth.) Working from center outward, follow **Quilting**, page 159, to stitch approx. $\frac{1}{8}$" outside appliqué designs, "in the ditch" (close to seamlines) on nine-patch blocks and inner border, and along marked lines on outer border.
10. Trim batting and backing even with edges of topper. Remove basting threads.
11. For binding, cut a 2$\frac{1}{4}$" x 5$\frac{3}{4}$ yd bias fabric strip (pieced as necessary). Press 1 end of strip $\frac{1}{2}$" to wrong side. Matching wrong sides, press strip in half lengthwise; unfold. Press long raw edges to center; refold.

12. To bind edges of table topper, unfold 1 long edge of binding. Beginning with pressed end of binding at least 3" from a corner and matching right side of binding to right side of topper, pin unfolded edge of binding along 1 edge of topper. Using pressing line closest to raw edge as a guide, sew binding to topper. Mitering binding at corners, continue pinning and sewing binding around topper until ends of binding overlap $\frac{1}{2}$"; trim excess binding. Fold binding over raw edges to back of topper; hand stitch in place.

TREE SKIRT

1. Follow Table Topper instructions.
2. For opening at back of tree skirt, use a pencil and ruler to mark a line from center of skirt to center of top edge. Use compass to draw a $\frac{3}{4}$" dia. circle at center of skirt. Cut along marked line and cut out circle. Make $\frac{3}{8}$" clips approx. $\frac{1}{2}$" apart into raw edge of circle.
3. For binding for skirt opening, follow Step 11 of Table Topper instructions, cutting a 2$\frac{1}{4}$" x 1$\frac{3}{4}$ yd bias fabric strip.
4. To bind edges of skirt opening, unfold 1 long edge of binding. Beginning with pressed end of binding at top of 1 opening edge and matching right side of binding to right side of skirt, pin unfolded edge of binding along opening edge of skirt. Using pressing line closest to raw edge as a guide, sew binding to skirt. Mitering binding at corners, continue pinning and sewing binding along opening in skirt. At top of remaining opening edge, trim binding to $\frac{1}{2}$" beyond skirt, press end of binding $\frac{1}{2}$" to wrong side, and sew remainder of binding to edge. Fold binding over raw edges to back of skirt; hand stitch in place.

DIAGRAM

TREE
TRUNK

CHRISTMAS TREE THROW (Shown on page 83)

You will need either an approx. 40" x 62" pre-laundered wool fabric piece and thread to match or an approx. 40" x 62" purchased wool afghan; ¼ yd of 44/45"w fabric for appliqué background; ¼ yd total of 44/45"w fabrics for pieced borders (we used 7 different fabrics); assorted fabrics for tree appliqués; a 5" fabric square for tree trunk appliqués; paper-backed fusible web; tear-away stabilizer; thread to match fabrics; clear nylon thread for appliqué; wool yarn to coordinate with afghan; tapestry needle; rotary cutter, cutting mat, and ruler (optional); and tracing paper.

1. (**Note:** If purchased afghan is used, begin with Step 2.) To bind edges of wool fabric piece, use matching thread and a wide zigzag stitch with a short stitch length to stitch over edges.

2. Wash, dry, and press fabrics.

3. For appliqué background, measure width of afghan; add 1". Cut a 6½"w fabric strip the determined length.

4. For pieced borders on background, follow Step 1 of Santa Pillow instructions, page 86, cutting seven 2½" x 14" strips from fabrics and cutting six 2¼"w strips from pieced panel. Matching right sides and ends, sew 3 strips together to make a 42½" long pieced strip; repeat for second pieced strip. Follow Step 2 of Santa Pillow instructions to sew borders to top and bottom of background.

5. Follow Steps 2 and 3 of Table Topper instructions, page 88, to make and apply 6 tree and tree trunk appliqués approx. 3" apart on appliqué background.

6. Fuse web to wrong side of appliquéd panel. Press short edges, then long edges of panel ½" to wrong side. Unfold edges and remove paper backing; refold edges and lightly fuse edges in place. With bottom of panel approx. 4" from 1 short edge (bottom) of afghan, arrange panel on afghan; fuse in place. Stitching very close to edges of panel and along inner edges of pieced borders, use a straight stitch to sew panel to afghan.

7. Using 2 strands of yarn, work Blanket Stitch, page 159, along bottom edge of afghan.

PATCHWORK DRESS (Shown on page 84)

You will need a ladies' long-sleeve shirt (we used a shirt without a collar); assorted fabrics for skirt, appliqués on skirt, collar band, cuffs, and dress clip (we used 8 different fabrics); paper-backed fusible web; tear-away stabilizer; thread to match fabrics; thread for appliqué (we used black); buttons to replace buttons on shirt (optional); two ¾" suspender clips and 6½" of ¾"w elastic for dress clip; fabric marking pencil; ruler; rotary cutter and cutting mat (optional); and tracing paper.

1. Wash, dry, and press shirt and fabrics.

2. Mark desired placement of top of skirt on shirt with a pin. Measure from pin to desired skirt length; record measurement.

3. (**Note:** We recommend using a rotary cutter for cutting shirt and fabric strips.) Button shirt placket. Use fabric marking pencil and ruler to draw a line across shirt ½" below pin. Cut off bottom of shirt along drawn line. Baste bottom 4" of shirt placket closed. Remove buttons from collar band and cuffs.

4. To determine width of pieced fabric panel for skirt, measure around bottom edge of shirt; multiply by 1½. To determine length of panel, subtract 5" from skirt length determined in Step 2.

5. (**Note:** Unless otherwise noted, use a ½" seam allowance for sewing steps.) For pieced panel, cut several 3"w and 7"w fabric strips the length determined in Step 4. Matching right sides and alternating strip widths, sew strips together along long edges. Continue to add strips until pieced panel is approx. same width as width determined in Step 4 (the skirt of our size medium dress is made from 8 narrow and 8 wide strips). Sew side edges of panel together to form a tube. Press seam allowances open.

6. To gather skirt, baste ½" and ¼" from 1 raw edge (top) of skirt. Pull basting threads, gathering skirt to fit bottom edge of shirt; knot threads and trim ends. Adjust gathers evenly. Matching right sides and raw edges, pin and sew gathered edge of skirt to bottom edge of shirt. Press seam allowance toward shirt.

7. For border, measure bottom edge of skirt; add 1". Cut a 10½"w fabric strip the determined length (piecing as necessary). Matching right sides and short edges, fold strip in half. Sew short edges together; press seam allowance open. With seam of border at 1 side, match right sides and raw edges and pin top edge of border to bottom edge of skirt; sew border to skirt. Press seam allowance toward border.

8. Follow Step 2 of Table Topper instructions, page 88, to make and apply desired number of tree and tree trunk appliqués along border with tops of trees approx. ½" from top of border (we used 1 appliqué for every wide strip in our skirt).

9. For each appliqué, cut a piece of stabilizer slightly larger than design; baste to wrong side of border under design. Using a medium width zigzag stitch with a very short stitch length, stitch over raw edges of appliqués. Remove stabilizer.

10. For hem, press bottom edge of skirt 2" to wrong side; press 2" to wrong side again and blindstitch in place.

11. To cover collar band, make a pattern by tracing shape of collar band onto tracing paper; cut out. Fuse web to wrong side of fabric. Use fabric marking pencil to draw around pattern on fabric. Cut out shape ¼" outside drawn lines. Press edges ¼" to wrong side. Remove paper backing.

12. Matching wrong side of fabric piece to right side of collar band, fuse fabric piece to collar band. Stitching close to edges, use a straight stitch to sew fabric piece to collar band. Make a new buttonhole in collar band.

13. To cover cuffs, make a pattern by tracing shape of 1 cuff onto tracing paper; cut out. Cut several 3" x 9" strips from fabrics. Matching right sides, sew strips together along long edges; press seam allowances to 1 side. Continue to add strips until cuff pattern will fit on pieced panel twice, allowing ¼" on all sides of pattern. Fuse web to wrong side of panel. Leaving at least ½" between shapes, draw around pattern twice on panel. Cut out shapes ¼" outside drawn lines. Press edges ¼" to wrong side. Remove paper backing. Repeat Step 12 to sew fabric pieces to cuffs.

14. Replace buttons on dress (with new buttons, if desired).

15. For dress clip, cut a 3" x 9" fabric strip. Matching right sides and long edges, fold strip in half. Sew long edges together to form a tube. Turn right side out; center seam at back of tube and press. Thread elastic through tube. Baste ends of elastic to ends of tube; adjust gathers of fabric evenly. Press ends of tube ¾" to back. With fronts of clips facing same direction as front of tube, thread suspender clips onto ends of tube. Stitching through all layers, sew across tube several times ½" from each pressed end to secure.

PINECONE WREATH (Shown on page 80)

You will need an 18" dia. wire-reinforced floral foam wreath form (available at craft stores and florist shops); assorted pinecones, dried pods, and nuts; ten 2¼" x 20" torn fabric strips for bows; florist wire; wire cutters; hot glue gun; and glue sticks.

1. For hanger, cut a 15" length of wire. Fold wire in half; twist wire 1" from fold to create a loop. With loop at back of wreath form, wrap wire around form and twist tightly. Push ends of wire into form and glue to secure.

2. Place wreath form right side up on a protected surface. Glue pinecones along inside and outside edges of form. Cover remainder of form with pinecones, dried pods, and nuts.

3. Tie fabric strips into bows. Glue bows to wreath.

PATCHWORK STOCKINGS (Shown on page 85)

For each stocking, you will need two 12" x 20" fabric pieces for stocking lining, two 12" x 20" pieces of fusible fleece for stocking lining backing, a 2" x 8" fabric strip for hanger, thread to match fabrics, tracing paper, fabric marking pencil, hot glue gun, and glue sticks.

For each stocking with Santa Ornament, you will **also** need two 12" x 20" fabric pieces for stocking, assorted fabrics for pieced border, a 7" x 11" fabric piece for toe and heel patches, paper-backed fusible web, tear-away stabilizer, clear nylon thread for appliqué, and 1 Santa Ornament (page 87) with hanger omitted.

For each stocking with Tree Ornament, you will **also** need fabrics for stocking and 1 Christmas Tree Ornament (page 86) with a 5" long twig for trunk and with bag and hanger omitted.

For each stocking with Patchwork Ornament, you will **also** need two 12" x 20" fabric pieces for stocking, a 6" x 8½" fabric piece for ornament background, assorted fabrics for pieced borders, a 7" x 11" fabric piece for toe and heel patches, paper-backed fusible web, tear-away stabilizer, clear nylon thread for appliqué, and 1 Patchwork Ornament (page 87) with button glued to center and with hanger omitted.

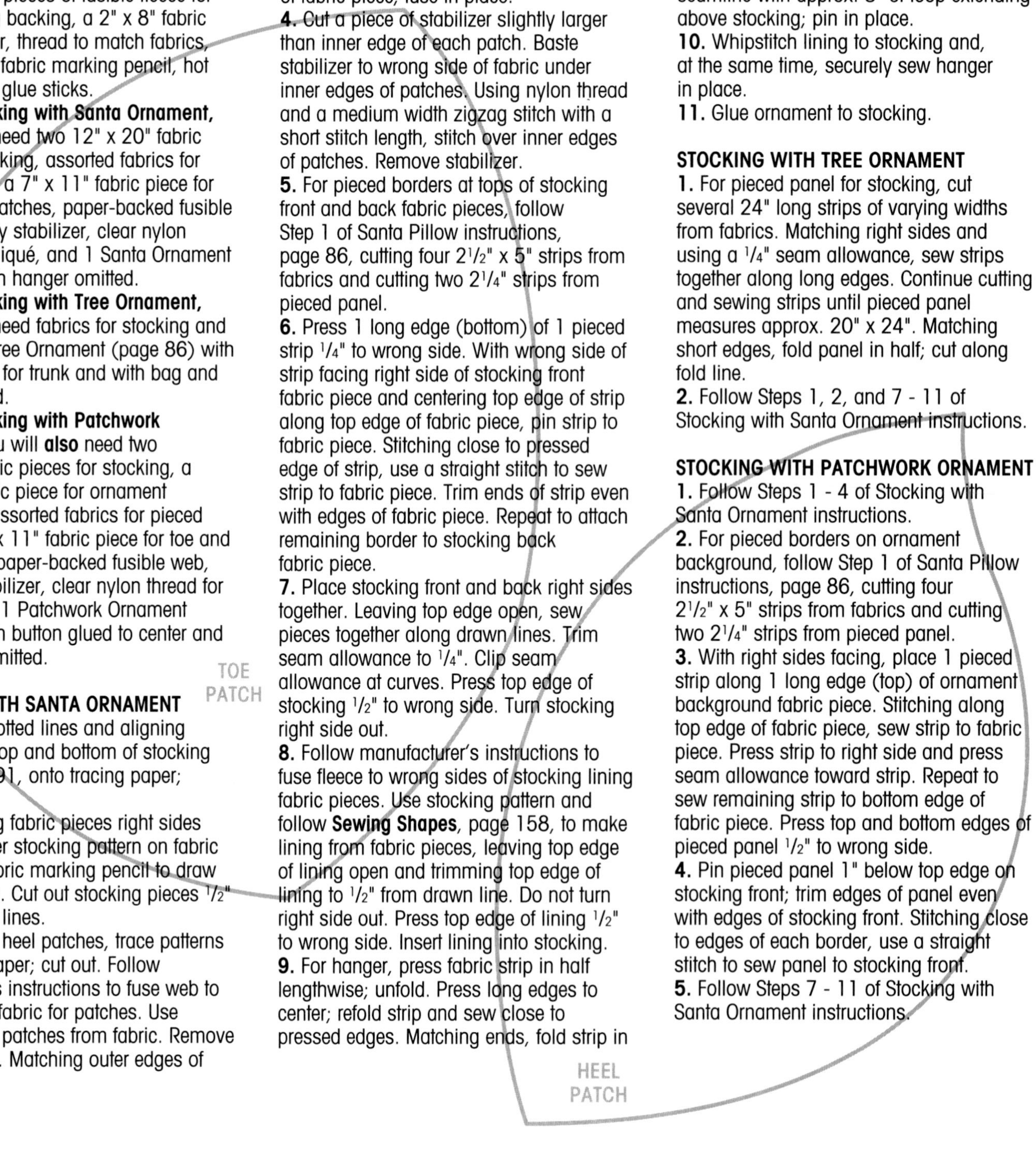

STOCKING WITH SANTA ORNAMENT

1. Matching dotted lines and aligning arrows, trace top and bottom of stocking pattern, page 91, onto tracing paper; cut out.

2. Pin stocking fabric pieces right sides together. Center stocking pattern on fabric pieces; use fabric marking pencil to draw around pattern. Cut out stocking pieces ½" outside drawn lines.

3. For toe and heel patches, trace patterns onto tracing paper; cut out. Follow manufacturer's instructions to fuse web to wrong side of fabric for patches. Use patterns to cut patches from fabric. Remove paper backing. Matching outer edges of patches to raw edges of stocking front fabric piece, arrange patches on right side of fabric piece; fuse in place.

4. Cut a piece of stabilizer slightly larger than inner edge of each patch. Baste stabilizer to wrong side of fabric under inner edges of patches. Using nylon thread and a medium width zigzag stitch with a short stitch length, stitch over inner edges of patches. Remove stabilizer.

5. For pieced borders at tops of stocking front and back fabric pieces, follow Step 1 of Santa Pillow instructions, page 86, cutting four 2½" x 5" strips from fabrics and cutting two 2¼" strips from pieced panel.

6. Press 1 long edge (bottom) of 1 pieced strip ¼" to wrong side. With wrong side of strip facing right side of stocking front fabric piece and centering top edge of strip along top edge of fabric piece, pin strip to fabric piece. Stitching close to pressed edge of strip, use a straight stitch to sew strip to fabric piece. Trim ends of strip even with edges of fabric piece. Repeat to attach remaining border to stocking back fabric piece.

7. Place stocking front and back right sides together. Leaving top edge open, sew pieces together along drawn lines. Trim seam allowance to ¼". Clip seam allowance at curves. Press top edge of stocking ½" to wrong side. Turn stocking right side out.

8. Follow manufacturer's instructions to fuse fleece to wrong sides of stocking lining fabric pieces. Use stocking pattern and follow **Sewing Shapes**, page 158, to make lining from fabric pieces, leaving top edge of lining open and trimming top edge of lining to ½" from drawn line. Do not turn right side out. Press top edge of lining ½" to wrong side. Insert lining into stocking.

9. For hanger, press fabric strip in half lengthwise; unfold. Press long edges to center; refold strip and sew close to pressed edges. Matching ends, fold strip in half to form a loop. Place ends of loop between stocking and lining at heel-side seamline with approx. 3" of loop extending above stocking; pin in place.

10. Whipstitch lining to stocking and, at the same time, securely sew hanger in place.

11. Glue ornament to stocking.

STOCKING WITH TREE ORNAMENT

1. For pieced panel for stocking, cut several 24" long strips of varying widths from fabrics. Matching right sides and using a ¼" seam allowance, sew strips together along long edges. Continue cutting and sewing strips until pieced panel measures approx. 20" x 24". Matching short edges, fold panel in half; cut along fold line.

2. Follow Steps 1, 2, and 7 - 11 of Stocking with Santa Ornament instructions.

STOCKING WITH PATCHWORK ORNAMENT

1. Follow Steps 1 - 4 of Stocking with Santa Ornament instructions.

2. For pieced borders on ornament background, follow Step 1 of Santa Pillow instructions, page 86, cutting four 2½" x 5" strips from fabrics and cutting two 2¼" strips from pieced panel.

3. With right sides facing, place 1 pieced strip along 1 long edge (top) of ornament background fabric piece. Stitching along top edge of fabric piece, sew strip to fabric piece. Press strip to right side and press seam allowance toward strip. Repeat to sew remaining strip to bottom edge of fabric piece. Press top and bottom edges of pieced panel ½" to wrong side.

4. Pin pieced panel 1" below top edge on stocking front; trim edges of panel even with edges of stocking front. Stitching close to edges of each border, use a straight stitch to sew panel to stocking front.

5. Follow Steps 7 - 11 of Stocking with Santa Ornament instructions.

TOE
PATCH

HEEL
PATCH

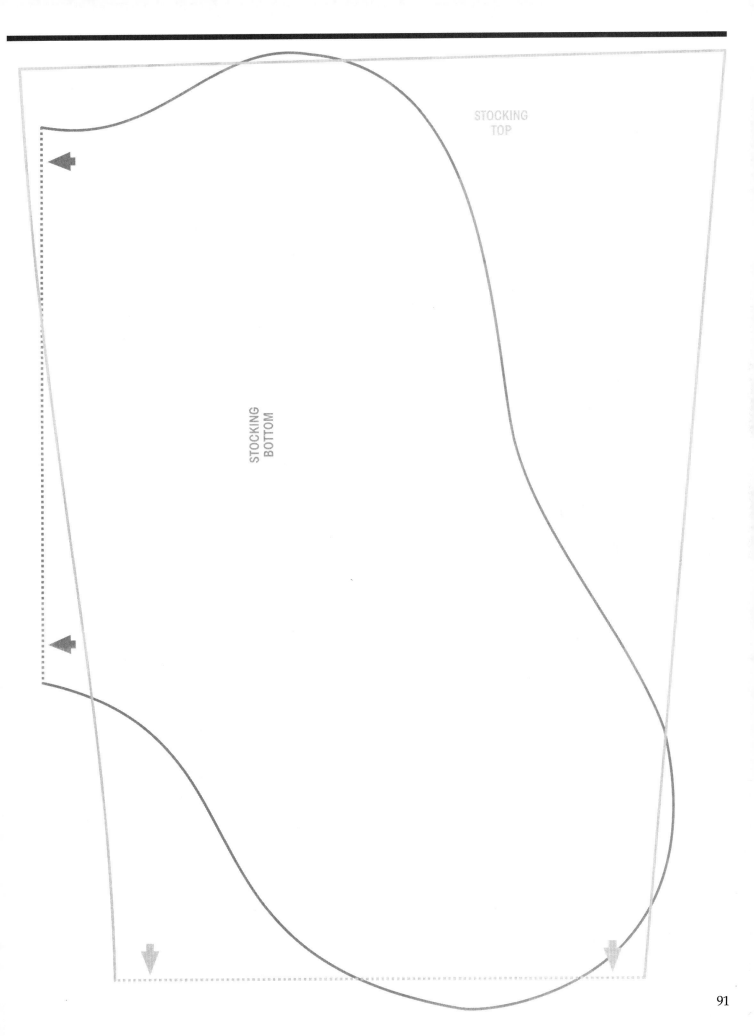

STOCKING
TOP

STOCKING
BOTTOM

THE SHARING
OF CHRISTMAS

Knowing the pleasure that a homemade gift can bring makes giving just as joyful as receiving. And the presents we create ourselves are often the most memorable ones. Our collection includes a variety of embellished wearables to make this Yuletide even merrier! From casual to dressy, you'll find festive trims and wintry designs to please the entire family. Let your loved ones know how dear they are to your heart with these handcrafted keepsakes for Christmas.

*S*prinkled with holiday magic, our **Hearts and Holly Sweater** (page 102) *is easy to make. Fused-on appliqués and embroidered accents add whimsical fun to the plain sweater.*

*B*rilliant sponge-painted blooms grace this Christmasy **Poinsettia Shirt** (page 104). *Fine detailing and the botanical name are added to the sweatshirt with a permanent pen.*

*A*n elegant **Christmas Vest** (page 107) *will add festive flair to a friend's holiday wardrobe. You'd never guess that this merry wear is fashioned from a men's suit vest! We simply used fusible web to cover it with colorful strip-pieced fabrics.*

*B*aby will stay toasty-warm in this adorable **Beary Elf Sweatshirt** (page 107). Cross stitched on a plain white sweatshirt, an elfin teddy is busily working on toys for good girls and boys.

*F*or your favorite little sweetheart, you'll find this **Holly Jumper** (page 110) a delight! The dress is embellished with machine-appliquéd holly leaves and peppermint "candies" crafted from covered buttons.

*L*ittle girls will love romping in our playful **Reindeer Jumper** (page 111). Corralled behind a red-ribbon fence, each reindeer wears a festive bow.

*I*t's so quick and easy to add Yuletide pizzazz to men's neckwear! To craft our **Festive Ties** (page 102), just fuse on a Santa or snowman cutout and embellish with simple stitches.

*R*oomy enough to carry holiday bundles, a purchased tote is bordered with festive fabric strips and wintry appliqués. The **Snowman Tote Bag** (page 111) is a handy gift for anyone who's on the go!

*O*ur cozy **Angel Thermal Shirt** (page 108) and **Santa Thermal Shirt** (page 110) are endearingly dressed up with simple appliqués. Accented with decorative blanket stitching and plaid fabric trims, the shirts offer lots of country appeal.

*D*imensional paints and fabric cutouts provide the cozy setting for our **Mom's Christmas Sweatshirt** (page 109). *Tiny poster-board stockings featuring the children's names are hung by the mantel using jewelry pin backs. A dove finds a holiday home on our* **Sweet Birdhouse Sweatshirt** *(page 104), which is hand painted.* (Opposite) *A white shirt is easily transformed into this snuggly* **Mr. Snowman Sweatshirt** *(page 106) using fusible cutouts and paints. This frosty friend is sure to spread cheer wherever he's worn.*

FESTIVE TIES (Shown on page 99)

For each tie, you will need a tie (we used flannel ties), thread to match tie, seam ripper, tracing paper, and thick craft glue.

For Santa tie, you will **also** need the following colors of felt for appliqués: white for beard, light tan for face, red for coat and hat, green for tree, brown for tree trunk, and black for mittens and boots; and desired embroidery floss to match felt.

For snowman tie, you will **also** need cotton batting for snowman, flannel for scarf, black felt for hat, and black embroidery floss.

SANTA TIE

1. Trace Santa appliqué patterns (shown in red) onto tracing paper; cut out. Use patterns to cut 1 of each shape from felt.
2. Use small dots of glue to glue appliqués to tie, overlapping appliqués as necessary; allow to dry.
3. Use seam ripper to open back seam of tie behind Santa.
4. Using 3 strands of floss to match appliqués, work Blanket Stitch, page 159, as desired along edges of appliqués.
5. Restitch back seam of tie.

SNOWMAN TIE

1. Using snowman appliqué patterns (shown in blue), follow Steps 1 - 3 of Santa Tie instructions, cutting appliqués from batting, flannel, and felt (place arrow on scarf pattern on grain of fabric).
2. (**Note:** Use 3 strands of floss for Step 2.) Work 1 Cross Stitch, page 158, for each eye. Work Running Stitch, page 158, for mouth. Work Blanket Stitch, page 159, along edges of appliqués, stopping approx. $1/8$" from ends of scarf. Fray ends of scarf.
3. Restitch back seam of tie.

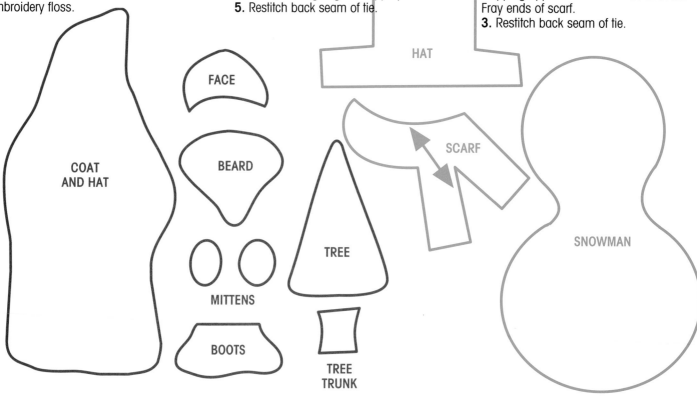

HEARTS AND HOLLY SWEATER (Shown on page 95)

You will need a long-sleeve cotton sweater; dark yellow, red, and rust fabrics for appliqués; paper-backed fusible web; Sulky® Heat-Away™ Brush-Off Stabilizer (available at fabric stores); fusible knit interfacing; sewing thread; red, yellow green, dark yellow green, and dark green tapestry yarn; brown and dark brown embroidery floss and floss to match appliqué fabrics; crewel needle; tracing paper; white vinegar; and a permanent felt-tip pen with fine point.

1. Wash, dry, and press sweater and fabrics. Unwrap yarn and floss skeins and soak yarn and floss for a few minutes in a mixture of 1 cup water and 1 tablespoon vinegar; allow to dry.

2. Matching dotted lines and aligning arrows, use permanent pen to trace large hearts and holly design onto a piece of stabilizer, adding heart portion of design to each side. Determine desired placement of design on sweater. Cut a piece of interfacing slightly larger than design and pin to wrong side of sweater under design area. Turn sweater wrong side out and follow manufacturer's instructions to fuse interfacing to sweater. Turn sweater right side out, position pattern on sweater, and baste pattern to sweater. Repeat for small heart and holly design on each sleeve.
3. (**Note:** Refer to **Embroidery** and **Cross Stitch** instructions, page 158, for Steps 3 and 6.) Follow stitch key, page 103, and use 1 strand of yarn or 3 strands of floss to work each design over stabilizer. Follow

manufacturer's instructions to remove stabilizer.
4. For appliqués, trace patterns shown in grey onto tracing paper; cut out. Follow manufacturer's instructions to fuse web to wrong sides of fabrics for appliqués. Use patterns to cut 2 hearts, 2 stars, and 1 gingerbread man for large design and 1 heart for each sleeve design from fabrics; remove paper backing.
5. Arrange appliqués on sweater; fuse in place.
6. Using 2 strands of floss to match appliqué, work Blanket Stitch along edges of appliqués. For gingerbread man, use dark brown floss to work French Knots for eyes and Cross Stitches for buttons.
7. To launder, turn sweater wrong side out and hand wash; dry flat.

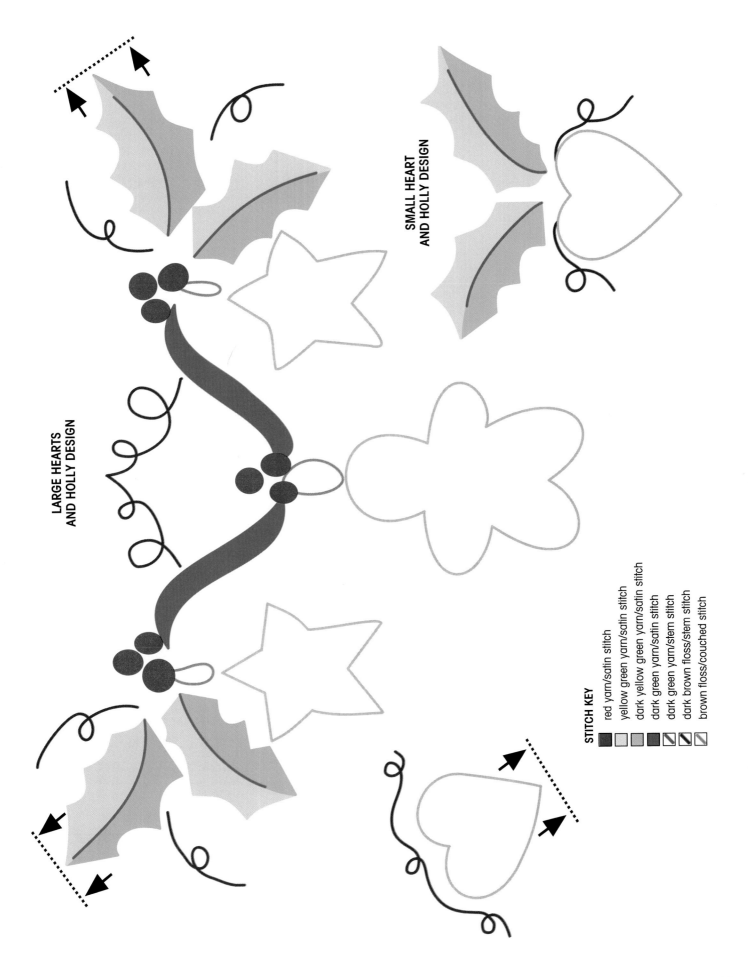

SMALL HEART
AND HOLLY DESIGN

LARGE HEARTS
AND HOLLY DESIGN

STITCH KEY

red yarn/satin stitch
yellow green yarn/satin stitch
dark yellow green yarn/satin stitch
dark green yarn/satin stitch
dark green yarn/stem stitch
dark brown floss/stem stitch
brown floss/couched stitch

POINSETTIA SHIRT (Shown on page 95)

You will need a sweatshirt; red, dark red, green, and dark green fabric paint; metallic gold dimensional fabric paint in squeeze bottle; Miracle Sponges™ (dry, compressed sponges available at craft stores); foam brushes; dark brown permanent felt-tip pen with fine point; hot-iron transfer pen; clear self-adhesive plastic (Con-tact® paper); tracing paper; and a T-shirt form or cardboard covered with waxed paper.

1. Wash and dry shirt according to paint manufacturers' recommendations; press. Insert T-shirt form into shirt.
2. Trace petal and leaf patterns onto tracing paper; cut out. Use permanent pen to draw around patterns on dry sponges; cut out shapes along drawn lines.
3. To sponge-paint poinsettias, lightly dampen large petal sponge shape. Use foam brush to apply red paint to center of sponge shape and dark red paint along edges; do not saturate. Reapplying paint to shape as necessary, stamp 5 large petals on shirt to form each poinsettia, overlapping petals as desired; allow to dry. Repeat to stamp small petals between large petals using small petal sponge.
4. To mask off each poinsettia for painting leaves, cut a piece of self-adhesive plastic approx. 1" larger on all sides than poinsettia. Lay plastic paper-backing side down over poinsettia. Use permanent pen to trace outline of poinsettia onto plastic; cut out shape along drawn lines. Remove paper backing. Matching edges, place plastic over poinsettia; press in place.
5. To sponge-paint leaves, use green and dark green paint and repeat Step 3 with leaf sponge, overlapping leaf sponge over flowers as desired.

6. Remove plastic from poinsettias. Remove T-shirt form from shirt. If necessary, follow manufacturer's instructions to heat-set paint.
7. Trace "Poinsettia" and "Euphorbia pulcherrima" patterns onto tracing paper. Following manufacturer's instructions, use transfer pen to transfer words to shirt.
8. Use permanent pen to outline petals and leaves, to draw veins on petals and leaves, and to draw over words.
9. Use gold paint to paint dots at center of each poinsettia; allow to dry.
10. To launder, turn shirt wrong side out and follow paint manufacturers' recommendations; hang to dry.

Poinsettia

Euphorbia pulcherrima

SWEET BIRDHOUSE SWEATSHIRT (Shown on page 100)

You will need a sweatshirt; a 1" x 18" torn fabric strip for bow; ivory, yellow, dark yellow, orange, red, green, light olive green, dark olive green, blue, dark blue, tan, and brown fabric paint; paintbrushes; tracing paper; hot-iron transfer pen; graphite transfer paper; black permanent felt-tip pen with fine point; safety pin; and a T-shirt form or cardboard covered with waxed paper.

1. Wash and dry shirt according to paint manufacturer's recommendations; press.
2. Trace patterns, page 105, onto separate pieces of tracing paper.
3. Following manufacturer's instructions, use transfer pen to transfer black lines of birdhouse pattern to sweatshirt. Repeat to transfer bird, moon, and star patterns to shirt as desired. Matching top of pole pattern to bottom of birdhouse and repeating design as necessary to reach top of waist ribbing, transfer birdhouse pole pattern to shirt.

4. (**Note:** Unless otherwise indicated, allow to dry after each paint color.) Insert T-shirt form into shirt. Paint beak of bird and several stars yellow. Paint moon yellow; while paint is still wet, shade with dark yellow. Paint star on birdhouse and remaining stars dark yellow. Paint birdhouse light olive green. Paint birdhouse perch, birdhouse opening, and roof tan. Paint side of birdhouse opening brown. Paint bird and snow on birdhouse ivory. Paint pole ivory and red.
5. For plaid pattern on birdhouse, reposition pattern over birdhouse and use transfer paper to transfer grey line on pattern to shirt. Use a pencil and ruler to draw horizontal and vertical lines approx. $3/4$" apart on front of birdhouse. Drawing lines parallel to bottom edge of side of birdhouse, draw lines approx. $5/8$" apart on side of birdhouse (lines should meet horizontal lines on front of birdhouse at corner). Drawing lines parallel to side edges of side of birdhouse, draw lines approx. $3/8$" apart on side of birdhouse.

Paint approx. $1/4$"w dark olive green stripes over drawn lines. Paint 1 approx. $1/16$"w light olive green stripe at center of each dark olive green stripe. Paint 1 approx. $1/16$"w dark blue stripe $1/8$" on each side of each dark olive green stripe.
6. For remaining details on birdhouse, reposition pattern over birdhouse and use transfer paper to transfer blue lines of pattern to shirt. Repeat for bird.
7. Paint lights on birdhouse yellow, orange, red, green, and blue.
8. Use black pen to outline all designs on shirt, drawing over all transferred details. Use pen to color in light sockets on birdhouse.
9. Remove T-shirt form from shirt. If necessary, heat-set designs according to paint manufacturer's instructions.
10. Tie fabric strip into a bow. Use safety pin on wrong side of shirt to pin bow to birdhouse pole.
11. To launder, turn shirt wrong side out, remove bow, and follow paint manufacturer's recommendations; hang to dry.

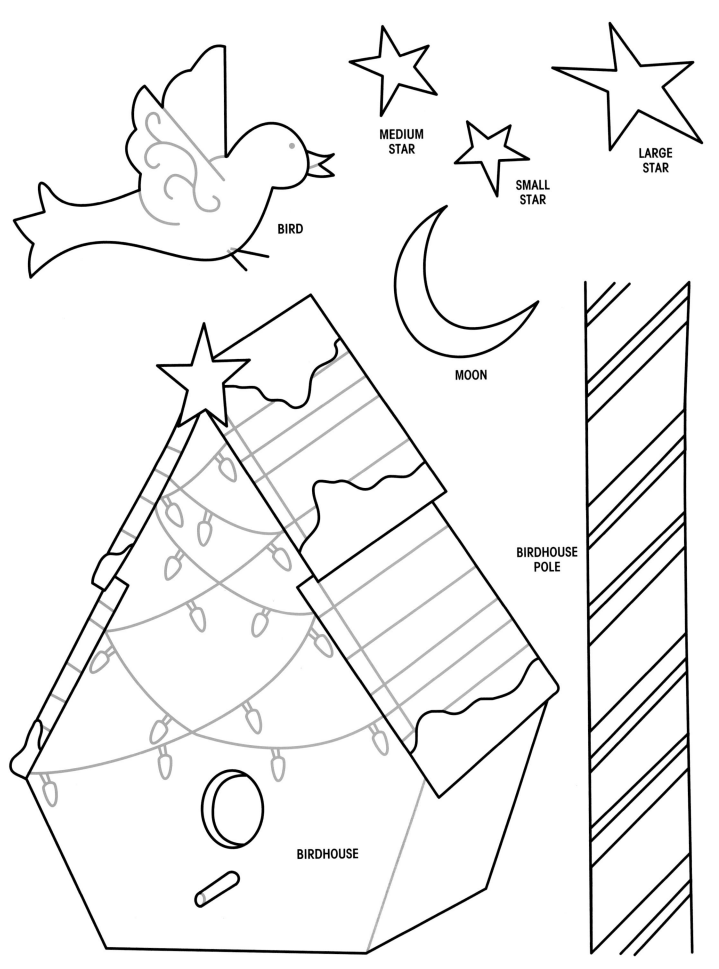

BIRD

MEDIUM STAR

SMALL STAR

LARGE STAR

MOON

BIRDHOUSE POLE

BIRDHOUSE

MR. SNOWMAN SWEATSHIRT (Shown on page 101)

You will need a sweatshirt large enough to accommodate an approx. 18" square design, fabrics for appliqués (we used flannel for our hatband and mitten), paper-backed fusible web, black embroidery floss, orange and black dimensional fabric paint in squeeze bottles, and tracing paper.

1. Wash and dry shirt and fabrics according to paint manufacturer's recommendations; press.
2. For hat and hatband patterns, follow **Tracing Patterns**, page 158. Trace eyebrow, nose, mitten, and pipe patterns onto tracing paper; cut out.
3. Follow manufacturer's instructions to fuse web to wrong sides of appliqué fabrics. Use patterns to cut appliqués from fabrics (we cut our hatband on the bias). Remove paper backing from appliqués. Arrange appliqués on shirt and fuse in place.
4. Use 4 strands of floss and work Blanket Stitch, page 159, along edges of hat and mitten.
5. For patterns for eyes and mouth, trace eye and coal patterns onto tracing paper; cut out.
6. For eyes, use a pencil to lightly draw around eye patterns on shirt. For mouth, draw around coal pattern 6 times on shirt with 1 coal positioned over end of pipe.
7. (**Note:** Allow to dry after each paint color.) Use orange paint to paint over edges of nose and to paint detail lines on nose. Use black paint to paint over edges of eyebrows and pipe and to fill in shapes for eyes and mouth.
8. To launder, turn shirt wrong side out and follow web and paint manufacturers' recommendations; hang to dry.

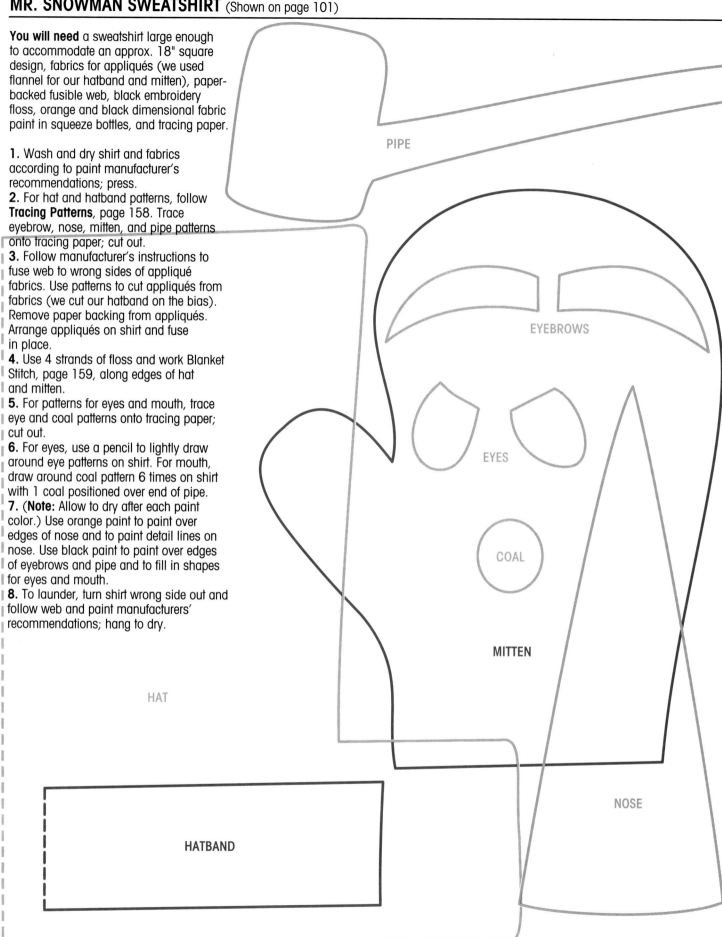

PIPE

EYEBROWS

EYES

COAL

MITTEN

HAT

NOSE

HATBAND

106

BEARY ELF SWEATSHIRT (Shown on page 96)

You will need a child's sweatshirt, one 7" square each of 11 mesh waste canvas and lightweight non-fusible interfacing, sewing thread, embroidery floss (see color key), masking tape, embroidery hoop, tweezers, and a spray bottle filled with water.

1. Wash, dry, and press shirt. Cover edges of canvas with masking tape. Mark center of stitching area on shirt with a pin. Match center of canvas to pin. Pin canvas to shirt. Pin interfacing to wrong side of shirt under canvas. Basting through all layers, baste around edges of canvas, from corner to corner, and from side to side. Center canvas in hoop.

2. (**Note:** Refer to **Cross Stitch** instructions, page 158, for Step 2.) Use a sharp needle to work design on shirt over canvas, stitching from large holes to large holes. Use 3 strands of floss for Cross Stitch and 2 strands for Backstitch and French Knots.

3. Remove basting threads, trim canvas to ³/₄" from design, and dampen canvas. Use tweezers to pull out canvas threads 1 at a time. Trim interfacing close to design.

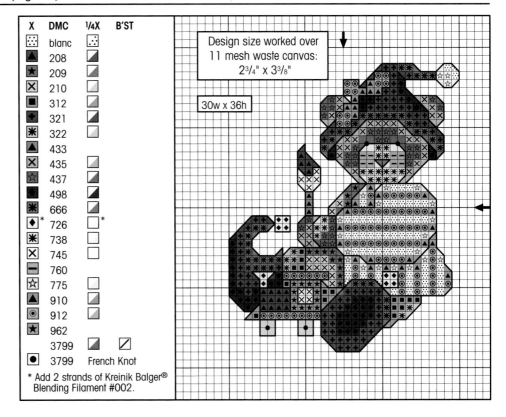

Design size worked over 11 mesh waste canvas: 2³/₄" x 3³/₈"

30w x 36h

X	DMC	1/4X	B'ST
	blanc		
▲	208	◢	
★	209	◢	
✕	210	◢	
■	312	◢	
✚	321	◢	
✳	322	◢	
▲	433		
✕	435	◢	
☆	437	◢	
■	498	◢	
✳	666	◢	
◆ *	726	▢	*
✳	738	▢	
✕	745	▢	
▬	760		
☆	775	◢	
▲	910	◢	
⊙	912	◢	
★	962		
	3799	◢	◿
●	3799	French Knot	

* Add 2 strands of Kreinik Balger® Blending Filament #002.

CHRISTMAS VEST (Shown on page 94)

You will need a men's suit vest (we found ours at a thrift store); approx. 1¹/₂ yds total of assorted fabrics for vest front; dry-cleanable paper-backed fusible web; thread to match fabrics and vest; metallic cord for bow, heavy metallic thread, embroidery floss, assorted trims, ¹/₈"w satin ribbon, and decorative beads (optional); buttons to replace buttons on vest (optional); lightweight cardboard for template; seam ripper; rotary cutter, cutting mat, and ruler (optional); and removable fabric marking pen.

1. Remove buttons from vest. Use seam ripper to take vest apart at shoulder and side seams. Set vest back aside.

2. (**Note:** We recommend using a rotary cutter for cutting strips. For sewing steps, match right sides and raw edges and use a ¹/₄" seam allowance unless otherwise indicated; press seam allowances to 1 side.) For pieced fabric panel for vest front squares, cut several 1"w to 3"w strips from fabrics, cutting from selvage to selvage. Alternating strip widths, sew strips together along long edges. Continue to add strips until pieced panel is approx. 36" wide.

3. For template, cut a 5" square of cardboard. Use template to cut approx. 36 squares from pieced panel (we cut some of our squares on the bias).

4. Turning squares as desired to alternate direction of fabric strips, sew squares together to form a pieced panel that vest front pieces will fit on, allowing at least ¹/₄" on all sides of vest front pieces (**Fig. 1**). Follow manufacturer's instructions to fuse web to wrong side of pieced panel.

Fig. 1

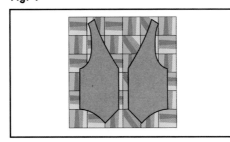

5. Leaving at least ¹/₂" between pieces, place vest front pieces right side down on paper side of pieced panel; draw around pieces. Cutting along drawn lines at shoulder and side and ¹/₄" outside remaining drawn lines, cut out each shape.

6. Clipping as necessary, press all edges except shoulder and side edges of each pieced shape ¹/₄" to wrong side. Unfold edges and remove paper backing. Refold edges and lightly press edges in place.

7. Matching edges, place pieced shapes on original vest front pieces; fuse in place. Topstitch along pressed edges.

8. To reassemble vest, press raw edges of right shoulder of vest back and vest back lining ¹/₂" to inside. Insert raw edges of right vest front shoulder ¹/₂" into pressed opening (**Fig. 2**); pin in place. Topstitch through all layers close to pressed edges of vest back. Repeat for remaining shoulder and each side of vest.

Fig. 2

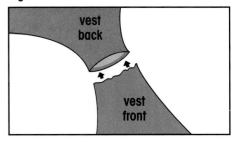

vest back

vest front

9. Use fabric marking pen to mark placement of original buttonholes on vest. Make a new buttonhole at each mark. Sew buttons to vest.

10. (**Note:** Refer to **Embroidery** instructions, page 158, for Step 10.) If desired, tie a length of cord into a bow; knot and fray ends. Arrange bow on vest and tack in place. Use metallic thread, floss, trims, and ribbon to embellish vest as desired. Sew beads to vest as desired.

11. Vest must be dry cleaned.

ANGEL THERMAL SHIRT (Shown on page 98)

You will need a ladies' thermal shirt with round neckline, fabrics for appliqués and trim at neckline, paper-backed fusible web, sewing thread or embroidery floss for appliqué, two 3/4"w star-shaped buttons (we used wooden buttons), thread to match trim fabric and thread to sew on buttons, and tracing paper.

1. Wash, dry, and press shirt and fabrics.
2. Follow manufacturer's instructions to fuse web to wrong sides of fabrics for appliqués.
3. Trace patterns onto tracing paper; cut out. Use patterns to cut indicated numbers of appliqués from fabrics. Remove paper backing and arrange appliqués on shirt, overlapping appliqués as necessary; fuse in place.
4. Either use sewing thread and machine blanket stitch or 3 strands of floss and hand Blanket Stitch, page 159, to stitch along edges of appliqués.
5. For trim at neckline, measure neckline of shirt; add 1". Cut a 1 3/4"w bias fabric strip the determined length (pieced as necessary). Press 1 end of strip 1/2" to wrong side. Press strip in half lengthwise; unfold. Press each long raw edge to center; refold strip. Beginning with unpressed end at 1 shoulder seam, pin strip along edge of neckline. Using a straight stitch, topstitch close to each edge of trim.
6. Sew 1 star button to shirt at top of each tree.

WINGS A (cut 2)

STAR A (cut 1)

WINGS B (cut 1)

STAR B (cut 1)

ROBE A (cut 2)

HEAD (cut 3)

STAR C (cut 2)

ROBE B (cut 1)

SLEEVE (cut 3)

HAND (cut 3)

FEET (cut 3 of each)

TREE A (cut 1)

TREE TRUNK (cut 2)

TREE B (cut 1)

MOM'S CHRISTMAS SWEATSHIRT (Shown on page 100)

You will need a sweatshirt; fabrics for fireplace (we used a mini-check), log, flame (we used metallic knit fabrics), mantel, and brick appliqués; paper-backed fusible web; shiny black and metallic gold dimensional fabric paint in squeeze bottles with very fine tips; orange glitter fabric paint; small round paintbrush; artist's tracing paper; and dressmaker's tracing paper.

For each stocking, you will **also** need heavy green poster board, red construction paper, 6" of ⅛" dia. gold twisted cord, a pin back, black permanent felt-tip pen with fine point, matte clear acrylic spray, hot glue gun, and glue sticks.

1. Wash, dry, and press shirt and non-metallic fabrics according to paint manufacturers' recommendations.

2. Follow manufacturer's instructions to fuse web to wrong sides of appliqué fabrics.

3. For fireplace pattern, use artist's tracing paper and follow **Tracing Patterns**, page 158. Trace remaining appliqué patterns (shown in grey) onto artist's tracing paper. For mantel pattern, draw a 1⅛" x 12¼" rectangle on artist's tracing paper. Cut out patterns.

4. Use patterns to cut 1 mantel and indicated numbers of remaining appliqués from fabrics. Remove paper backing and arrange appliqués on shirt, overlapping mantel approx. ¼" over fireplace and overlapping remaining appliqués as necessary; fuse in place.

5. For bricks on fireplace, cut approx. seventy ½" x 1" fabric pieces. Remove paper backing. Beginning at center of fireplace and working outward, arrange bricks on fireplace, trimming bricks as necessary to fit; fuse in place.

6. (**Note:** Allow to dry after each paint color.) Use black paint to paint over edges of bricks, fireplace, mantel, and logs. Use orange glitter paint and paintbrush to paint additional flames in fireplace.

7. Trace "the stockings were hung…" pattern onto artist's tracing paper. Use dressmaker's tracing paper to transfer words across shirt approx. ½" above mantel. Use gold paint to paint over words.

8. For stockings, trace outline and shaded areas of stocking pattern separately onto artist's tracing paper; cut out.

9. (**Note:** Follow Step 9 for each stocking.) Use patterns to cut stocking from poster board and stocking trim from red construction paper (if desired, turn patterns over for stocking in reverse). Glue stocking trim pieces to stocking. Use black pen to personalize stocking. Allowing to dry after each coat, apply 2 coats of acrylic spray to stocking. Tie gold cord into a bow; trim ends. Glue bow to stocking. Glue pin back to back of stocking. Pin stocking to sweatshirt.

10. To launder, remove stockings. Turn shirt wrong side out and follow web and paint manufacturers' recommendations; hang to dry.

FIREPLACE
(cut 1)

FLAME A
(cut 1)

FLAME B
(cut 2)

FLAME C
(cut 2)

LOGS
(cut 1)

STOCKING

the stockings were hung....

SANTA THERMAL SHIRT (Shown on page 98)

You will need a ladies' thermal shirt with round neckline, fabrics for appliqués and trim at neckline and sleeves, paper-backed fusible web, sewing thread or embroidery floss for appliqué, two 3/4"w star-shaped buttons (we used red wooden buttons), a 10mm jingle bell, thread to match trim fabric and thread to sew on buttons, and tracing paper.

1. Follow Steps 1 - 4 of Angel Thermal Shirt instructions, page 108.
2. For trim at neckline, measure neckline of shirt just below ribbing; add 1". Cut a 1 3/4"w bias fabric strip the determined length (pieced as necessary). Press 1 end of strip 1/2" to wrong side. Press strip in half lengthwise; unfold. Press each long raw edge to center; refold strip. Beginning with unpressed end at 1 shoulder seam, pin strip along neckline below ribbing. Using a straight stitch, topstitch close to each edge of trim.
3. For trim on sleeves, repeat Step 2, measuring and applying trim just above ribbing on each sleeve.
4. Sew 1 star button to shirt at top of each tree. Sew jingle bell to shirt at point of Santa's hat.

STAR A
(cut 1)

STAR B
(cut 1)

FACE
(cut 1)

SMALL TREE
(cut 1)

BEARD
(cut 1)

SMALL
TREE TRUNK
(cut 1)

LARGE
TREE TRUNK
(cut 2)

MITTEN
(cut 2)

COAT
AND HAT
(cut 1)

LARGE TREE
(cut 2)

BOOTS
(cut 1)

HOLLY JUMPER
(Shown on page 96)

You will need a jumper, white fabric for "candies," green fabrics for leaf appliqués (we used 4 different fabrics), paper-backed fusible web, tear-away stabilizer, 12" of 5/8"w red satin ribbon, thread to match jumper and appliqué fabrics, 7/8" dia. covered button hardware for each "candy," liquid fray preventative, red permanent fabric marker, a safety pin, and tracing paper.

1. Wash, dry, and press jumper and fabrics.
2. Follow manufacturer's instructions to fuse web to wrong sides of appliqué fabrics.
3. Trace leaf pattern onto tracing paper; cut out. Use pattern to cut 3 holly leaves for holly design on bodice and desired number of leaves for holly designs on skirt from fabrics. Remove paper backing and arrange appliqués on jumper; fuse in place.
4. Cut a piece of stabilizer slightly larger than each holly design. Baste stabilizer to wrong side of jumper under each design. Use a medium width zigzag stitch with a very short stitch length to stitch over edges of leaves. For veins in leaves, use a narrow width zigzag stitch with a very short stitch length to stitch along center of each leaf. Remove stabilizer.
5. For each "candy," use a pencil to lightly trace candy design onto white fabric. Use red marker to color alternating segments of design. Use pattern supplied with covered button hardware to cut out design. Follow manufacturer's instructions to cover button with fabric piece.
6. Sew 1 "candy" at center of each holly design.
7. Tie ribbon into a bow; trim ends. Apply fray preventative to ribbon ends; allow to dry. Use safety pin on wrong side of jumper to pin bow behind "candy" in holly design on bodice.
8. Remove bow before laundering.

CANDY

SNOWMAN TOTE BAG (Shown on page 99)

You will need a tote bag large enough to accommodate a 14¹/₂" x 12¹/₂" design, fabrics for borders and appliqués (we used a star-print fabric for corner blocks of borders), paper-backed fusible web, sewing thread or embroidery floss for appliqué, two ³/₄"w star shaped buttons (we used wooden buttons), thread to sew on buttons, black permanent felt-tip pen with fine point, and tracing paper.

1. Wash, dry, and press tote and fabrics.
2. Follow manufacturer's instructions to fuse web to wrong sides of fabrics.
3. For borders, cut two 1¹/₄" x 12¹/₂" strips, two 1¹/₄" x 14¹/₂" strips, and four 1¹/₄" squares from fabrics. Remove paper backing. With short strips at sides and long strips at top and bottom, arrange strips on bag, overlapping ends; fuse in place. Fuse squares over overlapped ends of strips.

4. For appliqués, trace patterns onto tracing paper; cut out. Use patterns to cut indicated numbers of appliqués from fabrics. Remove paper backing and arrange appliqués on bag, overlapping appliqués as necessary; fuse in place.
5. Either use sewing thread and machine blanket stitch or 3 strands of floss and hand Blanket Stitch, page 159, to stitch along edges of borders and appliqués.
6. Sew 1 star button to tote at top of each tree.
7. Use black pen to draw eyes, nose, mouth, and buttons on each snowman.

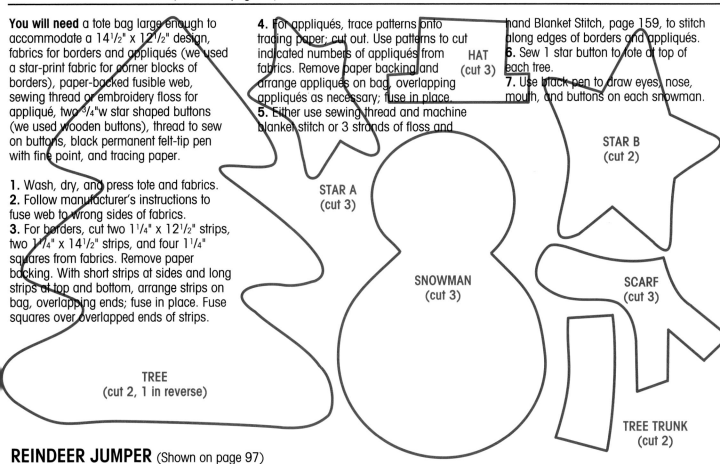

STAR A (cut 3)

STAR B (cut 2)

HAT (cut 3)

SNOWMAN (cut 3)

SCARF (cut 3)

TREE (cut 2, 1 in reverse)

TREE TRUNK (cut 2)

REINDEER JUMPER (Shown on page 97)

We placed our jumper over a white shirt embellished with Blanket Stitch, page 159, worked with red embroidery floss along the collar and cuffs.

You will need a jumper with bib large enough to accommodate a 7¹/₂" x 4¹/₂" design, tan fabric for reindeer, 16" of ¹/₄"w red satin ribbon and 20" of ⁵/₈"w red grosgrain ribbon for fence, 1 yd of ³/₈"w plaid ribbon for bows, thread to match jumper and plaid ribbon, paper-backed fusible web, covered button hardware for five ⁷/₈" dia. buttons, one ¹/₄" dia. red shank button with shank removed, tan embroidery floss, white and black fabric paint, small round paintbrushes, black permanent felt-tip pen with fine point, fabric marking pencil, tracing paper, graphite transfer paper, liquid fray preventative, fabric glue, hot glue gun, and glue sticks.

1. Wash and dry jumper, ribbons, and fabric according to paint and glue manufacturers' recommendations; press.
2. For fence, cut two 7¹/₂" lengths from satin ribbon for rails and six 3" lengths from grosgrain ribbon for pickets; trim each 3" length to a point at 1 end. Apply fray preventative to ribbon ends and allow to dry.

3. Use fabric marking pencil and a ruler to draw a 7¹/₂" long horizontal line at center front of bib ³/₄" above bottom of bib. Repeat to draw another line 1³/₄" above bottom of bib.
4. Matching 1 long edge (bottom) of 1 satin ribbon length to each drawn line, use fabric glue to glue ribbon lengths across front of bib. Beginning ¹/₂" from ends of satin ribbons and spacing lengths ¹/₂" apart, glue grosgrain ribbon lengths across satin ribbon lengths with square ends at bottom of bib. Allow to dry.
5. For reindeer, follow manufacturer's instructions to cover buttons with tan fabric.
6. Trace face pattern onto tracing paper.
7. (**Note:** Leaving 1 reindeer's nose untransferred and unpainted, follow Step 7 for each reindeer. Allow to dry after each paint color.) Use transfer paper to transfer black lines of face pattern to 1 covered button. Paint eyes white with black pupils. Paint nose black. Highlight nose and pupils of eyes with white. Use black pen to draw over transferred lines for mouth.
8. For ears, cut two 3" x 5" pieces of tan fabric. Follow manufacturer's instructions to fuse web to wrong side of 1 fabric piece; remove paper backing. Matching wrong sides, fuse fabric pieces together.

9. Trace ears pattern onto tracing paper; cut out. Use pattern to cut 5 ears pieces from fused fabric. Knot a length of floss tightly around center of each ears piece; trim ends of floss.
10. Hot glue 1 ears piece to top back of each reindeer. Hot glue red button to reindeer with unpainted nose.
11. Cut five 7" lengths from plaid ribbon. Tie each length into a bow; trim ends. Apply fray preventative to ribbon ends and allow to dry.
12. Tack bows to jumper between tops of fence pickets. Sewing reindeer with red nose above center bow, sew reindeer to jumper above bows.
13. Use 4 strands of floss and long stitches to stitch antlers above each reindeer.
14. To launder, turn jumper wrong side out and follow paint and glue manufacturer's recommendations.

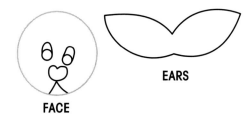

FACE

EARS

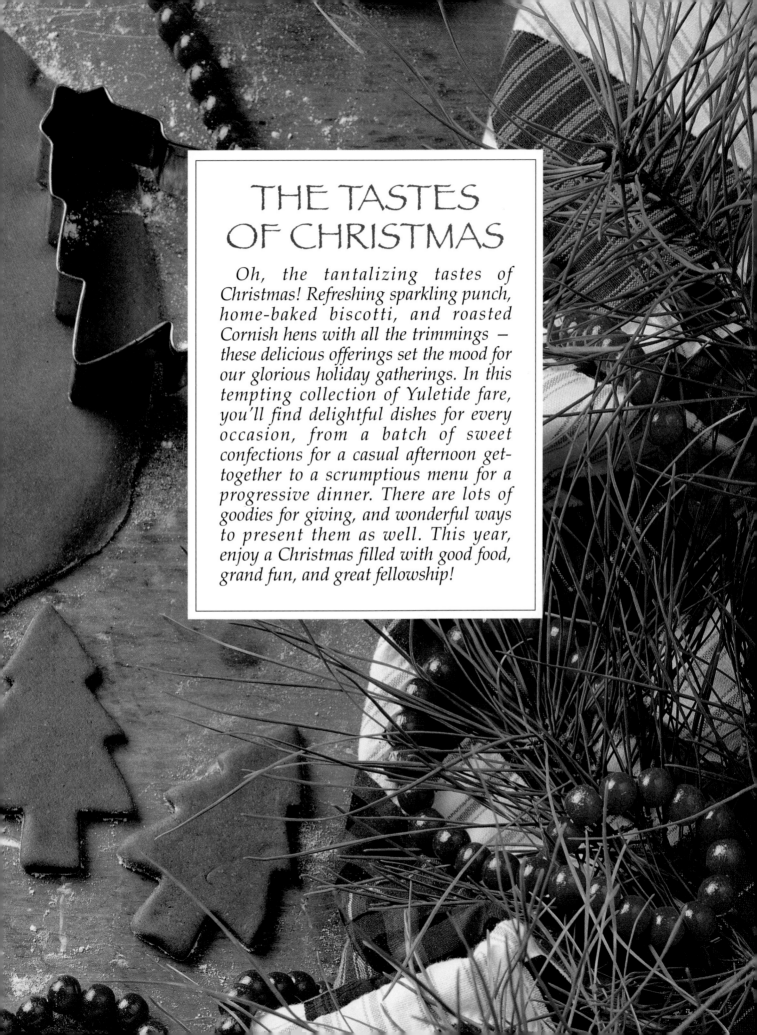

THE TASTES OF CHRISTMAS

Oh, the tantalizing tastes of Christmas! Refreshing sparkling punch, home-baked biscotti, and roasted Cornish hens with all the trimmings — these delicious offerings set the mood for our glorious holiday gatherings. In this tempting collection of Yuletide fare, you'll find delightful dishes for every occasion, from a batch of sweet confections for a casual afternoon get-together to a scrumptious menu for a progressive dinner. There are lots of goodies for giving, and wonderful ways to present them as well. This year, enjoy a Christmas filled with good food, grand fun, and great fellowship!

HOME FOR THE HOLIDAYS

As nature ushers in wintry weather, our hearts are warmed by happy thoughts of Christmas — family reunions around a crowded dinner table, Yuletide toasts, and lasting memories. In this collection, you'll find a scrumptious sampling of recipes that will soon become family favorites. What a wonderful way to welcome loved ones home for the holidays and make your Christmas meal the most memorable one ever!

Dressed in a colorful medley of chopped greens, cabbage, sweet red pepper, and savory spices, Stuffed Holiday Ham is cooked to succulent perfection.

STUFFED HOLIDAY HAM

- 1 small head green cabbage, coarsely chopped
- 1/2 pound mustard greens, spinach, or other fresh greens
- 1 medium onion, quartered
- 1 rib celery, coarsely chopped
- 1 small sweet red pepper, quartered
- 2 cloves garlic
- 2 teaspoons crushed red pepper flakes
- 8 to 9 pound fully cooked butt portion bone-in ham

Combine first 7 ingredients in small batches in a food processor; pulse process until finely chopped. Place ham in center of 2 layers of cheesecloth large enough to cover ham. Make random cuts in ham down to the bone. Open cuts with fingers and stuff as much vegetable mixture as possible into each cut. Press remaining vegetable mixture onto surface of ham. Gather cheesecloth around ham; tie with kitchen string. Place stuffed ham in a large stockpot or roasting pan; add water to cover at least half of ham. Cover and bring water to a boil over high heat. Reduce heat to medium-low and simmer 1 1/2 to 2 hours or until vegetables are tender and ham is heated through, adding hot water as needed. Remove from heat and cool 1 hour. Remove ham from stockpot. Carefully unwrap cheesecloth, leaving vegetables on ham. Cover ham and refrigerate overnight. Serve chilled.
Yield: about 22 servings

ORANGE-CARROT SOUP

- 1/4 cup finely chopped onion
- 1 tablespoon butter or margarine
- 4 cups chicken or vegetable stock
- 1 pound carrots, shredded
- 1 can (11 ounces) mandarin oranges in syrup, undrained
- 1/2 cup orange juice
- 2 teaspoons grated orange zest
- 2 teaspoons honey
- 1/4 teaspoon ground ginger
- 1/4 cup cold water
- 1 tablespoon cornstarch
- 1/2 cup half and half

In a Dutch oven over medium heat, cook onion and butter about 5 minutes or until onion is clear. Add chicken stock and carrots. Increase heat to medium-high and bring to a boil. Reduce heat to medium; cook about 15 minutes or until carrots are almost tender. Remove from heat.

Lightly toasted Dill Crackers are great sprinkled atop bowls of tasty Orange-Carrot Soup. Served hot, the flavorful combo will chase away winter chills.

Remove 1 cup carrots from liquid using a slotted spoon; set aside. Add oranges and syrup, orange juice, orange zest, honey, and ginger to soup. Batch process soup in a food processor until puréed. Return soup to Dutch oven over medium heat. Add reserved carrots to soup; bring to a simmer. Combine cold water and cornstarch in a small bowl. Add cornstarch mixture and half and half to soup; stir until thickened. Serve warm with Dill Crackers.
Yield: about 8 cups soup

DILL CRACKERS

- 1 package (10 ounces) oyster crackers
- 1/4 cup vegetable oil
- 2 teaspoons dried dill weed

Preheat oven to 300 degrees. Place crackers in a large bowl. Combine oil and dill weed in a small bowl. Pour oil mixture over crackers; stir until well coated. Transfer to an ungreased jellyroll pan. Bake 15 minutes, stirring every 5 minutes. Place pan on a wire rack to cool. Store in an airtight container.
Yield: about 6 cups crackers

A rich side dish, Cheesy Spinach Soufflé *(clockwise from left)* is loaded with Parmesan cheese. Inspired by two old-fashioned favorites — yeast rolls and corn bread — Cornmeal Yeast Muffins offer whole kernels of sweet golden corn in every bite. It's easy to make crunchy Pickled Yellow Squash just like grandmother's! Ours is seasoned with green peppers, onions, and mustard and celery seeds. Cream cheese, milk, and butter make Creamy Garlic Mashed Potatoes extra smooth and delicious.

CHEESY SPINACH SOUFFLÉ

- 1 container (16 ounces) cottage cheese
- 1 1/2 cups (about 6 ounces) shredded Parmesan cheese
- 2 packages (10 ounces each) frozen chopped spinach, cooked and well drained
- 2 eggs, separated
- 1/4 cup butter or margarine, melted
- 2 tablespoons minced onion
- 1 clove garlic, minced
- 2 tablespoons all-purpose flour
- 1/2 teaspoon baking powder
- 1/2 teaspoon lemon pepper

Preheat oven to 350 degrees. In a medium bowl, combine cottage cheese, Parmesan cheese, spinach, egg yolks, melted butter, onion, and garlic. In a small bowl, combine flour, baking powder, and lemon pepper. Add dry ingredients to spinach mixture; stir until well blended. In a small bowl, beat egg whites until stiff; fold into spinach mixture. Pour into a greased 2-quart soufflé dish. Bake uncovered 50 to 60 minutes or until center is set. Serve warm.

Yield: about 10 servings

CREAMY GARLIC MASHED POTATOES

- 4 pounds russet potatoes, peeled and cut into 2-inch pieces
- 6 cloves garlic
- 2 teaspoons salt, divided
- 2 packages (3 ounces each) cream cheese, softened
- 1/2 cup butter or margarine
- 1 cup warm milk

Place potatoes in a Dutch oven. Cover with water; add garlic and 1 teaspoon salt. Cover and bring to a boil over medium-high heat. Reduce heat to medium and continue cooking 10 minutes or until potatoes are just tender; drain. Return potatoes and garlic to low heat. Add cream cheese, butter, and remaining 1 teaspoon salt; mash until cream cheese and butter are melted. Add milk and continue mashing until coarsely mashed. Serve warm.

Yield: about 14 servings

CORNMEAL YEAST MUFFINS

    1 package dry yeast
  1/4 cup plus 1 teaspoon sugar, divided
  1/3 cup warm water (105 to
         115 degrees)
    1 cup milk
  1/2 cup butter or margarine
 1 1/2 teaspoons salt
    1 can (15.25 ounces) whole kernel
         corn, drained
    1 cup cream-style corn
    2 eggs, beaten
 1 1/2 cups yellow cornmeal
    3 cups all-purpose flour

In a small bowl, dissolve yeast and 1 teaspoon sugar in warm water. In a small saucepan, combine milk, butter, remaining 1/4 cup sugar, and salt over medium heat; whisk until butter melts and sugar is dissolved. Remove from heat and pour into a large bowl. Add whole kernel corn, cream style corn, eggs, and yeast mixture; stir until well blended. Add cornmeal and flour, 1 cup at a time; stir until a thick batter forms. Cover and let rise in a warm place (80 to 85 degrees) 1 to 1 1/2 hours or until almost doubled in size. Stir batter down. Spoon batter into greased muffin tins, filling each two-thirds full. Let rise uncovered in a warm place about 45 minutes.

Preheat oven to 375 degrees. Bake 20 to 25 minutes or until golden brown. Allow muffins to cool in pan 5 minutes. Serve warm or transfer to a wire rack to cool completely.

Yield: about 2 dozen muffins

PICKLED YELLOW SQUASH

    2 quarts cold water
    1 cup canning and pickling salt
    8 cups sliced yellow squash
    4 green peppers, chopped
    2 cups chopped white onions
    3 cups sugar
    2 cups white vinegar (5% acidity)
    1 teaspoon celery seed
    1 teaspoon mustard seed

Follow manufacturer's instructions to prepare canning jars, lids, and bands.

Sweet and tangy Overnight Fruit Salad combines pineapple chunks, cherries, mandarin orange slices, and miniature marshmallows in a creamy dressing.

In a large nonmetallic bowl, combine water and salt; stir until well blended. Place squash in salt mixture. Cover and allow to stand 2 hours. Using a colander, drain and thoroughly rinse squash with cold water. In a large bowl, combine squash, peppers, and onions.

Combine sugar, vinegar, celery seed, and mustard seed in a large Dutch oven (preferably enamelware). Bring vinegar mixture to a boil over high heat. Add vegetables; bring to a boil again. Fill sterilized jars to within 1/2 inch of tops. Wipe jar rims and threads. Quickly cover with lids and screw bands on tightly. Using water-bath method as directed by the USDA, process jars 15 minutes. When jars have cooled, check seals. Lids should be curved down or remain so when pressed. Refrigerate all unsealed jars.

Yield: about 5 pints pickled squash

OVERNIGHT FRUIT SALAD

    1 can (20 ounces) pineapple
         chunks in heavy syrup, drained,
         reserving 2 tablespoons syrup
    3 egg yolks, beaten
    2 tablespoons sugar
    2 tablespoons white vinegar
    1 tablespoon butter or margarine
  1/8 teaspoon salt
    2 cans (17 ounces each) pitted white
         Royal Anne cherries, drained
    2 cans (11 ounces each) mandarin
         oranges, drained
 1 1/2 cups miniature marshmallows
    1 cup whipping cream

Chill a small bowl and beaters from an electric mixer in freezer. Place pineapple chunks in a large bowl; set aside. In the top of a double boiler over hot water, combine egg yolks, sugar, vinegar, reserved pineapple syrup, butter, and salt. Stirring constantly, cook mixture about 4 minutes or until thickened. Remove from heat and allow to cool; chill 30 minutes.

Add cherries, mandarin oranges, and marshmallows to pineapple chunks. Stir in chilled dressing. In chilled bowl, beat whipping cream until stiff peaks form; fold into fruit mixture. Chill fruit salad overnight.

Yield: about 16 servings

Coconut-Orange Cake *(left)* is a dreamy dessert featuring an orange-flavored filling between two layers of moist goodness. Iced with fluffy frosting sweetened with orange juice, the cake is covered with coconut and mandarin orange segments. A new twist on a traditional treat, Eggnog Custard Pie is laced with bourbon and ground nutmeg.

EGGNOG CUSTARD PIE

CRUST
- 1 1/2 cups all-purpose flour
- 1/4 teaspoon salt
- 1/2 cup vegetable shortening
- 1/4 cup water

FILLING
- 4 eggs
- 1/2 cup sugar
- 2 cups half and half
- 2 tablespoons bourbon
- 1 teaspoon vanilla extract
- 1/4 teaspoon ground nutmeg
- 1/8 teaspoon salt

TOPPING
- 1/2 cup whipping cream
- 1 1/2 tablespoons sugar
- 1 teaspoon bourbon

For crust, combine flour and salt in a medium bowl. Using a pastry blender or 2 knives, cut in shortening until mixture resembles coarse meal. Sprinkle with water; mix until a soft dough forms. On a lightly floured surface, use a floured rolling pin to roll out dough to 1/8-inch thickness. Transfer to a 9-inch pie plate. Crimp edges of crust; use a sharp knife to trim excess crust.

Preheat oven to 450 degrees. For filling, beat eggs and sugar in a medium bowl until well blended. Add half and half; beat until smooth. Stir in bourbon, vanilla, nutmeg, and salt. Pour filling into crust. Bake 10 minutes. Reduce heat to 325 degrees and bake an additional 35 to 40 minutes or until a knife inserted in center of pie comes out clean. Cool pie on a wire rack.

For topping, beat whipping cream and sugar in a small bowl until stiff peaks form. Beat in bourbon. To serve, spoon topping onto each piece of pie.
Yield: about 8 servings

COCONUT-ORANGE CAKE

CAKE
- 1 package (18.25 ounces) yellow cake mix
- 3 eggs
- 1/3 cup vegetable oil
- 1 can (8 1/2 ounces) cream of coconut
- 1 cup sour cream

ORANGE FILLING
- 1/2 cup sugar
- 1 1/2 tablespoons all-purpose flour
- 1 can (11 ounces) mandarin oranges, drained
- 2 egg yolks (reserve egg whites for icing)
- 1/2 teaspoon butter or margarine
- 1/2 teaspoon vanilla extract

ICING
- 1 1/2 cups sugar
- 1/4 cup orange juice
- 2 egg whites
- 1 tablespoon light corn syrup
- 1/4 teaspoon cream of tartar
- 1 teaspoon vanilla extract
- 1 cup sweetened shredded coconut

   Mandarin orange segments
   to decorate

Preheat oven to 350 degrees. For cake, combine cake mix, eggs, and oil in a large bowl; beat until well blended. Add cream of coconut and sour cream; beat until smooth. Cut circles of waxed paper to line bottoms of two 9-inch round cake pans. Grease paper and sides of pans. Pour batter into prepared pans. Bake 32 to 36 minutes or until a toothpick inserted in center of cake comes out clean. Cool in pans 10 minutes on a wire rack. Run knife around edge of pans to loosen cake; remove from pans and place on wire rack to cool completely.

For orange filling, combine sugar and flour in a heavy small saucepan. Add oranges, egg yolks, butter, and vanilla. Stirring constantly, place over medium heat and cook about 15 minutes or until mixture thickens. Cool to room temperature. Spread filling between cake layers.

For icing, combine sugar, orange juice, egg whites, corn syrup, and cream of tartar in top of a double boiler. Beat with a mixer until sugar is well blended. Place over boiling water and continue beating about 7 minutes or until soft peaks form. Remove from heat and add vanilla. Continue beating 2 minutes or until icing is desired consistency. Ice cake. Sprinkle coconut on top and sides of cake. Decorate with orange segments. Store in an airtight container in refrigerator.

Yield: about 16 servings

BANANA-NUT CREAM TART

FILLING
- ½ cup sugar
- 3 tablespoons all-purpose flour
- 3 cups half and half
- 3 eggs, beaten
- 3 tablespoons butter or margarine
- ¾ teaspoon vanilla extract
- ¼ teaspoon butter flavoring

CRUST
- 1 cup vanilla wafer crumbs (about 20 cookies)
- 1 cup chopped pecans, toasted and coarsely ground
- ¼ cup butter or margarine, softened
- ¼ cup sugar

TOPPING
- 1 egg white
- 2 teaspoons water
- 1 cup chopped pecans
- ¼ cup firmly packed brown sugar
- 2 tablespoons apple jelly
- 6 medium bananas

For filling, combine sugar and flour in the top of a double boiler. Add half and half, eggs, and butter; place over simmering water. Stirring frequently, cook about 20 minutes or until thick enough to coat back of a spoon. Stir in vanilla and butter flavoring. Remove from heat and pour into a medium bowl. Place plastic wrap directly on surface of pudding; chill.

Preheat oven to 350 degrees. For crust, combine all ingredients in a medium bowl. Press mixture into bottom and up sides of a lightly greased 8 x 11-inch tart pan with a removable bottom. Bake 10 to 12 minutes or until crust is firm; chill.

For our Banana-Nut Cream Tart, a light pudding filling covers a layer of banana slices on a crust of vanilla wafer crumbs and chopped pecans. Alternating rows of banana slices and caramelized nuts top the yummy delight.

Reduce oven to 225 degrees. For topping, combine egg white and water in a small bowl; beat until foamy. Stir in pecans and brown sugar. Spread coated pecans on an ungreased baking sheet. Bake 45 minutes, stirring every 15 minutes, or until golden brown. Cool pan on a wire rack.

To serve, melt apple jelly in a small saucepan over medium heat. Slice 2 bananas and place a single layer in pie crust. Spoon half of chilled filling over bananas. Place another single layer of 2 sliced bananas on filling. Top with remainder of filling. Alternate rows of caramelized nuts and slices of remaining bananas on top of filling. Brush melted apple jelly over bananas.

Yield: about 12 servings

Dashing Through The Snow

For an enjoyable evening of laughter and reminiscing with longtime friends and new neighbors, try an old-fashioned progressive dinner. As the group travels from one home to the next, they'll be ushered in from the cold with welcoming aromas and samplings of delicious appetizers, soup and salad, a main course, and desserts. On the following pages, you'll discover wonderful make-ahead recipes to help you plan a merry menu for all!

Filled with shrimp, crabmeat, and mild cheeses, Seafood Crêpes are a scrumptious appetizer. Guests can choose from two delicious toppings — Creamy Lemon-Dill Sauce or hearty Basil Red Sauce.

SEAFOOD CRÊPES WITH CREAMY LEMON-DILL AND BASIL RED SAUCES

FILLING

- 3 tablespoons butter
- 1/4 cup finely minced green onion
- 1 clove garlic, minced
- 1/2 pound boiled shrimp, shelled, deveined, and cut into bite-size pieces
- 2 cans (6 ounces each) lump crabmeat, drained
- 1/2 cup ricotta cheese
- 2 tablespoons grated Parmesan cheese
- 1/8 teaspoon ground white pepper

CRÊPES

- 1 1/2 cups sifted all-purpose flour
- 1/4 teaspoon salt
- 4 eggs
- 1 1/4 cups milk
- 1 cup cold water
- 2 tablespoons vegetable oil

For filling, melt butter in a medium saucepan over medium-low heat. Add onion and garlic; sauté until onion is tender. Transfer onion mixture to a medium bowl. Stir in shrimp, crabmeat, cheeses, and white pepper until well blended. Place in an airtight container in refrigerator until ready to use.

For crêpes, combine flour and salt in a medium bowl. Add eggs, milk, water, and oil; beat until well blended.

Preheat and lightly grease a griddle or large skillet over medium heat. For each crêpe, spoon about 1 tablespoon batter onto griddle, using back of spoon to smooth into a 4-inch circle. Cook until edges are lightly browned; remove from griddle. Place crêpes in a single layer between sheets of waxed paper. Repeat with remaining batter.

Fill each crêpe with about 1 tablespoon of filling; roll up crêpe. Serve with Creamy Lemon-Dill Sauce and Basil Red Sauce.
Yield: about 50 appetizers

CREAMY LEMON-DILL SAUCE

- 1/2 cup whipping cream
- 4 cloves garlic, minced
- 1/4 cup fresh lemon juice
- 3/4 cup olive oil
- 1/4 cup minced fresh dill weed
- 1/4 teaspoon salt
- 1/8 teaspoon ground white pepper

In a heavy small saucepan, heat whipping cream over medium heat until it comes to a boil. Reduce heat to low and

Tickle your guests' fancies with the bubbly flavor of Sparkling Wine Punch. It's a spirited combination of red grape juice, club soda, white wine, and orange liqueur. A fruited ice ring makes the beverage especially festive.

add garlic. Simmer mixture about 15 minutes or until garlic is tender and cream has reduced in volume almost by half. Place warm cream mixture in a food processor. With processor running, add lemon juice and process until well blended. Continue processing and gradually add oil; process until an emulsion is formed. Stir in dill weed, salt, and white pepper. Serve with Seafood Crêpes.
Yield: about 1 cup sauce

BASIL RED SAUCE

- 2 cans (14.5 ounces each) plum tomatoes, undrained and coarsely chopped
- 1 package (3 ounces) sun-dried tomatoes
- 1/3 cup chopped fresh basil leaves
- 1/4 cup minced onion
- 4 cloves garlic, minced
- 1/4 teaspoon salt
- 1/4 teaspoon ground black pepper
- 1/4 teaspoon sugar
- 1 tablespoon seasoned rice wine vinegar
- 1 tablespoon olive oil

Place canned tomatoes and sun-dried tomatoes in a medium saucepan over medium heat. Bring to a boil and cook

2 minutes. Remove from heat and allow to cool 5 minutes.

Place tomato mixture, basil, onion, garlic, salt, pepper, and sugar in a food processor; pulse process briefly to blend ingredients. With processor running, gradually add vinegar and oil; process until well blended. Serve with Seafood Crêpes.
Yield: about 3 2/3 cups sauce

SPARKLING WINE PUNCH

Make ice ring at least 24 hours in advance.

- Seedless red grapes
- 1 bottle (48 ounces) red grape juice, chilled and divided
- 1 bottle (32 ounces) club soda, chilled
- 1 fifth (750 ml) sparkling white wine, chilled
- 1/4 cup orange-flavored liqueur

Make ice ring by placing grapes in a 4-cup ring mold. Add 3 cups grape juice; cover and freeze.

To serve, combine remaining grape juice, club soda, wine, and liqueur in punch bowl. Float ice ring on top and serve.
Yield: about eighteen 6-ounce servings

121

ROASTED GARLIC

- 6 large heads garlic
- 1 loaf (8 ounces) 2¹/₂-inch-diameter French bread, cut into ¹/₄-inch slices

Preheat oven to 375 degrees. Remove the outermost papery skin from each head of garlic, leaving cloves of garlic intact. Slice across stem end of each garlic head. Place garlic heads in a baking dish; cover with heavy aluminum foil. Bake about 1 hour. Allow garlic to cool 10 to 15 minutes before serving. Place French bread slices on a baking sheet. Toast in a 375-degree oven 5 minutes, turning slices over after 3 minutes. To serve, press garlic pulp out of each clove and spread on toast.
Yield: about 50 servings

CURRIED BLUE CHEESECAKE

- 1¹/₄ cups butter-flavored cracker crumbs
- ¹/₄ cup freshly grated Parmesan cheese
- ¹/₄ cup butter or margarine, melted
- 3 packages (8 ounces each) cream cheese, softened
- 4 eggs
- ¹/₂ cup mayonnaise
- ¹/₂ cup finely minced onion
- 1 tablespoon lemon juice
- ³/₄ teaspoon curry powder
- ¹/₂ teaspoon Worcestershire sauce
- 8 ounces blue cheese, crumbled

  Chutney to garnish
  Crackers to serve

Preheat oven to 300 degrees. In a medium bowl, combine cracker crumbs, Parmesan cheese, and melted butter. Press into bottom of a greased 9-inch springform pan. In a large bowl, beat cream cheese until fluffy. Add eggs, 1 at a time, beating 2 minutes after each addition. Continue beating while adding mayonnaise, onion, lemon juice, curry powder, and Worcestershire sauce; beat until well blended. Stir in blue cheese. Pour filling over crust. Bake 1¹/₂ hours. Turn oven off. With oven door partially open, leave cheesecake in oven 1 hour. Transfer to a wire rack to cool. Remove sides of pan. Spoon chutney over top of cheesecake. Serve chilled or at room temperature with crackers.
Yield: about 50 servings

Garnished with chutney and served with crackers, Curried Blue Cheesecake *(clockwise from top left)* is a robust blend of Parmesan, cream, and blue cheeses spiced with curry powder. Simple Roasted Garlic is a sweet, buttery-soft spread for toasted slices of French bread. Marinated in a soy sauce and brown sugar mixture, Beef Saté is terrific grilled or broiled. Our Hot Peanut Dipping Sauce is the perfect condiment for these tender skewered tidbits.

BEEF SATÉ WITH HOT PEANUT DIPPING SAUCE

- ³/₄ cup seasoned rice wine vinegar
- ¹/₃ cup peanut oil
- ¹/₃ cup soy sauce
- 3 cloves garlic, minced
- 1 tablespoon firmly packed brown sugar
- 1 tablespoon grated fresh ginger
- 1 teaspoon crushed red pepper flakes
- 2 pounds flank steak, trimmed of fat and thoroughly chilled

  Six-inch-long bamboo skewers

In a large bowl, combine vinegar, oil, soy sauce, garlic, brown sugar, ginger, and red pepper flakes; stir until well blended. Slice chilled meat across the grain, at an angle, into thin slices. Place beef strips in marinade and refrigerate overnight. Soak bamboo skewers in water overnight.

Thread marinated beef strips onto skewers. Broil or grill about 4 inches from heat 5 to 6 minutes; turning once after 3 minutes. Serve warm with Hot Peanut Dipping Sauce.
Yield: about 4 dozen appetizers

HOT PEANUT DIPPING SAUCE

- ¹/₄ cup smooth peanut butter
- ¹/₄ cup beef broth
- 2 tablespoons peanut oil
- 1 tablespoon soy sauce
- 1 tablespoon seasoned rice wine vinegar
- 1 teaspoon dark sesame oil
- 1 teaspoon freshly grated ginger
- ¹/₂ teaspoon crushed red pepper flakes

Combine all ingredients in a food processor; process until well blended. Transfer to a small bowl; cover and store at room temperature 2 hours to allow flavors to blend. Serve at room temperature with warm Beef Saté.
Yield: about ¹/₂ cup sauce

Warm up holiday guests with a steaming bowl of Mushroom Soup. Seasoned with onion, celery, and garlic, the soup is loaded with fresh sliced mushrooms in a well-seasoned beef broth. Your bread basket won't stay filled for long with the homemade goodness of our Herbed Breadsticks.

MUSHROOM SOUP

 1 pound fresh mushrooms
 1/4 cup butter or margarine
 1 onion, coarsely chopped
 2 stalks celery, coarsely chopped
 2 cloves garlic, minced
 6 cups beef broth
 1 teaspoon dried thyme leaves
 1/2 teaspoon dried parsley flakes
 1 bay leaf

 Chopped fresh parsley to garnish

Separate mushroom caps from stems; set aside. Coarsely chop mushroom stems. In a Dutch oven over medium heat, combine mushroom stems, butter, onion, celery, and garlic; sauté about 8 minutes or until tender. Add beef broth, thyme, dried parsley, and bay leaf. Cover and reduce heat to medium-low; simmer about 45 minutes. Strain and return liquid to Dutch oven. Discard cooked vegetables. Slice mushroom caps and add to soup. Cover and simmer over medium-low heat about 15 minutes or until mushrooms are just tender. Garnish with fresh parsley and serve warm.
Yield: about 8 servings

HERBED BREADSTICKS

 2 packages dry yeast
 4 tablespoons sugar, divided
 1/4 cup warm water
 2 cups milk
 4 tablespoons butter or margarine
 2 teaspoons salt
 6 cups all-purpose flour, divided
 1 egg white, beaten
 3 tablespoons dried Italian herb
  seasoning

In a small bowl, dissolve yeast and 1 tablespoon sugar in warm water. Set aside. In a small saucepan, warm milk, butter, remaining 3 tablespoons sugar, and salt over medium heat until butter melts. In a large bowl, combine 5 cups flour, yeast mixture, and milk mixture; stir until a soft dough forms. Turn onto a lightly floured surface. Adding remaining flour as needed, knead 10 to 15 minutes or until dough becomes smooth and elastic. Place in a large greased bowl, turning once to coat top of dough. Cover and let rise in a warm place (80 to 85 degrees) 1 hour or until doubled in size.

Turn dough onto a lightly floured surface and punch down. Divide dough in half. Shape half of dough into 12 equal pieces. Roll each piece into a 15-inch-long rope. Twist each rope of dough several times. Place breadsticks on a well-greased baking sheet. Repeat with remaining dough. Cover and let rise in a warm place 20 to 30 minutes or until dough has risen slightly.

Preheat oven to 400 degrees. Lightly brush breadsticks with beaten egg white and sprinkle with herb seasoning. Bake about 15 minutes or until golden brown. Serve warm or transfer to a wire rack to cool.
Yield: about 2 dozen breadsticks

BLOOD ORANGE SORBET

Blood oranges have red meat and are available in a limited supply from November to July.

- 4 cups blood orange juice (about 8 to 10 blood oranges) **or** another variety of juice oranges
- 1 cup sugar
- 2 teaspoons grated blood orange zest

    Blood orange segments and mint leaves to garnish

In a medium bowl, combine orange juice, sugar, and orange zest; stir until sugar has dissolved. Chill mixture. Freeze mixture in a 2-quart ice-cream freezer according to manufacturer's instructions. To serve, garnish with orange segments and mint leaves.
Yield: about 20 servings

PEAR AND BLUE CHEESE SALAD WITH TOASTED WALNUT DRESSING

Salad may be prepared ahead of time and refrigerated; prepare dressing immediately before serving.

SALAD
- 8 to 10 cups mixed salad greens
- 1 small red onion, thinly sliced
- 2 red pears, quartered, cored, and thinly sliced (dip pears in a mixture of 3 tablespoons **each** water and lemon juice)

DRESSING
- 1 cup coarsely chopped walnuts
- 1/2 cup vegetable oil
- 6 tablespoons red wine vinegar
- 1 teaspoon sugar
- 1/2 teaspoon salt
- 1/8 teaspoon ground white pepper

- 4 ounces Gorgonzola cheese, crumble to serve

For salad, arrange salad greens and onion and pear slices on 8 salad plates. Cover and refrigerate until ready to serve.
For dressing, toast walnuts in oil over medium heat in a heavy medium skillet about 5 minutes or until lightly browned. Reserving oil in skillet, place walnuts on a paper towel to drain. Add vinegar, sugar, salt, and white pepper to oil in skillet; stir over medium heat until well blended. Spoon dressing over salads and sprinkle with toasted walnuts and cheese.
Yield: 8 servings

Blood Orange Sorbet *(top)* combines three simple ingredients for an icy-sweet treat between courses. Thin red pear slices, crumbled cheese, and onion are nestled on a bed of mixed salad greens for our deliciously tangy Pear and Blue Cheese Salad with Toasted Walnut Dressing.

SMOKED CORNISH HENS WITH RED CURRANT SAUCE

- 1 jar (10 ounces) red currant jelly
- 1/4 cup dry white wine
- 2 tablespoons orange juice
- 1/2 teaspoon ground allspice
- 1/8 teaspoon salt
- 1/8 teaspoon ground black pepper
- 4 Cornish hens, smoked, halved, and chilled

Preheat oven to 275 degrees. Combine jelly, wine, orange juice, allspice, salt, and pepper in a food processor. Process until well blended. Place hens in a single layer in a deep roasting pan. Baste with jelly mixture. Cover and heat in the same oven with Stuffed Deviled Onions 1 1/2 to 2 hours or until temperature registers 165 degrees on a meat thermometer. Baste hens with jelly mixture while baking. Serve warm.
Yield: 8 servings

Note: If not used as part of a progressive dinner, heat hens in a 350-degree oven 45 minutes or until heated through; baste frequently.

WHOLE GREEN BEANS WITH DILLED BUTTER CURLS

Make butter curls several hours before serving.

- 1/2 cup butter, softened
- 2 tablespoons chopped fresh dill weed **or** 1 teaspoon dried dill weed
- 1 teaspoon lemon juice
- 1 teaspoon minced onion
- 3 cans (14 1/2 ounces each) vertical pack whole green beans

In a small bowl, combine butter, dill weed, lemon juice, and onion. Shape mixture into a stick of butter slightly wider than a butter curler. Wrap in plastic wrap and chill until firm.

To prepare butter curls, dip butter curler in warm water. Pull curler across surface of seasoned butter to make each curl. Place curls in ice water. Store in refrigerator until ready to serve.

Pour 3/4 cup green bean liquid into a large saucepan over medium-high heat. Place vegetable steamer in saucepan. Drain remaining liquid from green beans. Place green beans in steamer; cover and steam until heated through. Serve warm with chilled butter curls.
Yield: about 8 servings

Succulent Smoked Cornish Hens are slow-roasted and basted with flavorful Red Currant Sauce. Whole Green Beans with Dilled Butter Curls and Stuffed Deviled Onions are the perfect side dishes to complete this delightful entrée.

STUFFED DEVILED ONIONS

- 8 whole white onions (about 3 inches in diameter)
- 2 tablespoons olive oil
- 2 cloves garlic, minced
- 8 medium fresh mushrooms, finely chopped
- 1/3 cup Dijon-style mustard
- 1/4 cup white wine
- 3/4 cup chicken broth, divided
- 1/2 teaspoon hot pepper sauce
- 3/4 cup (3 ounces) shredded Cheddar cheese
- 1 package (8 ounces) seasoned corn bread stuffing

Cut a small slice off bottom of each onion to flatten. Cut an "X" in bottom of each onion about 1/4-inch deep. In a Dutch oven, cook onions in boiling water 15 minutes. Drain onions; allow to cool enough to handle. Make a thin slice across top to level and scoop out center of each onion, leaving a 1/2-inch shell; reserve onion centers. Finely chop reserved onion centers to yield 1/2 cup.

Preheat oven to 275 degrees. Stirring frequently, cook oil, garlic, and chopped onion in a large saucepan over medium heat until onion is almost soft but not brown. Add mushrooms and continue to cook 2 to 3 minutes or until mushrooms are soft. Add mustard, wine, 1/4 cup chicken broth, and hot pepper sauce; stir until well blended. Remove from heat. Stir in cheese and corn bread stuffing. Fill each onion with stuffing mixture. Place onions in a 9 x 13-inch baking dish. In a microwave-safe cup, microwave remaining 1/2 cup chicken broth on high power (100%) 1 minute. Pour broth into baking dish. Cover and bake in the same oven with Smoked Cornish Hens 1 1/2 to 2 hours. Serve warm.
Yield: 8 servings

Note: If not used as part of a progressive dinner, cover and bake onions in a 350-degree oven 45 minutes or until heated through.

STEAMED CRANBERRY PUDDING WITH ORANGE HARD SAUCE

ORANGE HARD SAUCE
- 1/2 cup butter, softened
- 1 1/2 cups sifted confectioners sugar
- 1 1/2 tablespoons brandy
- 2 teaspoons grated orange zest
- 1 teaspoon orange extract
- 1/2 teaspoon vanilla extract

CRANBERRY PUDDING
- 1 cup raisins
- 1/2 cup brandy
- 1/2 cup butter or margarine, softened
- 1/2 cup granulated sugar
- 1/2 cup firmly packed brown sugar
- 1 cup whole berry cranberry sauce
- 2 eggs
- 3/4 teaspoon butter flavoring
- 2 cups all-purpose flour
- 1 1/2 teaspoons baking powder
- 1 teaspoon ground cinnamon
- 1/2 teaspoon ground allspice
- 1/2 teaspoon baking soda
- 1/2 teaspoon salt
- 1 cup coarsely chopped fresh cranberries
- 3/4 cup finely chopped toasted pecans

For orange hard sauce, cream butter in a medium bowl. Gradually add remaining ingredients while continuing to beat; beat until fluffy. Spoon into serving dish and chill.

For cranberry pudding, combine raisins and brandy in a small saucepan over medium-low heat. Heat 5 minutes; remove from heat and set aside. In a large bowl, cream butter and sugars. Add cranberry sauce, eggs, and butter flavoring; beat until smooth. In a small bowl, combine flour, baking powder, cinnamon, allspice, baking soda, and salt. Add dry ingredients to creamed mixture; stir until well blended. Stir in cranberries, pecans, and brandied raisin mixture. Spoon batter into a greased and floured 8-cup pudding mold. Cover with mold lid or aluminum foil. Set mold on a rack inside a large stockpot. Add boiling water to stockpot to come halfway up sides of mold. Cover stockpot and keep water at a gentle boil, adding boiling water as necessary. Steam 2 to 2 1/4 hours or until a toothpick inserted in center comes out clean. Unmold steamed pudding onto serving plate and serve warm with orange hard sauce.

Yield: about 14 servings

Bavarian Creams with Raspberry Sauce *(in cups)* is a dreamy custard dessert sprinkled with chocolate shavings. A decorative mold gives our Steamed Cranberry Pudding its elegant shape. Laced with brandy, raisins, cranberries, and toasted pecans, it's especially sumptuous served with creamy Orange Hard Sauce.

BAVARIAN CREAMS WITH RASPBERRY SAUCE

CUSTARD
- 1 envelope unflavored gelatin
- 1/3 cup cold orange juice
- 3/4 cup sugar
- 4 egg yolks
- 1/8 teaspoon salt
- 1 3/4 cups milk, scalded
- 1 cup whipping cream

RASPBERRY SAUCE
- 1 tablespoon cornstarch
- 2 tablespoons cold water
- 1 package (12 ounces) frozen red raspberries, partially thawed
- 4 tablespoons raspberry jelly
- 1 tablespoon orange-flavored liqueur

Shaved bittersweet chocolate to garnish

For custard, soften gelatin in orange juice in a small bowl. Combine sugar, egg yolks, and salt in a small bowl; beat until well blended. Whisking constantly, add egg mixture to scalded milk in a heavy medium saucepan. Stirring constantly, cook over medium-low heat about 20 minutes or until custard thickens enough to thinly coat the back of a spoon. Stir gelatin mixture into hot custard, stirring until well blended. Pour custard into a medium bowl; cover and chill 1 1/2 hours.

Beat whipping cream until stiff; fold into chilled custard. Spoon into individual serving dishes; cover and chill 30 minutes.

For raspberry sauce, combine cornstarch and cold water in a small bowl. In a heavy medium saucepan, combine raspberries and jelly. Bring to a boil over medium-high heat. Stirring constantly, add cornstarch mixture; stir until thickened. Press raspberry mixture through a sieve into a medium bowl; discard seeds and pulp. Stir liqueur into raspberry liquid; spoon over custard. Garnish with shaved chocolate.

Yield: about 8 servings

HOT FRUITED TEA

- 1 whole orange
- 10 cups water
- 4 regular-size tea bags
- 2 cinnamon sticks
- 1 teaspoon whole cloves
- 2 cans (12 ounces each) frozen cranberry-raspberry-strawberry juice beverage concentrate
- 1 cup firmly packed brown sugar

  Orange slices to serve

Peel whole orange in one continuous strip; set peel aside and reserve orange meat for another use. Place water, tea bags, cinnamon sticks, cloves, and orange peel in a heavy large saucepan. Bring to a simmer over medium-high heat. Cover and continue to simmer 15 minutes. Strain tea into a Dutch oven; discard tea bags, orange peel, and spices. Add concentrate and brown sugar; stir over medium-low heat until sugar dissolves and tea is hot. Serve hot with orange slices.
Yield: about seventeen 6-ounce servings

SPICY CHRISTMAS TREES

COOKIES
- $1/3$ cup butter or margarine, softened
- $1/3$ cup vegetable shortening
- $1 1/4$ cups sugar
- 1 cup sour cream
- $1/2$ cup molasses
- 2 eggs
- 1 teaspoon vanilla extract
- $5 1/4$ cups all-purpose flour
- $1/4$ cup cocoa
- 1 tablespoon ground cinnamon
- 2 teaspoons baking powder
- 2 teaspoons ground ginger
- 1 teaspoon ground allspice
- 1 teaspoon baking soda
- 1 teaspoon salt

ICING
- 1 cup sifted confectioners sugar
- 1 tablespoon plus 1 teaspoon milk

For cookies, cream butter, shortening, and sugar in a large bowl until fluffy. Add sour cream, molasses, eggs, and vanilla; beat until smooth. In another large bowl, combine flour, cocoa, cinnamon, baking powder, ginger, allspice, baking soda, and salt. Add half of dry ingredients to creamed mixture; stir until a soft dough forms. Stir remaining dry ingredients, 1 cup at a time, into dough; use hands if necessary to mix well. Divide dough into fourths. Wrap in plastic wrap and chill 2 hours or until dough is firm.

Our Spicy Christmas Trees are a yummy after-dinner snack. Their old-fashioned gingerbread flavor is sure to please! Serve these soft cookies with Hot Fruited Tea — a heartwarming concoction of fruit juices, cinnamon, cloves, brown sugar, and tea.

Preheat oven to 350 degrees. On a lightly floured surface, use a floured rolling pin to roll out one fourth of dough to slightly less than $1/4$-inch thickness. Use $3 1/4$ x 4-inch and $2 1/4$ x $3 1/4$-inch Christmas tree-shaped cookie cutters to cut out cookies. Transfer to a greased baking sheet. Bake 7 to 9 minutes or until firm to the touch. Transfer cookies to a wire rack to cool. Repeat with remaining dough.

For icing, combine confectioners sugar and milk in a small bowl; stir until smooth. Spoon icing into a pastry bag fitted with a small round tip. Pipe outline onto each cookie. Allow icing to harden. Store in an airtight container.
Yield: about 7 dozen cookies

VISIONS OF SUGARPLUMS

Inspired by the enchanting Nutcracker ballet, our collection of dreamy confections, cookies, and candies will magically transport you to the Kingdom of Sweets where the Sugarplum Fairy presides over mountains of chocolate, swirls of icing, and stacks of sugar-coated yummies. These sumptuous visions will surely delight young and old alike this holiday season!

Crushed peppermint candies add a refreshing minty flavor to an old favorite. Cut into squares, our Peppermint Divinity *(left, on plate)* is simply divine! Miniature Toffee Cheesecakes are rich and yummy bite-size morsels. Holly Mints are sweet little confections embellished with cinnamon candies.

MINIATURE TOFFEE CHEESECAKES

CRUST
- 1/2 cup butter or margarine, softened
- 1/2 cup firmly packed brown sugar
- 1 teaspoon vanilla extract
- 1 1/4 cups all-purpose flour
- 1/2 cup finely chopped pecans

FILLING
- 2 packages (8 ounces each) cream cheese, softened
- 1/2 cup firmly packed brown sugar
- 2 eggs
- 1 teaspoon vanilla-butter-nut flavoring
- 1 package (6 ounces) milk chocolate-covered toffee bits

For crust, cream butter, brown sugar, and vanilla in a medium bowl until fluffy. Add flour; stir until well blended. Stir in pecans. Press 1 teaspoon crust mixture into bottom of each paper-lined tin of a miniature muffin pan.

Preheat oven to 350 degrees. For filling, beat cream cheese and brown sugar in a medium bowl until fluffy. Add eggs and vanilla-butter-nut flavoring; beat until well blended. Stir in toffee bits. Spoon 1 tablespoon filling mixture over each crust. Bake 16 to 18 minutes or until filling is set in center. Place pan on a wire rack to cool. Store in refrigerator in an airtight container.

Yield: about 5 dozen miniature cheesecakes

PEPPERMINT DIVINITY

- 1 jar (7 ounces) marshmallow creme
- 2 cups sugar
- 1/2 cup water
- 2 tablespoons light corn syrup
- 1/8 teaspoon salt
- 1/2 teaspoon vanilla extract
- 3/4 cup finely crushed peppermint candies (about 6 ounces)

Spoon marshmallow creme into a large bowl; set aside. Butter sides of a heavy medium saucepan. Combine sugar, water, corn syrup, and salt in saucepan. Stirring constantly, cook over medium heat until sugar dissolves. Using a pastry brush dipped in hot water, wash down any sugar crystals on sides of pan. Attach a candy thermometer to pan, making sure thermometer does not touch bottom of pan. Increase heat to medium-high and bring to a boil. Cook, without stirring, until syrup reaches hard-ball stage (approximately 250 to 268 degrees). Test about

Creamy cherry-flavored fondant is wrapped around candied cherry centers and drenched in luscious dark chocolate to create Cherry Sugarplums. A box or tin of these goodies will make a great gift!

1/2 teaspoon syrup in ice water. Syrup will roll into a hard ball in ice water and will remain hard when removed from the water. Remove from heat. While beating with an electric mixer on medium speed, slowly pour syrup over marshmallow creme. Add vanilla and increase speed of mixer to high. Continue to beat just until mixture holds its shape. Quickly stir in crushed candies. Press into a greased 8-inch square pan. Allow to harden. Cut into 1-inch squares. Store in an airtight container.

Yield: about 4 dozen candies

HOLLY MINTS

- 4 1/2 cups sifted confectioners sugar
- 5 tablespoons butter, softened
- 3 tablespoons evaporated milk
- 12 drops peppermint-flavored oil
  Green liquid food coloring

  Small red cinnamon candies to garnish

In a large bowl, combine confectioners sugar, butter, evaporated milk, and flavored oil; tint green. Knead mixture until smooth and color is well blended. Firmly press mixture into a 1 1/2-inch-long rubber leaf-shaped candy mold. Immediately remove from mold and place on waxed paper. Garnish mints with cinnamon candies for holly berries. Store in a cool place in a container with a loose-fitting lid.

Yield: about 9 dozen mints

CHERRY SUGARPLUMS

- 1/3 cup butter, softened
- 1/3 cup light corn syrup
- 1 teaspoon cherry flavoring
  Liquid red food coloring
- 4 cups sifted confectioners sugar
- 4 ounces candied cherries, halved
- 6 ounces chocolate-flavored candy coating
- 4 ounces bittersweet baking chocolate

In a medium bowl, cream butter and corn syrup until fluffy. Stir in cherry flavoring; tint pink. Beating with an electric mixer, gradually add confectioners sugar to butter mixture until too stiff to beat. Stir in remaining sugar. Pour mixture onto a dampened smooth surface. Knead until very smooth and creamy. Using teaspoonfuls of candy mixture, shape balls around cherry halves. Place balls on waxed paper. Lightly cover with waxed paper and allow to dry overnight at room temperature.

In a heavy medium saucepan over low heat, melt candy coating and bittersweet chocolate. Remove chocolate from heat. Placing each ball on a fork and holding over saucepan, spoon chocolate over balls. Place balls on a baking sheet covered with waxed paper. Place in refrigerator to allow chocolate to harden. Store in an airtight container in a cool place.

Yield: about 5 1/2 dozen candies

Sprinkled with confectioners sugar, our flaky Christmas Rosettes *(clockwise from lower left)* resemble little snow-covered Christmas trees. Mint leaves are stirred into the batter of Fresh Mint Cookies for a light, delicious treat. Loaded with chopped walnuts and candied cherries, Cherry-Walnut Fudge is a colorful Yuletide sweet.

CHRISTMAS ROSETTES

- ³/₄ cup evaporated milk
- 2 eggs
- 2 teaspoons vanilla extract
- 1 cup sifted all-purpose flour
- 2 tablespoons granulated sugar
- ¹/₈ teaspoon salt
  Vegetable oil
  Sifted confectioners sugar

In a medium bowl, combine evaporated milk, eggs, and vanilla; whisk until well blended. In a small bowl, combine flour, granulated sugar, and salt. Gradually add dry ingredients to milk mixture; whisk until smooth. Cover and chill mixture 30 minutes.

Place ³/₄ inch of oil in a heavy medium saucepan over medium-high heat. Preheat rosette iron in hot oil. Remove iron from heat and blot on paper towel. Dip bottom of iron into batter and immediately into hot oil. Batter should release from iron. If not, gently shake iron to release batter. Cook about 30 seconds or until lightly browned; drain on paper towels. Sprinkle warm rosettes with confectioners sugar. Store in a single layer between sheets of waxed paper in an airtight container.

Yield: about 8 dozen rosettes

FRESH MINT COOKIES

Prepare dough one day in advance to allow flavors to blend.

- 1¹/₂ cups butter or margarine, softened
- ²/₃ cup superfine granulated sugar
- 1 egg
- 2 tablespoons minced fresh mint leaves
- 1 tablespoon grated orange zest
- ¹/₂ teaspoon vanilla extract
- 2 cups all-purpose flour
  Granulated sugar

In a large bowl, cream butter and superfine sugar until fluffy. Add egg, mint leaves, orange zest, and vanilla; beat until smooth. Add flour to creamed mixture; stir until a soft dough forms. Cover dough and chill overnight.

Preheat oven to 350 degrees. Shape dough into 1-inch balls. Place balls 1 inch apart on an ungreased baking sheet; flatten balls with bottom of a glass dipped in granulated sugar. Bake 7 to 9 minutes or until edges are lightly browned. Transfer cookies to a wire rack to cool. Store in an airtight container.

Yield: about 6 dozen cookies

CHERRY-WALNUT FUDGE

- 2¹/₄ cups sugar
- ¹/₂ cup sour cream
- ¹/₄ cup milk
- 2 tablespoons butter or margarine
- 1 tablespoon light corn syrup
- ¹/₄ teaspoon salt
- 2 teaspoons vanilla extract
- 1 cup coarsely chopped walnuts
- ¹/₂ cup candied cherries, quartered

Line a 7 x 11-inch baking pan with aluminum foil, extending foil over ends of pan. Grease foil and set pan aside. Butter sides of a heavy large saucepan. Combine sugar, sour cream, milk, butter, corn syrup, and salt. Stirring constantly, cook over medium-low heat until sugar dissolves. Using a pastry brush dipped in hot water, wash down any sugar crystals on sides of pan. Attach a candy thermometer to pan, making sure thermometer does not touch bottom of pan. Increase heat to medium and bring to a boil. Cook, without stirring, until syrup reaches soft-ball stage (approximately 234 to 240 degrees). Test about ¹/₂ teaspoon syrup in ice water. Syrup will easily form a ball in ice water but will flatten when held in your hand. Place pan in 2 inches of cold water in sink.

Add vanilla; do not stir. Cool to approximately 110 degrees. Using medium speed of an electric mixer, beat fudge until thickened and no longer glossy. Stir in walnuts and cherries. Spread mixture into prepared pan. Cool completely. Use ends of foil to lift fudge from pan. Cut into 1-inch squares. Store in an airtight container in a cool place.

Yield: about 5 dozen pieces fudge

BRANDIED FRUIT COOKIES

- 2 packages (8 ounces each) chopped dates
- 1 cup raisins
- 3/4 cup brandy
- 3/4 cup butter or margarine, softened
- 1 cup sugar
- 1/4 cup hot water
- 1 teaspoon baking soda
- 2 eggs
- 2 cups all-purpose flour
- 1 teaspoon ground cloves
- 4 cups chopped pecans
- 1 cup candied cherries, coarsely chopped
- 1 cup candied pineapple, coarsely chopped

Preheat oven to 350 degrees. In a large bowl, combine dates, raisins, and brandy; set aside.

In another large bowl, cream butter and sugar until fluffy. In a small bowl, combine hot water and baking soda. Add baking soda mixture and eggs to butter mixture; beat until smooth. In a small bowl, combine flour and cloves. Add dry ingredients to creamed mixture; stir until a soft dough forms. Stir in brandied fruit mixture, pecans, cherries, and pineapple. Drop teaspoonfuls of dough 2 inches apart onto a greased baking sheet. Bake 9 to 11 minutes or until edges are lightly browned. Transfer cookies to a wire rack to cool. Store in a single layer between sheets of waxed paper in an airtight container.

Yield: about 8 dozen cookies

NUTTY CARAMELS

- 2 cups sugar
- 2 cups whipping cream, divided
- 1 1/2 cups light corn syrup
- 3/4 cup butter
- 1 1/2 cups finely chopped toasted pecans
- 1 teaspoon vanilla extract

Butter sides of a heavy Dutch oven. Combine sugar, 1 cup whipping cream, corn syrup, and butter in pan. Stirring constantly, cook over medium-low heat

Nutty Caramels *(left)* are chewy little tidbits packed with buttery flavor and toasted pecans. Brandied Fruit Cookies have all the goodness of traditional fruitcake — with a little added punch.

until sugar dissolves. Using a pastry brush dipped in hot water, wash down any sugar crystals on sides of pan. Attach a candy thermometer to pan, making sure thermometer does not touch bottom of pan. Continuing to stir, increase heat to medium and bring to a boil. Gradually add remaining 1 cup whipping cream. Stirring frequently without touching sides of pan, cook until syrup reaches firm-ball stage (approximately 242 to 248 degrees). Test about 1/2 teaspoon syrup in ice water.

Syrup will roll into a firm ball in ice water but will flatten if pressed when removed from the water. Remove from heat and stir in pecans and vanilla. Immediately pour into a buttered 10 1/2 x 15 1/2-inch jellyroll pan. Cool at room temperature several hours. Cut into 1-inch squares using a lightly oiled heavy knife. Wrap each candy piece in a foil candy wrapper and store in a cool place.

Yield: about 12 1/2 dozen caramels

Three layers of gooey goodness, Turtle Brownies *(left)* feature a dark brownie "crust," a layer of rich caramel, and a topping of semisweet chocolate and chopped walnuts. Using only a few basic ingredients, you can make our cinnamon- and spearmint-flavored Stained Glass Candy. A light dusting of confectioners sugar gives the "glass" candy a frosted appearance.

TURTLE BROWNIES

BROWNIES
- 1 cup butter or margarine
- 4 ounces unsweetened baking chocolate
- 4 eggs
- 2 cups sugar
- 1 teaspoon vanilla-butter-nut flavoring
- 1½ cups all-purpose flour
- ½ teaspoon salt

TOPPING
- 1 package (14 ounces) caramels
- 2 tablespoons milk
- 1½ cups finely chopped toasted walnuts
- 1 package (6 ounces) semisweet chocolate chips
- 2 teaspoons vegetable shortening

Preheat oven to 350 degrees. For brownies, melt butter and chocolate in a double boiler over simmering water; remove from heat and allow to cool. In a large bowl, lightly beat eggs. Add sugar and vanilla-butter-nut flavoring; beat until smooth. Combine chocolate mixture with sugar mixture. In a small bowl, combine flour and salt. Add dry ingredients to chocolate mixture; stir until smooth. Spread batter into a greased and floured 9 x 13-inch baking pan. Bake 25 to 30 minutes or until set in center. Place pan on a wire rack to cool.

For topping, place caramels and milk in top of a double boiler over medium heat. Stir until caramels melt. Stir in walnuts. Spoon caramel mixture over warm brownies, spreading evenly. Allow brownies to cool. In a small microwave-safe bowl, microwave chocolate chips on high power (100%) 2 minutes, stirring after each minute. Add shortening; stir until well blended. Spread over caramel topping. Allow chocolate to harden. Cut into 1½-inch squares. Store in an airtight container.

Yield: about 3 dozen brownies

STAINED GLASS CANDY

- 1 cup sifted confectioners sugar
- 3¾ cups granulated sugar
- 1¼ cups light corn syrup
- 1 cup water
- ⅛ teaspoon **each** of spearmint- and cinnamon-flavored oils
- Green and red liquid food coloring

Spread confectioners sugar evenly into two 10½ x 15½-inch jellyroll pans. In a heavy large saucepan, combine granulated sugar, corn syrup, and water. Stirring constantly, cook over medium-low heat until sugar dissolves. Using a pastry brush dipped in hot water, wash down any sugar crystals on sides of pan. Attach a candy thermometer to pan, making sure thermometer does not touch bottom of pan. Increase heat to medium-high and bring to a boil. Cook, without stirring, until syrup reaches soft-crack stage (approximately 270 to 290 degrees). Test about ½ teaspoon syrup in ice water. Syrup will form hard threads in ice water but will soften when removed from the water. Remove from heat; immediately pour half of syrup into a second heated saucepan. Add spearmint oil and green food coloring to half of syrup; add cinnamon oil and red food coloring to remaining syrup. Pour each flavored candy into separate jellyroll pans. Allow candy to cool completely; break into pieces. Store in an airtight container.

Yield: about 2 pounds candy

132

WINTER FOREST CHRISTMAS TREES

COOKIES

1 cup butter or margarine, softened
1½ cups sifted confectioners sugar
1 egg
1½ teaspoons vanilla extract
2½ cups all-purpose flour
½ teaspoon baking soda
¼ teaspoon cream of tartar

DECORATING ICING

3½ cups sifted confectioners sugar
⅓ cup milk
¾ teaspoon liquid green food coloring
½ teaspoon mint extract

White coarse decorating sugar to decorate

ROYAL ICING

½ cup sifted confectioners sugar
2¼ teaspoons water
1 teaspoon meringue powder
Yellow and red paste food coloring

For cookies, cream butter and confectioners sugar in a large bowl until fluffy. Add egg and vanilla; beat until smooth. In a medium bowl, combine flour, baking soda, and cream of tartar. Add dry ingredients to creamed mixture; stir until a soft dough forms. Divide dough in half. Wrap in plastic wrap and chill 3 hours.

Preheat oven to 375 degrees. On a lightly floured surface, use a floured rolling pin to roll out half of dough to ⅛-inch thickness. Use a 3 x 5¼-inch tree-shaped cookie cutter to cut out cookies. Transfer cookies to a lightly greased baking sheet. Bake 5 to 7 minutes or until bottoms are lightly browned. Transfer to a wire rack with waxed paper underneath to cool. Repeat with remaining dough.

For decorating icing, combine confectioners sugar, milk, food coloring, and mint extract in a medium bowl; stir until smooth. Ice cookies. Before icing is completely dry, sprinkle with coarse decorating sugar. Allow icing to harden.

For royal icing, beat confectioners sugar, water, and meringue powder in a small bowl with an electric mixer 7 to 10 minutes or until stiff. Place 2 tablespoons icing in a small bowl; tint yellow. Tint remaining icing red. Spoon red icing into a pastry bag fitted with a medium round tip. Pipe red birds onto trees. Spoon yellow icing into a pastry bag fitted with a very small round tip. Pipe small beaks onto birds. Allow icing to harden.

Store in single layers between sheets of waxed paper in an airtight container.
Yield: about 2 dozen cookies

Delightful cookies that are as sweet to look at as they are to eat, Winter Forest Christmas Trees *(top)* are decorated with minty green icing and tiny frosting cardinals. A sprinkling of coarse sugar "snow" adorns the trees' boughs. Butter-Pecan Brittle is packed with nuts for delicious snacking during the holiday season.

BUTTER-PECAN BRITTLE

2 cups sugar
¾ cup light corn syrup
¼ cup water
3 cups coarsely chopped toasted pecans
¼ cup butter
1 teaspoon vanilla extract
½ teaspoon salt
1 teaspoon baking soda

Butter sides of a heavy large saucepan. Combine sugar, corn syrup, and water in saucepan. Stirring constantly, cook over medium-low heat until sugar dissolves. Using a pastry brush dipped in hot water, wash down any sugar crystals on sides of pan. Attach a candy thermometer to pan, making sure thermometer does not touch bottom of pan. Increase heat to medium and bring to a boil. Cook, without stirring, until syrup reaches hard-crack stage (approximately 300 to 310 degrees) and turns light golden in color. Test about ½ teaspoon syrup in ice water. Syrup will form brittle threads in ice water and will remain brittle when removed from the water. Remove from heat and stir in pecans, butter, vanilla, and salt; stir until butter melts. Add baking soda (syrup will foam); stir until soda dissolves. Pour syrup onto a large piece of buttered aluminum foil. Using a buttered spatula, pull edges of warm candy until stretched thin. Cool completely. Break into pieces. Store in an airtight container.
Yield: about 2 pounds brittle

133

Laced with coffee-flavored liqueur and crunchy pecans, Mocha-Nut Fudge *(left)* is a chocolate lover's dream come true! Lemon-Pecan Cookies combine the tangy flavor of lemon and the nutty richness of pecans to create these tummy-tempting yummies.

MOCHA-NUT FUDGE

    4   cups sugar
  1/2   teaspoon salt
    1   cup evaporated milk
  1/3   cup light corn syrup
    6   tablespoons butter, divided
  1/2   cup coffee-flavored liqueur
    2   teaspoons vanilla extract
1 1/2   cups semisweet chocolate chips,
          melted
    1   cup finely chopped toasted pecans

Butter sides of a heavy large saucepan. Combine sugar and salt in saucepan. Add evaporated milk, corn syrup, and 3 tablespoons butter. Stirring constantly, cook over medium-low heat until sugar dissolves. Using a pastry brush dipped in hot water, wash down any sugar crystals on sides of pan. Attach a candy thermometer to pan, making sure thermometer does not touch bottom of pan. Increase heat to medium and bring to a boil. Cook, without stirring, until syrup reaches soft-ball stage (approximately 234 to 240 degrees). Test about 1/2 teaspoon syrup in ice water. Syrup will easily form a ball in ice water but will flatten when held in your hand. Remove from heat. Add remaining 3 tablespoons butter, liqueur, and vanilla; do not stir. Place pan in 2 inches of cold water in sink. Cool to approximately 110 degrees. Add melted chocolate. Using medium speed of an electric mixer, beat until thickened and no longer glossy. Stir in pecans. Drop teaspoonfuls of mixture onto waxed paper. Cool completely. Store in an airtight container in a cool place.

Yield: about 8 dozen pieces fudge

LEMON-PECAN COOKIES

  1/2   cup butter or margarine, softened
  1/4   cup vegetable shortening
    1   cup sugar
    1   egg
    2   tablespoons honey
    1   teaspoon grated lemon zest
  1/2   teaspoon lemon extract
    2   cups all-purpose flour
  1/2   teaspoon baking soda
  1/2   teaspoon cream of tartar
  1/4   teaspoon salt
    1   cup finely chopped toasted pecans

Preheat oven to 375 degrees. In a large bowl, cream butter, shortening, and sugar until fluffy. Add egg, honey, lemon zest, and lemon extract; beat until smooth. In a small bowl, combine flour, baking soda, cream of tartar, and salt. Add dry ingredients to creamed mixture; stir until a soft dough forms. Stir in pecans. Drop tablespoonfuls of dough 3 inches apart onto a lightly greased baking sheet. Bake 6 to 8 minutes or until bottoms are lightly browned. Transfer cookies to a wire rack to cool. Store in an airtight container.

Yield: about 3 1/2 dozen cookies

PUMPKIN BISCOTTI

2¼ cups all-purpose flour
1½ cups whole-wheat flour
1 cup sugar
1 teaspoon pumpkin pie spice
½ teaspoon baking soda
½ teaspoon baking powder
¼ teaspoon salt
1 cup canned pumpkin
2 eggs
¼ cup vegetable oil
1 tablespoon grated orange zest
½ teaspoon vanilla extract
½ teaspoon orange extract
1½ cups coarsely chopped toasted
   walnuts

Preheat oven to 300 degrees. Combine flours, sugar, pumpkin pie spice, baking soda, baking powder, and salt in a large bowl. In a small bowl, whisk pumpkin, eggs, oil, orange zest, and extracts. Add pumpkin mixture to flour mixture; beat until a soft dough forms. Turn onto a lightly floured surface. Add walnuts and knead 3 minutes or until walnuts are evenly distributed. Divide dough into thirds. On a lightly greased baking sheet, shape each piece of dough into a slightly flattened 2½ x 10-inch loaf, flouring hands as necessary. Allow 3 inches between loaves on baking sheet. Bake 45 to 47 minutes or until loaves are lightly browned; cool 10 minutes on baking sheet. Cut loaves diagonally into ½-inch slices. Lay slices flat on a baking sheet. Bake 15 to 17 minutes, turn slices over, and bake 15 to 17 minutes longer. Transfer cookies to a wire rack to cool completely. Store in an airtight container.
Yield: about 3½ dozen cookies

LEMON-GINGER CREAMS

1¾ cups sugar
1 cup whipping cream
1½ tablespoons light corn syrup
¾ cup miniature marshmallows
2 tablespoons lemon juice
½ tablespoon grated lemon zest
2 tablespoons finely chopped
   crystallized ginger

Butter sides of a heavy large saucepan. Combine sugar, whipping cream, and corn syrup in saucepan. Stirring constantly, cook over medium-low heat until sugar dissolves. Using a pastry brush dipped in hot water, wash down any sugar crystals on sides of pan. Attach a candy thermometer to pan, making sure thermometer does not touch bottom of pan.

Lemon-Ginger Creams *(left, on plate)* are a rich concoction of marshmallows, lemon zest, and bits of winter-warming ginger. You'll find lots of toasted walnuts in our spicy Pumpkin Biscotti — it's great for dipping in a hot drink.

Increase heat to medium and bring to a boil. Cook, without stirring, until syrup reaches soft-ball stage (approximately 234 to 240 degrees). Test about ½ teaspoon syrup in ice water. Syrup will easily form a ball in ice water but will flatten when held in your hand. Remove from heat and stir in marshmallows until melted. Pour mixture into a medium heat-resistant nonmetallic bowl. Add lemon juice and lemon zest. Beat 10 to 12 minutes or until creamy. Stir in ginger. Spoon mixture into a pastry bag fitted with a large round tip (#12). Pipe candy mixture into small paper candy cups placed on a baking sheet. Chill until firm. Store in an airtight container in a cool place.
Yield: about 3½ dozen candies

CHRISTMAS FIESTA

Spice up your holiday get-togethers with a menu from South of the Border!
From zesty posole casserole to tasty tamales, the robust recipes in this collection offer
everything you need for an authentic Yuletide fiesta. Our carnival of fun Mexican
fare will guarantee a Feliz Navidad for friends, family, and guests!

Steamed in corn shucks to seal in the flavor, savory Pork Tamales offer a shredded-meat filling in a traditional masa harina dough. To accompany the entrée, there are two wonderful toppings, Red Pepper and Green Chile Cream Sauces. The first is a milder mixture of sweet red pepper and green onions, while the latter includes green chiles and jalapeños for those who like a fiery meal!

PORK TAMALES WITH RED PEPPER AND GREEN CHILE CREAM SAUCES

Prepare meat mixture a day ahead for easy assembly of tamales.

- 7 pound pork shoulder roast, boned, saving bone
- 2 heads garlic, separated into cloves
- 9 cups water
- 1/3 cup plus 1/4 cup chili powder, divided
- 4 teaspoons cumin seed
- 3 teaspoons salt, divided
- 1 package (8 ounces) dried corn shucks
- 1 package (4.4 pounds) masa harina (about 16 cups)
- 2 pounds (4 cups) shortening or lard
- 1 can (14.5 ounces) beef broth

Cut pork into 3-inch pieces. Place meat, bone, and garlic in a stockpot. Add 9 cups water, and more if necessary, to cover meat; bring to a boil over medium-high heat. Reduce heat to medium-low; cover and simmer about 2 hours or until meat is tender. Place meat and liquid in separate containers; discard bone. Shred meat by hand or in a food processor. Place meat in a heavy Dutch oven and stir in 1/3 cup chili powder, cumin seed, and 1 teaspoon salt. Add about 3 cups of reserved liquid to Dutch oven. Stirring frequently, cover and simmer over low heat 1 hour to allow flavors to blend. If necessary, add additional liquid to prevent meat from sticking to pan. Cover and chill meat and reserved liquid overnight in separate containers.

Place corn shucks in warm water about 30 minutes to soften. Clean and separate corn shucks.

For tamale dough, combine masa harina, remaining 1/4 cup chili powder, and remaining 2 teaspoons salt in a large bowl. Cut shortening into masa mixture until it resembles coarse meal. Skim fat from chilled liquid. If necessary, add beef broth to reserved liquid to make 8 cups. Gradually add liquid to mixture, stirring until a soft dough forms that will stick together.

To assemble each tamale, place a softened corn shuck on a flat surface with a long side facing you. Spread about 1/4 cup dough from wide end about 4 1/2 inches along one side. Continue to spread dough, forming a rectangle that covers about two-thirds of the wide end of corn shuck (**Fig. 1**).

Fig. 1

Spread a heaping tablespoon of meat down center of dough (**Fig. 2**).

Fig. 2

Roll edge closest to you over meat, rolling back corn shuck enough to expose a small amount of dough (**Fig. 3**).

Fig. 3

Bring far side toward you until dough edges overlap; wrap corn shuck around tamale. Fold narrow end of corn shuck over tamale. Stand individual tamales in a container or tie in bundles with kitchen string and stand with open ends up (**Fig. 4**).

Fig. 4

(**Note:** Tamales may be chilled or frozen at this point and steamed at a later time).

To steam tamales, stand tamales with open ends up in a steamer basket placed over hot water in a stockpot. Cover and steam 1 to 1 1/2 hours. Serve warm with Red Pepper Cream Sauce and Green Chile Cream Sauce.
Yield: about 5 1/2 dozen tamales

RED PEPPER CREAM SAUCE
- 1/4 cup butter or margarine
- 1 large sweet red pepper, chopped
- 1/4 cup thinly sliced green onions
- 3 tablespoons all-purpose flour
- 1/2 teaspoon salt
- 1/4 teaspoon ground white pepper
- 1 1/2 cups half and half
- 1 tablespoon freshly squeezed lemon juice

  Sweet red pepper strips to garnish

In a medium saucepan, melt butter over medium heat. Add red pepper and onions; cook until almost tender. Reserve 2 tablespoons pepper mixture. Place remaining pepper mixture in a food processor and purée. Return mixture to saucepan and reduce heat to medium-low. Stirring constantly, add flour, salt, and white pepper to mixture. Cook 2 minutes or until flour is well blended and sauce thickens. While whisking mixture, gradually add half and half and lemon juice. Stir in reserved pepper mixture. Increase heat to medium; continue cooking 5 minutes or until mixture thickens. Garnish with sweet red pepper strips. Serve warm over Pork Tamales.
Yield: about 2 1/2 cups sauce

GREEN CHILE CREAM SAUCE
- 1/4 cup butter or margarine
- 1/4 cup thinly sliced green onions
- 3 cans (4.5 ounces each) chopped green chiles, undrained
- 2 tablespoons finely chopped fresh, seeded jalapeño peppers
- 2 tablespoons all-purpose flour
- 1/4 teaspoon salt
- 1/4 teaspoon ground white pepper
- 1 1/2 cups half and half
- 2 teaspoons freshly squeezed lime juice

In a medium saucepan, melt butter over medium heat. Add onions; cook until almost tender. Add green chiles and jalapeño peppers; stirring frequently, cook 2 minutes. Reduce heat to medium-low; stirring constantly, add flour, salt, and white pepper to mixture. Cook 1 minute or until flour is well blended and sauce thickens. While whisking mixture, gradually add half and half and lime juice; continue cooking 5 minutes or until mixture thickens. Serve warm over Pork Tamales.
Yield: about 3 1/4 cups sauce

RASPBERRY LEMONADE

- 3 cups sugar
- 1 cup water
- 1 package (12 ounces) frozen whole red raspberries, thawed **or** 1 cup raspberry juice
- 1½ cups freshly squeezed lemon juice (about 10 to 12 small lemons)
- 1 tablespoon grated lemon zest
- 5 to 6 cups club soda, chilled

    Lemon slices to garnish

In a medium saucepan, combine sugar and water over medium heat; stir until sugar dissolves. Increase heat to medium-high and bring to a boil. Stirring constantly, boil 1 minute. Pour sugar syrup into a heat-resistant medium bowl and allow to cool.

Press raspberries through a sieve over another medium bowl. Discard seeds and pulp. Add lemon juice, raspberry juice, and lemon zest to sugar syrup; cover and chill.

To serve, combine juice mixture and club soda to taste. Garnish with lemon slices.

Yield: about thirteen 6-ounce servings

JíCAMA AND ORANGE SALAD WITH LIME DRESSING

LIME DRESSING
- ½ cup sugar
- 1 tablespoon dry mustard
- ¾ cup peanut oil
- 6 tablespoons freshly squeezed lime juice
- ¼ cup honey
- 3 tablespoons water
- ¼ cup white wine vinegar
- 2 tablespoons chopped fresh cilantro

SALAD
- Leaf lettuce
- 4 to 5 cups peeled, matchsticked jícama
- 5 navel oranges, peeled and sectioned
- Seeds of 2 pomegranates
- Finely chopped unsalted dry-roasted peanuts

For lime dressing, combine sugar and dry mustard in a medium bowl. Add oil, lime juice, honey, water, and vinegar; stir until well blended. Stir in cilantro.

For salad, layer ingredients in order given. Serve with lime dressing.

Yield: about 14 servings

Garnished with lemon slices, tangy Raspberry Lemonade will have your guests asking for more. Jícama and Orange Salad with Lime Dressing is a crisp and colorful combination of sweet, tart pomegranate seeds, orange sections, nutty slivers of Mexican jícama, and leaf lettuce. It's great with our tamales!

Fresh, hand-rolled Flour Tortillas are just right for dipping in our delicious Chicken and Rice Soup. Chopped green chiles and cumin give the soup a hot, peppery flavor.

FLOUR TORTILLAS

2 cups all-purpose flour
3/4 teaspoon baking powder
1/2 teaspoon salt
1/4 cup vegetable shortening or lard
8 tablespoons water

In a medium bowl, combine flour, baking powder, and salt. Using a pastry blender or 2 knives, cut in shortening until mixture resembles coarse meal. Add water, stirring until well blended.

Turn dough onto a lightly floured surface. Gradually sprinkle dough with additional water as necessary to shape into a ball. Knead dough 3 to 5 minutes or until smooth and elastic. Divide dough into 12 balls. Cover with plastic wrap and let rest at room temperature 30 minutes.

Heat a griddle or large skillet over medium-high heat. Working with 1 ball of dough at a time on a very lightly floured surface, roll into a 7-inch circle. To form a circle, rotate dough and turn over every few strokes of the rolling pin. On hot griddle, cook tortilla about 1 minute on each side or until lightly browned. Transfer tortilla onto a platter and cover with a lid or wrap in a kitchen towel and aluminum foil to retain moisture. Repeat with remaining dough. Wrapped tortillas may be placed in a 200-degree oven for a short period of time to remain warm. To reheat, place foil-wrapped tortillas in a 325-degree oven 15 to 20 minutes.

Yield: twelve 7-inch tortillas

CHICKEN AND RICE SOUP

3 pound broiler-fryer chicken, discarding giblets
6 1/2 cups water
1 medium onion, cut into large pieces
2 ribs celery with leaves, cut into pieces
1 clove garlic
1 bay leaf
1 cup thinly sliced carrots
2/3 cup uncooked long-grain rice
1/2 cup finely chopped onion
1 can (4.5 ounces) chopped green chiles
2 chicken bouillon cubes
1/4 teaspoon salt
1/4 teaspoon ground white pepper
1/4 teaspoon ground cumin

Chopped green onions to garnish

Place chicken, water, onion pieces, celery, garlic, and bay leaf in a stockpot over high heat; bring to a boil. Cover and reduce heat to medium-low; simmer 1 hour or until chicken is tender. Strain chicken stock and chill; discard vegetables. Skin and bone chicken. Cut meat into bite-size pieces; chill.

Skim fat from chicken stock. Combine chicken stock, carrots, rice, chopped onion, green chiles, bouillon, salt, white pepper, and cumin in a Dutch oven over medium-high heat; bring mixture to a boil. Reduce heat to low; cover and simmer 30 minutes, adding chicken pieces during last 10 minutes. Garnish with green onions and serve warm.

Yield: about 9 cups soup

Inspired by an authentic Mexican Christmas dish, Posole Casserole is a spicy concoction of zucchini, hominy, and onions stirred together with a generous portion of Monterey Jack and Cheddar cheeses.

POSOLE CASSEROLE

2 medium onions, coarsely chopped
3 tablespoons vegetable oil
1 medium zucchini, diced
4 cloves garlic, minced
1 tablespoon chili powder
2 teaspoons ground cumin
2 cans (15$\frac{1}{2}$ ounces each) yellow hominy, drained
1 tablespoon freshly squeezed lime juice
$\frac{1}{2}$ teaspoon salt
$\frac{1}{2}$ teaspoon ground black pepper
1 cup (4 ounces) shredded Monterey Jack and Cheddar cheeses
$\frac{1}{4}$ cup fresh cilantro leaves, chopped

Fresh cilantro leaves to garnish

Cook onions in oil in a heavy large skillet over medium-high heat 5 minutes or until onions begin to soften. Stirring frequently, add zucchini, garlic, chili powder, and cumin; cook about 5 minutes or until onions begin to brown. Reduce heat to medium-low. Add hominy, lime juice, salt, and pepper; stir until well blended. Continue cooking until hominy is heated through. Remove from heat. Stir in cheeses and chopped cilantro. Garnish with cilantro leaves and serve warm.
Yield: about 12 servings

PECAN PRALINES

2 cups sugar
1 teaspoon baking soda
1 cup buttermilk
1 tablespoon light corn syrup
$\frac{3}{4}$ cup butter, cut into small pieces
2 cups chopped pecans
1 teaspoon vanilla extract

Butter sides of a heavy Dutch oven. Combine sugar and baking soda in buttered pan. Add buttermilk and corn syrup. Stirring constantly, cook over medium-low heat until sugar dissolves. Using a pastry brush dipped in hot water, wash down any sugar crystals on sides of pan. Attach a candy thermometer to pan, making sure thermometer does not touch bottom of pan. Increase heat to medium and bring to a boil. Cook, stirring constantly, until syrup reaches 210 degrees on thermometer; add butter. Continue stirring and cooking mixture until syrup reaches soft-ball stage (approximately 234 to 240 degrees). Test about 1/2 teaspoon syrup in ice water. Syrup will easily form a ball in ice water but will flatten when held in your hand. Place pan in 2 inches of cold water in sink. Cool to approximately 140 degrees. Using medium speed of an electric mixer, beat candy until thickened and no longer glossy. Quickly stir in pecans and vanilla. Drop by tablespoonfuls onto lightly greased waxed paper. Allow pralines to cool completely. Wrap pralines individually in cellophane or plastic wrap and store in an airtight container.

Yield: about 2 1/2 dozen pralines

CANDIED PUMPKIN

8	cups 1-inch cubes of fresh pumpkin (about a 5-pound pumpkin)
1/2	cup firmly packed brown sugar
1/4	cup granulated sugar
1 1/2	tablespoons all-purpose flour
1/2	teaspoon ground cinnamon
1/2	teaspoon salt
1/4	teaspoon ground allspice
3/4	cup orange juice
1/4	cup maple syrup
3	tablespoons butter or margarine, softened

Chopped toasted pecans to serve

Preheat oven to 350 degrees. Place pumpkin pieces in a single layer on a lightly greased 10 1/2 x 15 1/2 x 1-inch jellyroll pan; set aside. In a medium saucepan, combine sugars, flour, cinnamon, salt, and allspice. Add orange juice, maple syrup, and butter, stirring until well blended. Stirring occasionally, cook over medium heat about 5 minutes. Pour over pumpkin. Spooning syrup over pumpkin every 15 minutes, bake 1 hour or until pumpkin is hot and syrup is bubbly. Sprinkle with pecans to serve.

Yield: about 12 servings

MEXICAN SUGAR COOKIES

3/4	cup vegetable oil
2	eggs
1 1/2	teaspoons vanilla extract
1 1/4	cups sugar, divided
2	cups all-purpose flour
1	teaspoon baking powder
1/4	teaspoon salt
1 1/2	teaspoons ground cinnamon

Pecan Pralines *(bottom, on plate)* are irresistible caramelized candy patties packed with lots of crunchy nuts. Mexican Sugar Cookies offer an old-fashioned favorite flavored with cinnamon. Served hot and bubbly, Candied Pumpkin *(in dessert cup)* starts with chunks of fresh pumpkin that are baked in a sauce of brown sugar and maple syrup, then sprinkled with chopped pecans.

Preheat oven to 400 degrees. In a large bowl, beat oil, eggs, and vanilla until well blended. Add 1 cup sugar; beat until smooth. In a small bowl, combine flour, baking powder, and salt. Add flour mixture to oil mixture; stir until a soft dough forms. In a small bowl, combine remaining 1/4 cup sugar and cinnamon. Drop teaspoonfuls of dough into cinnamon-sugar mixture; roll into balls. Place balls 2 inches apart on a greased baking sheet. Flatten cookies with bottom of a glass dipped in cinnamon-sugar mixture. Bake 4 to 6 minutes or until bottoms are lightly browned. Transfer cookies to a wire rack to cool. Store in a cookie tin.

Yield: about 4 1/2 dozen cookies

CHRISTMAS CASUAL

Christmas is a wonderful time to open your home for a casual afternoon or evening of fun and refreshments. Warming drinks and tantalizing sweets are sure to inspire Yuletide spirit in all who partake of your easygoing hospitality. The assortment of festive recipes collected here is ideal for get-togethers spent sharing two of life's simple pleasures — lively conversation and delicious foods!

Our Spicy Cranberry-Nut Cake offers a tart filling of whole cranberries and crushed pineapple nestled between moist layers of nutty spice cake. It's decorated with pecans and sweetened whipped cream touched with cinnamon and mace. A warm cup of Christmas cheer, Mulled Cranberry Port is a spirited beverage made with orange and cranberry juices, wine, and spices.

SPICY CRANBERRY-NUT CAKE

CAKE
- 8 eggs
- 1 tablespoon vanilla extract
- 2 cups sugar
- 1 cup all-purpose flour
- 4 teaspoons baking powder
- 1 teaspoon ground cinnamon
- 5 cups chopped pecans

FILLING
- 1 can (8$\frac{1}{4}$ ounces) crushed pineapple in heavy syrup, drained with $\frac{1}{4}$ cup of syrup reserved
- 3 tablespoons cornstarch
- 1 can (16 ounces) whole berry cranberry sauce
- Red liquid food coloring

ICING
- 1$\frac{1}{2}$ cups whipping cream
- 2 tablespoons sifted confectioners sugar
- $\frac{1}{4}$ teaspoon ground cinnamon
- $\frac{1}{8}$ teaspoon ground mace

Preheat oven to 350 degrees. For cake, grease three 9-inch cake pans and line bottoms with waxed paper. In a large bowl, beat eggs and vanilla 5 minutes at high speed of an electric mixer. In a small bowl, combine sugar, flour, baking powder, and cinnamon. Reduce mixer to medium speed and add dry ingredients to egg mixture; beat 5 minutes. Reduce speed to low and stir in pecans. Pour batter into prepared pans. Bake 25 to 30 minutes or until a toothpick inserted in center of cake comes out clean. Cool in pans on a wire rack 5 minutes. Transfer cakes to wire rack to cool completely.

For filling, combine $\frac{1}{4}$ cup reserved pineapple syrup with cornstarch in a heavy medium saucepan. Add drained pineapple and cranberry sauce. Stirring constantly, cook over medium-high heat until mixture comes to a boil and thickens; reduce heat to medium and boil 2 minutes. Add 5 drops food coloring. Transfer filling to a covered container and chill 2 hours.

For icing, place a small bowl and beaters from electric mixer in freezer to chill. Spread filling between layers and on top of cake. In chilled bowl, beat icing ingredients until stiff peaks form. Ice sides of cake. Transfer remaining icing to a pastry bag fitted with a medium open star tip; pipe shell borders. Store in refrigerator until ready to serve.

Yield: about 12 servings

Easy as pie, Hot Fudge Sundae Cake is ready in minutes. The fudge topping is baked right in! Garnish individual servings with whipped cream, chopped nuts, and cherries, and you have an old-fashioned soda-fountain favorite to share.

MULLED CRANBERRY PORT

- 4 cups cranberry juice cocktail
- 1 can (6 ounces) frozen orange juice concentrate
- $\frac{1}{2}$ cup sugar
- 1 tablespoon whole cloves
- $\frac{1}{2}$ teaspoon whole allspice
- 1 cinnamon stick
- 2 medium oranges, sliced
- 1 bottle (750 ml) tawny or ruby port wine

Cinnamon sticks and orange slices to serve

Combine cranberry juice cocktail, orange juice concentrate, and sugar in a Dutch oven over medium-high heat. Place cloves and allspice in a coffee filter tied with kitchen string and add to juice mixture. Add cinnamon stick and orange slices. Bring to a boil. Reduce heat to low; add wine and stir until mixture is heated through. Serve hot with additional cinnamon sticks and orange slices.

Yield: about ten 6-ounce servings

HOT FUDGE SUNDAE CAKE

- 1 cup all-purpose flour
- $\frac{3}{4}$ cup granulated sugar
- $\frac{1}{2}$ cup cocoa, divided
- 2 teaspoons baking powder
- $\frac{1}{4}$ teaspoon salt
- $\frac{1}{2}$ cup milk
- 2 tablespoons vegetable oil
- 1 teaspoon vanilla extract
- 1 cup firmly packed brown sugar
- 1$\frac{3}{4}$ cups hot brewed coffee

Whipped cream, chopped pecans, and maraschino cherries to serve

Preheat oven to 350 degrees. In a medium bowl, combine flour, sugar, $\frac{1}{4}$ cup cocoa, baking powder, and salt. In a large bowl combine milk, oil, and vanilla; stir in flour mixture. Spread batter into an ungreased 9-inch square baking pan; sprinkle with brown sugar and remaining $\frac{1}{4}$ cup cocoa. Slowly pour hot coffee over mixture. Bake 35 to 40 minutes or until cake begins to crack on top and pull away from sides. Cool in pan on a wire rack 15 minutes. To serve, spoon cake into serving dishes; top with whipped cream, pecans, and cherries.

Yield: about 10 servings

GINGERBREAD SQUARES

CAKE
- ¼ cup butter or margarine, softened
- ½ cup sugar
- ½ cup sour cream
- ½ cup molasses
- 2 eggs
- ¾ teaspoon vanilla extract
- ¼ teaspoon orange extract
- 1¼ cups all-purpose flour
- ½ cup whole-wheat flour
- 1 teaspoon baking soda
- 1 teaspoon ground cinnamon
- 1 teaspoon ground ginger
- ½ teaspoon ground allspice
- ¼ teaspoon salt

ICING
- ½ cup butter or margarine
- 1 cup firmly packed brown sugar
- ¼ cup whipping cream
- 1 tablespoon light corn syrup
- 1 cup sifted confectioners sugar
- 1 teaspoon vanilla extract
- ½ cup finely chopped walnuts

Preheat oven to 350 degrees. For cake, cream butter and sugar in a large bowl. Add sour cream, molasses, eggs, and extracts; beat until smooth. In a small bowl, combine flours, baking soda, cinnamon, ginger, allspice, and salt. Add dry ingredients to creamed mixture; stir until well blended. Line bottom of a greased 9-inch square pan with waxed paper; grease waxed paper. Spread batter into prepared pan. Bake 24 to 28 minutes or until a toothpick inserted in center of cake comes out clean. Cool in pan on a wire rack.

For icing, melt butter in a heavy medium saucepan over medium heat. Stirring constantly, add brown sugar, whipping cream, and corn syrup; cook until mixture comes to a boil. Boil 1 minute. Remove from heat; pour into a heat-resistant medium bowl. Add confectioners sugar and vanilla; beat until smooth. Stir in walnuts. Spread icing over cake. Cut into 2-inch squares.

Yield: about 16 servings

CINNAMON MOCHA
- 6 ounces semisweet baking chocolate, coarsely chopped
- ½ cup half and half
- ¼ cup sugar
- ½ teaspoon ground cinnamon
- 1½ quarts hot brewed coffee

Combine chocolate, half and half, sugar, and cinnamon in the top of a double boiler

Topped with a creamy brown sugar icing that's loaded with walnuts, our yummy Gingerbread Squares are flavored with molasses, ginger, cinnamon, and allspice. These tasty treats are perfect to serve with aromatic Cinnamon Mocha.

over hot water; stir until chocolate melts. Transfer chocolate mixture to a large heat-resistant container. Pour brewed coffee over chocolate mixture; whisk until frothy. Pour into cups and serve hot.

Yield: about ten 6-ounce servings

CHOCOLATE-NUT COFFEE CAKE

1/2 cup firmly packed brown sugar
1/2 cup semisweet chocolate mini chips
1/2 cup finely chopped walnuts
1 tablespoon ground cinnamon
3/4 cup butter or margarine, softened
1 1/2 cups granulated sugar
3 eggs
1 tablespoon instant coffee granules dissolved in 1 tablespoon hot water
2 teaspoons vanilla extract
3 cups all-purpose flour
1 1/2 teaspoons baking powder
1 1/2 teaspoons baking soda
1/4 teaspoon salt
1 1/2 cups sour cream

Preheat oven to 350 degrees. In a medium bowl, combine brown sugar, chocolate chips, walnuts, and cinnamon; set aside. In a large bowl, cream butter and granulated sugar until fluffy. Add eggs, 1 at a time, beating well after each addition. Add coffee mixture and vanilla; beat until well blended. In a medium bowl, combine flour, baking powder, baking soda, and salt. Alternately stir dry ingredients and sour cream into creamed mixture, stirring just until well blended. Spoon one-third of batter into bottom of a greased and floured 10-inch tube pan with a removable bottom. Spoon one-third of chocolate chip mixture over batter. Repeat layers, ending with chocolate chip mixture. Bake 1 hour or until a toothpick inserted in center of cake comes out clean. Cool cake in pan on a wire rack 10 minutes. Run a knife around edge of pan; remove sides of pan. Allow to cool completely. Run knife around bottom of cake and remove bottom of pan. Store in an airtight container.
Yield: about 16 servings

PRALINE COFFEE

1 1/2 quarts strongly brewed coffee
2 cans (12 ounces each) evaporated milk
1 1/2 cups firmly packed brown sugar
1 1/2 cups pecan-flavored liqueur

In a Dutch oven, combine coffee, evaporated milk, and brown sugar. Stirring occasionally, cook over medium-high heat until sugar dissolves and mixture is heated through; remove from heat. Stir in liqueur. Serve hot.
Yield: about fourteen 6-ounce servings

Warm your guests with our creamy homemade Praline Coffee laced with liqueur. To accompany this delicious drink, we suggest Chocolate-Nut Coffee Cake, which is swirled and topped with chocolate chips, brown sugar, chopped walnuts, and cinnamon. Bite-size Pumpkin-Walnut Pies are tasty morsels, too!

PUMPKIN-WALNUT PIES

CRUST
2 1/4 cups all-purpose flour
1/2 teaspoon salt
1/2 cup vegetable shortening, chilled
1/4 cup butter or margarine, chilled
1/4 cup ice water

FILLING
3/4 cup canned pumpkin
1/3 cup granulated sugar
1/4 cup firmly packed brown sugar
2 eggs
1/4 cup dark corn syrup
1/2 teaspoon vanilla extract
2 teaspoons all-purpose flour
3/4 teaspoon pumpkin pie spice
1/4 cup evaporated milk
3/4 cup finely chopped walnuts

For crust, combine flour and salt in a medium bowl. Using a pastry blender or 2 knives, cut in shortening and butter until mixture resembles coarse meal. Sprinkle with water; mix until a soft dough forms. Shape dough into a ball. Wrap in plastic wrap and chill.

Preheat oven to 350 degrees. For filling, beat pumpkin, sugars, eggs, corn syrup, and vanilla in a medium bowl until well blended. In a small bowl, combine flour and pumpkin pie spice. Add dry ingredients and evaporated milk to pumpkin mixture; beat until well blended. Stir in walnuts.

Shape dough into 1-inch balls; press 1 ball into bottom and up sides of each tin of an ungreased miniature muffin pan. Place 1 tablespoon pumpkin mixture in each crust. Bake 15 to 20 minutes or until center is almost set. Cool pies in pan on a wire rack 5 minutes. Serve warm or transfer to wire rack to cool completely. Store in an airtight container in refrigerator.
Yield: about 3 dozen mini pies

CRANBERRY-APPLE STRUDEL

- 5 cups peeled, cored, and very thinly sliced baking apples (about 2 pounds)
- 2 cups granulated sugar
- 1¼ cups fresh cranberries
- ¼ cup apple juice
- 2 tablespoons cornstarch
- 2 teaspoons grated lemon zest
- ¾ teaspoon ground cinnamon
- ¼ teaspoon ground allspice
- ⅛ teaspoon salt
- 1 package (16 ounces) frozen phyllo dough, thawed
- ½ cup butter or margarine, melted and divided
  Confectioners sugar

Preheat oven to 375 degrees. For filling, combine apple slices, granulated sugar, cranberries, apple juice, cornstarch, lemon zest, cinnamon, allspice, and salt in a large saucepan over medium-high heat; stir constantly until mixture begins to boil. Reduce heat to medium and continue stirring until mixture thickens. Remove from heat and cool to room temperature.

To assemble strudel, place a large damp cloth (about 14 x 36 inches) on a flat surface. Working quickly, place short sides of 2 sheets of phyllo dough along one short side of cloth. Overlapping short edges 2 inches, place next 2 sheets of dough on towel. Brush dough with melted butter. Continue layering dough and brushing with butter, reserving 1 tablespoon butter. Beginning 4 inches from one short edge of dough, spread filling to cover an area about 5 inches wide and 12 inches long (**Fig. 1**).

Fig. 1

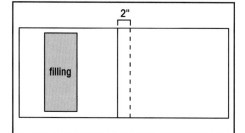

Beginning at filled edge of dough, hold short edge of cloth and pull dough over filling. Continue to fold dough and filling. Using cloth, transfer strudel, seam side down, to a greased 10½ x 15½-inch jellyroll pan.

A favorite German treat, Cranberry-Apple Strudel features layers of flaky pastry with a tart cranberry and apple filling tucked inside. The strudel is brushed with melted butter and baked until golden brown, then sprinkled with confectioners sugar. Honey adds sweetness to full-bodied Honey-Rum Coffee.

Make cuts with a knife across strudel at about 1 inch intervals. Brush top of strudel with reserved butter.

Bake 30 to 40 minutes or until golden brown. Place pan on a wire rack. Sift confectioners sugar over warm strudel. Slice strudel at cuts; serve warm or cool completely.
Yield: about 12 servings

HONEY-RUM COFFEE

- 1 can (12 ounces) evaporated milk
- 6 tablespoons honey
- 1½ quarts strongly brewed hot coffee
- ½ cup dark rum

In a Dutch oven, combine evaporated milk and honey. Stirring occasionally, cook over medium-high heat until milk is warm. Add coffee; stir until well blended. Remove from heat. Stir in rum. Serve hot.
Yield: about ten 6-ounce servings

Topped with raspberry sauce and plump whole berries, Raspberry-Cream Cheese Brownie Pie is a fudgy delight. It begins with a brownie layer that's topped with a rich chocolate-cream cheese mixture.

RASPBERRY-CREAM CHEESE BROWNIE PIE

  1 package (10 ounces) raspberry-
       flavored semisweet chocolate
       chips, divided
  1 cup butter or margarine, softened
  2 cups sugar, divided
  3 eggs
  2 teaspoons vanilla extract, divided
  2 cups all-purpose flour
  $^{1}/_{2}$ teaspoon baking powder
 11 ounces (one 8-ounce package and
       one 3-ounce package) cream
       cheese, softened
  1 egg
  1 jar (12 ounces) seedless raspberry
       jam

  Frozen red raspberries to garnish

Preheat oven to 350 degrees. In a small microwave-safe bowl, microwave 1 cup chocolate chips on medium-high power (80%) 2 minutes, stirring after 1 minute. In a large bowl, beat butter and $1^{2}/_{3}$ cups sugar until fluffy. Beat in 3 eggs, 1 at a time. Stir in melted chocolate and 1 teaspoon vanilla. In a small bowl, combine flour and baking powder. Add dry ingredients to creamed mixture; stir until well blended. Line a 9-inch springform pan with aluminum foil; grease foil. Spread chocolate mixture into prepared pan. Bake 40 minutes.

In a small microwave-safe bowl, microwave remaining $^{2}/_{3}$ cup chocolate chips on medium-high power (80%)

2 minutes, stirring after 1 minute. In a large bowl, beat cream cheese and remaining $^{1}/_{3}$ cup sugar until smooth. Add 1 egg and remaining 1 teaspoon vanilla; beat until smooth. Stir in melted chocolate. Gently spread cream cheese mixture over warm brownie layer. Bake 15 minutes or until cream cheese mixture is set. Cool in pan on a wire rack. Cover and chill.

To serve, melt raspberry jam in a heavy small saucepan over medium heat. Remove from heat; cool 10 minutes. Remove sides of springform pan. Spoon melted raspberry jam over each piece of brownie pie. Garnish with frozen raspberries.
Yield: about 16 servings

APRICOT WINE CORDIAL

12 ounces dried apricots
1 bottle (1.5 liters) dry white wine
2 cups sugar
1 cup apricot-flavored brandy

In a food processor, process apricots until finely chopped. Place apricots in a non-metal container. Stir in wine, sugar, and brandy. Cover and allow to stand at room temperature 1 to 4 weeks. Strain wine and pour into gift bottles. Reserve fruit for Lemon Cakes with Apricot Sauce.
Yield: about 7 cups wine

LEMON CAKES WITH APRICOT SAUCE

CAKE
1 cup butter or margarine, softened
1 cup sugar
4 eggs
3/4 cup sour cream
1/4 cup fresh lemon juice
1 tablespoon grated lemon zest
1 teaspoon vanilla extract
2 1/4 cups cake flour
1 teaspoon baking powder
1/4 teaspoon salt

SAUCE
1 cup water
3/4 cup sugar
3 cups reserved fruit from Apricot Wine Cordial **or** combine 12 ounces finely chopped dried apricots and 1/2 cup apricot brandy

Preheat oven to 350 degrees. For cake, cream butter and sugar in a large bowl until fluffy. Add eggs, 1 at a time, beating well after each addition. Add sour cream, lemon juice, lemon zest, and vanilla; beat until well blended. In a medium bowl, combine dry ingredients; add to creamed mixture, stirring until smooth. Spoon about 1/4 cup batter into each tin of a greased shortcake pan. Bake 17 to 19 minutes or until a toothpick inserted in center of cake comes out clean. Cool in pan 5 minutes. Turn cakes onto a wire rack to cool completely.

For sauce, combine water and sugar in a medium saucepan on medium-high heat. Cook until sugar dissolves and mixture comes to a boil. Reduce heat to medium; cover and cook 2 minutes. Remove from heat; cool 20 minutes. Stir fruit into sugar syrup. Spoon sauce over individual cakes to serve.
Yield: about 18 cakes

For flavorful Apricot Wine Cordial, chopped apricots are marinated in white wine, brandy, and sugar for several weeks. Scrumptious little Lemon Cakes are served with candied Apricot Sauce made from the reserved fruit pieces. Baked in shortcake pans, the cakes are just right for individual servings.

CHOCOLATE CREAM PIE

CRUST
- 1 1/2 cups all-purpose flour
- 1/2 teaspoon salt
- 1/2 cup shortening
- 1/4 cup cold water

FILLING
- 1 cup sugar
- 1/4 cup cocoa
- 1/4 cup cornstarch
- 1 3/4 cups milk
- 3 tablespoons butter or margarine
- 3 egg yolks, beaten (reserve egg whites for meringue)
- 2 tablespoons orange-flavored liqueur
- 1 teaspoon vanilla extract

MERINGUE
- 4 egg whites
- 1/2 teaspoon cream of tartar
- 1 teaspoon orange-flavored liqueur
- 1/2 cup sifted confectioners sugar

For crust, combine flour and salt in a medium bowl. Using a pastry blender or 2 knives, cut in shortening until mixture resembles coarse meal. Sprinkle with water; mix until a soft dough forms. On a lightly floured surface, use a floured rolling pin to roll out dough to 1/8-inch thickness. Transfer to a 9-inch pie plate and use a sharp knife to trim edge of dough. Prick bottom of crust with a fork. Chill 30 minutes.

Preheat oven to 450 degrees. Bake crust 10 to 12 minutes or until lightly browned. Cool completely on a wire rack.

For filling, combine sugar, cocoa, and cornstarch in a heavy medium saucepan. Stir in milk and butter. Stirring constantly, cook over medium heat until mixture thickens and begins to boil. Continuing to stir, boil 1 minute. Remove from heat. Add about 1/2 cup chocolate mixture to egg yolks; stir until well blended. Gradually add egg mixture to chocolate mixture in saucepan, stirring until well blended. Return to medium heat and bring to a boil; boil 1 minute or until thick enough to coat back of a spoon. Stir in liqueur and vanilla. Remove filling from heat; pour into crust.

Preheat oven to 350 degrees. For meringue, beat egg whites and cream of tartar in a medium bowl until foamy. Add liqueur. Gradually add confectioners sugar, beating until stiff peaks form. Spread meringue over filling. Bake 10 to 15 minutes or until golden brown. Serve warm or chilled. Store in an airtight container in refrigerator.
Yield: about 10 servings

Fluffy meringue tops a chocolaty filling for our Chocolate Cream Pie. Generously crowned with coconut, crushed pineapple, pecans, and preserves, Orange Marmalade Cake is a moist and tangy dessert.

ORANGE MARMALADE CAKE

CAKE
- 3/4 cup butter or margarine, softened
- 1 cup sugar
- 3 eggs
- 1 teaspoon vanilla extract
- 3/4 cup orange marmalade
- 2 1/2 cups all-purpose flour
- 1 teaspoon baking soda
- 1/2 cup buttermilk

ICING
- 1 cup sugar
- 1/3 cup milk
- 1 can (15 1/2 ounces) crushed pineapple, drained
- 1/2 cup sweetened shredded coconut
- 1/2 cup finely chopped toasted pecans
- 2 tablespoons orange marmalade

Preheat oven to 350 degrees. For cake, cream butter and sugar in a large bowl until fluffy. Add eggs and vanilla; beat until smooth. Stir in marmalade. In a medium bowl, sift flour and baking soda together. Alternately beat dry ingredients and buttermilk into butter mixture. Pour batter into a greased and floured 8 1/2-inch fluted tube pan. Bake 40 to 45 minutes or until a toothpick inserted in center of cake comes out clean. Cool in pan on a wire rack 10 minutes; invert onto a serving plate.

For icing, combine sugar and milk in a heavy medium saucepan. Stirring constantly, cook over medium-low heat until sugar dissolves. Using a pastry brush dipped in hot water, wash down any sugar crystals on sides of pan. Attach a candy thermometer to pan, making sure thermometer does not touch bottom of pan. Bring to a boil. Cook, without stirring, until syrup reaches 230 degrees. Remove from heat; pour into a heat-resistant bowl. Using medium speed of an electric mixer, beat mixture until thickened and creamy. Stir in pineapple, coconut, pecans, and marmalade. Spoon over cake. Store in an airtight container in refrigerator.
Yield: about 16 servings

Our Chocolate-Pecan Tart is loaded with chocolate chips baked in a sweet filling and topped with an eye-pleasing arrangement of pecan halves.

CHOCOLATE-PECAN TART

CRUST

- 1¼ cups all-purpose flour
- 2 tablespoons sugar
- ¼ teaspoon ground cinnamon
- ¼ cup butter or margarine, softened
- ¼ cup shortening
- 1 egg yolk
- ½ teaspoon vanilla extract

FILLING

- ½ cup semisweet chocolate mini chips
- 1¼ cups pecan halves
- 3 tablespoons granulated sugar
- 3 tablespoons firmly packed brown sugar
- ⅛ teaspoon salt
- 3 tablespoons butter or margarine, melted
- ½ cup dark corn syrup
- 3 eggs
- 1 teaspoon vanilla extract

For crust, combine flour, sugar, and cinnamon in a medium bowl. Using a pastry blender or 2 knives, cut in butter and shortening until mixture resembles coarse meal. Add egg yolk and vanilla; mix just until blended. Firmly press pastry into bottom and up sides of a 9-inch-diameter tart pan with a removable bottom. Chill 30 minutes.

Preheat oven to 400 degrees. Prick bottom of tart shell with a fork. Bake 5 minutes. Allow to cool 15 minutes.

For filling, reduce oven temperature to 350 degrees. Sprinkle chocolate chips over cooled crust. Arrange pecan halves on chocolate chips. In a medium bowl, combine sugars and salt. Stir in melted butter and corn syrup. Add eggs and vanilla; whisk until well blended. Slowly pour mixture over pecans in crust. Bake 40 to 45 minutes or until filling is almost set. Place tart on a wire rack to cool. Remove sides of pan to serve.

Yield: about 10 servings

CHOCOLATE FRUITCAKE

CAKE

- ½ cup butter
- ½ cup granulated sugar
- ½ cup firmly packed brown sugar
- 2 eggs
- 1 teaspoon vanilla extract
- ½ cup buttermilk
- 4 ounces semisweet baking chocolate, melted
- 2½ cups all-purpose flour
- 1 teaspoon baking powder
- 1 teaspoon baking soda
- 1 teaspoon salt
- ¾ cup cherry preserves
- ¼ cup brandy
- 1 cup chopped red candied cherries
- 1 cup chopped dates
- 1 cup coarsely chopped pecans

GLAZE

- ¼ cup water
- 1½ tablespoons cornstarch
- ½ cup sugar
- 3 tablespoons cocoa
- 2½ tablespoons butter
- 2 tablespoons brandy
- ½ teaspoon vanilla extract

     Candied cherry and pecan halves
        to decorate

Preheat oven to 350 degrees. For cake, cream butter and sugars in a large bowl. Add eggs and vanilla; beat until smooth. Stir in buttermilk and melted chocolate. In a medium bowl, combine flour, baking powder, baking soda, and salt. Add dry ingredients to creamed mixture; stir until well blended. Add preserves and brandy; stir until well blended. Stir in cherries, dates, and pecans. Spoon batter into a well-greased 10-inch fluted tube pan. Bake 50 to 60 minutes or until a toothpick inserted in center of cake comes out clean. Cool in pan 10 minutes. Invert cake onto a serving plate.

For glaze, combine water and cornstarch in a small saucepan; stir until cornstarch dissolves. Stir in sugar and cocoa. Stirring frequently, cook over medium heat until mixture starts to boil; add butter, brandy, and vanilla. Remove from heat and stir until butter melts; allow glaze to cool 5 minutes. Pour glaze over warm cake. Decorate with cherry and pecan halves. Cool completely. Store in an airtight container.

Yield: about 16 servings

Flavored with semisweet chocolate, spirited Chocolate Fruitcake is like the traditional holiday favorite — only better! A decadent chocolate glaze laced with brandy covers the cake, which is sweetly garnished with candied cherries and pecan halves.

Gifts from the Kitchen

Handmade gifts are a heartfelt way to express your appreciation or simply wish someone a happy holiday. Our collection of delicious recipes offers scrumptious candies, a spirited beverage, and much more to share with others. From sweet to spicy, each tasty treat is packed with yummy goodness and wrapped in Yuletide cheer. Basic containers are dressed up with paints and merry trims for festive presentations that will be enjoyed long after the season has passed.

For a memorable gift that teachers will love, moist and delicious Apple-Cinnamon-Nut Bread is tucked inside this cute basket. Each little loaf is packed with crunchy pecans and features a sweet layer of apples and cinnamon. A personalized message on the basket's chalkboard lid is sure to earn high marks!

APPLE-CINNAMON-NUT BREAD

1 1/2 cups all-purpose flour
1 cup sugar, divided
1/2 cup chopped pecans
1 1/2 teaspoons baking powder
1/2 teaspoon salt
1/2 teaspoon ground cinnamon
1/3 cup vegetable oil
1 egg
1/4 cup orange juice
1 teaspoon vanilla extract
1 medium Granny Smith apple, peeled, cored, and thinly sliced

Preheat oven to 350 degrees. In a medium bowl, combine flour, 3/4 cup sugar, pecans, baking powder, and salt. Combine remaining 1/4 cup sugar and cinnamon in a small bowl; set aside. In another small bowl, whisk oil, egg, orange juice, and vanilla. Add oil mixture to dry ingredients; stir just until moistened. Spread half of batter into 4 greased and floured 2 1/2 x 5-inch baking pans. Place a single layer of apple slices over batter. Sprinkle cinnamon-sugar mixture over apples. Spread remaining batter over apples. Bake 30 to 35 minutes or until a toothpick inserted in center of bread comes out clean and tops are lightly browned. Cool bread in pans on a wire rack 10 minutes. Transfer bread to wire rack to cool completely. Store in an airtight container.

Yield: 4 mini bread loaves

TEACHER'S BASKET

You will need a basket with handle, a chalkboard to fit over top of basket, red and green acrylic paint, medium flat and small round paintbrushes, white colored pencil, two 3/4 yd lengths of 7/8"w ribbon, artificial greenery with berries, matte clear acrylic spray, masking tape, hot glue gun, and glue sticks.

1. For basket lid, use tape to mask edges of chalkboard next to frame. Paint frame green; allow to dry. Paint red dots on frame; allow to dry. Remove tape. Use white pencil to write message on chalkboard. Spray chalkboard with acrylic spray; allow to dry.
2. For ties on lid, match ends and fold 1 ribbon length in half. Glue 1/2" at fold to back of chalkboard at center of 1 side. Repeat for remaining tie. Trim ribbon ends.

3. Glue a length of greenery to basket handle; glue a sprig of greenery to basket lid.
4. Place gift in basket. Place lid on basket; tie ribbons into bows around each end of basket handle.

Irish Cream Liqueur is a rich and smooth after-dinner drink spiked with whiskey. Presented in decorative bottles with festive trims and gift tags, the spirited beverage will spread Christmas cheer.

IRISH CREAM LIQUEUR

2 cans (14 ounces each) sweetened condensed milk
2 cups Irish whiskey
2 cups half and half
1/4 cup instant coffee granules
2 tablespoons chocolate syrup
1 teaspoon vanilla extract

Combine all ingredients in a large bowl; whisk until coffee granules dissolve and mixture is well blended. Pour liqueur into containers with lids. Chill at least 3 weeks before serving. Store in refrigerator.

Yield: about 6 cups liqueur

It's a snap to make our light and tasty Cheese Straws using a handy cookie press. A touch of red pepper adds a wonderfully piquant flavor to the snacks. Topped with a crazy-quilt design, our hand-painted tin is the perfect gift container.

CHEESE STRAWS

- 2 cups all-purpose flour
- 1/2 cup butter or margarine, melted
- 1 1/2 teaspoons salt
- 3/4 teaspoon ground red pepper
- 1 pound sharp Cheddar cheese, finely shredded (4 cups)

Preheat oven to 350 degrees. In a medium bowl, combine flour, melted butter, salt, and red pepper. Add cheese; mix with a pastry blender until well blended.

Place dough in a cookie press fitted with a 1 1/2-inch ribbon disc. Press dough in long strips onto an ungreased baking sheet. Cut strips into 3 1/2-inch lengths.

Bake 8 to 9 minutes or until bottoms are lightly browned. Transfer cheese straws to a wire rack to cool. Store in a tin.
Yield: about 7 1/2 dozen cheese straws

PAINTED TIN

You will need a tin with lid (ours is 8" dia. x 3 1/4"h), white spray paint, matte clear acrylic spray, desired colors of acrylic paint, small round paintbrushes, black permanent felt-tip pens with medium and fine points, and tracing paper.

1. Spray paint tin and lid white; allow to dry.
2. For lid, use a pencil and a ruler to divide top of lid into several areas; continue lines

onto sides of lid. Use acrylic paint to paint several areas of lid solid colors; allow to dry.
3. Trace star and tree patterns onto tracing paper; cut out. Use pencil to draw around patterns on lid. Use pencil to lightly sketch freehand designs on lid (we sketched straight and zigzag stripes and squares on our lid). Allowing to dry between colors, paint designs on lid (in 1 area we used the tip of a paintbrush handle to paint dots).
4. Use medium-point black pen to outline areas of color and designs. Use fine-point black pen to draw lines on lid to resemble stitches.
5. Allowing to dry after each coat, apply 2 coats of acrylic spray to tin and lid.

Heavenly Pickled Onions

Accented with a star-shaped label, a jar of Pickled Onions is packed with zesty old-fashioned goodness. Precious clothespin angels with raffia wings add heavenly touches to plain paper gift bags.

PICKLED ONIONS

    8 pints pearl onions (about
          5 pounds), peeled
  3/4 cup salt
    7 cups white vinegar (5% acidity)
    1 cup sugar
       Small bay leaves
       Whole red peppercorns
       Whole green peppercorns
       Mustard seed

Place onions in a large bowl; sprinkle with salt. Cover onions with water. Cover and refrigerate overnight.

Follow manufacturer's instructions to prepare half-pint canning jars, lids, and bands.

Combine vinegar and sugar in a small stockpot over high heat; bring to a boil. Reduce heat and keep mixture hot. Drain onions and rinse with cold water. Fill sterilized jars with onions. Add a bay leaf and 1 teaspoon each of red peppercorns, green peppercorns, and mustard seed to each jar. Add hot vinegar mixture to each jar to within 1/2 inch of top. Wipe jar rims and threads. Quickly cover with lids and screw bands on tightly. Using water-bath method as directed by the USDA, process jars 10 minutes. When jars have cooled, check seals. Lids should be curved down or remain so when pressed. Refrigerate all unsealed jars.
Yield: about 12 half-pints onions

ANGEL BAGS AND STAR JAR LID LABELS

For each bag and label, you will need a paper bag, cream-colored heavy paper, spring-type clothespin, several 1 yd lengths of natural raffia, colored pencils, black felt-tip pen with medium point, tracing paper, graphite transfer paper, hot glue gun, and glue sticks.

ANGEL BAG
1. Trace angel pattern onto tracing paper. Use transfer paper to transfer design onto cream-colored paper.
2. Use colored pencils to color angel as desired. Use black pen to draw over transferred lines. Cut out angel.
3. Center clothespin on back of angel with clip at bottom and glue in place.
4. Tie raffia lengths together into a bow. Glue center of bow inside top of clothespin above spring. Place gift in bag. Fold top of bag to front. Clip clothespin to top of bag.

STAR JAR LID LABEL
1. Trace star pattern onto tracing paper; cut out. Use pattern to cut star from cream-colored paper.
2. Use colored pencil to color edges of star. Use black pen to outline star, to draw dashed lines on star to resemble stitches, and to write "pickled onions" on star.
3. Glue star to jar lid.

155

Delight a friend with tangy Candied Citrus Peel dipped in decadent dark chocolate. The gourmet treat makes a great gift, especially when given in our decorated canister. A wooden snowflake and buttons are hot glued to the top of a glass jar, which is finished with a tied-on fabric bow.

CANDIED CITRUS PEEL

6	navel oranges
2	cups sugar
1	cup water
1	tablespoon light corn syrup
	Sugar
1 1/4	cups semisweet chocolate chips
2 1/2	teaspoons vegetable shortening

Peel oranges and cut peel into 1/4-inch-wide x 3-inch-long strips. In a large saucepan, combine orange peel and enough water to cover; place over high heat and bring to a boil. Drain peel and repeat boiling process 2 more times. In a heavy medium saucepan, combine 2 cups sugar, 1 cup water, and corn syrup. Stirring constantly, cook over medium-low heat until sugar dissolves. Using a pastry brush dipped in hot water, wash down any sugar crystals on sides of pan. Attach a candy thermometer to pan, making sure thermometer does not touch bottom of pan. Increase heat to medium and bring to a boil. Cook, without stirring, until syrup reaches soft-ball stage (approximately 234 to 240 degrees). Test about 1/2 teaspoon syrup in ice water. Syrup will easily form a ball in ice water but will flatten when held in your hand. Add fruit peel. Stirring often, allow peel to simmer over medium-low heat 30 minutes. Drain peel; if desired, reserve syrup for another use (good as a flavored sweetener). Place peel on a wire rack with waxed paper underneath to dry 15 minutes. Roll peel in sugar to coat. Place pieces of candied peel on wire rack and dry overnight.

In a small heavy saucepan, melt chocolate chips and shortening over low heat. Dip one end of each piece of candied peel into chocolate; place on a baking sheet lined with waxed paper. Chill until chocolate hardens. Store in an airtight container in a cool place.
Yield: about 1 1/4 pounds candy

No-bake Chocolate-Nut Truffles are easy to make with rich chocolate liqueur, vanilla wafer crumbs, and toasted pecans. Rolled in confectioners sugar, the yummy sweets are melt-in-your-mouth good! Terra-cotta flowerpots are embellished with country fabrics, jute twine, and artificial berries for unique containers. This gift will help friendship bloom long after the truffles are all gone.

CHOCOLATE-NUT TRUFFLES

 2 cups vanilla wafer crumbs
 2 cups sifted confectioners sugar
 1 cup finely chopped toasted pecans
 2 tablespoons cocoa
 4 1/2 tablespoons whipping cream
 4 1/2 tablespoons chocolate-flavored liqueur
 Sifted confectioners sugar

In a large bowl, combine vanilla wafer crumbs, 2 cups confectioners sugar, pecans, and cocoa. Add whipping cream and liqueur; stir until well blended. Shape into 1-inch balls; roll in confectioners sugar. Store in an airtight container in a cool place.
Yield: about 5 dozen candies

FLOWERPOT CONTAINERS

For each container, you will need a clay flowerpot and saucer, scraps of fabric, paper-backed fusible web, poster board, jute twine, artificial greenery with berries, heavy paper for tag (we used handmade paper), brown felt-tip pen with fine point, pinking shears, 1/8" hole punch, craft glue, and cellophane.

1. For fabric trim on rim of pot, measure width of rim. Cut several strips of fabric the determined width by various lengths. Overlapping ends of strips slightly and cutting additional strips as necessary to cover rim, glue strips to rim of pot. Allow to dry.
2. For top of lid, follow manufacturer's instructions to fuse web to wrong sides of 2 fabrics. Fuse 1 fabric piece to poster board. Draw around bottom of saucer on fabric-

covered poster board. Cutting approx. 1/8" inside drawn circle, cut out circle. Use pinking shears to cut a circle from remaining fabric piece approx. 1/2" smaller on all sides than first circle; fuse small circle to center of first circle. Glue circle to bottom of saucer (top of lid).
3. Line pot with cellophane. Place gift in pot. Place lid on pot. Wrap twine securely around pot and lid and knot at top; trim ends close to knot. Tie 2 lengths of twine together into a bow around knot at top of lid; trim ends.
4. Tuck a sprig of greenery under bow; glue to secure.
5. For tag, tear a rectangle from heavy paper and punch a hole in 1 corner. Use brown pen to write message on tag. Thread tag onto 1 streamer of bow.

TRACING PATTERNS

When entire pattern is shown, place tracing paper over pattern and trace pattern. Cut out pattern. For a more durable pattern, use a permanent pen to trace pattern onto acetate; cut out.

When only half of pattern is shown (indicated by dashed line on pattern), fold tracing paper in half and place fold along dashed line of pattern. Trace pattern half; turn folded paper over and draw over traced lines on remaining side of paper. Unfold pattern and cut out. For a more durable pattern, use a permanent pen to trace pattern half onto acetate; turn acetate over and trace pattern half again, aligning dashed lines to form a whole pattern. Cut out.

SEWING SHAPES

1. Center pattern on wrong side of 1 fabric piece and use fabric marking pencil or pen to draw around pattern. **DO NOT CUT OUT SHAPE.**
2. Place fabric pieces right sides together. Leaving an opening for turning, carefully sew pieces together **directly on drawn line.**
3. Leaving a ¹⁄₄" seam allowance, cut out shape. Clip seam allowance at curves and corners. Turn shape right side out.

CROSS STITCH

COUNTED CROSS STITCH (X)

Work 1 Cross Stitch to correspond to each colored square in the chart. For horizontal rows, work stitches in 2 journeys (**Fig. 1**). For vertical rows, complete each stitch as shown in **Fig. 2**. When working over 2 fabric threads, work Cross Stitch as shown in **Fig. 3**. When the chart shows a Backstitch crossing a colored square (**Fig. 4**), a Cross Stitch (**Fig. 1, 2, or 3**) should be worked first; then the Backstitch (**Fig. 6**) should be worked on top of the Cross Stitch.

Fig. 1

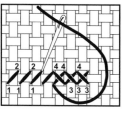

Fig. 2

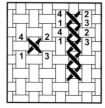

Fig. 3

Fig. 4

QUARTER STITCH (¹⁄₄X)

Quarter Stitches are denoted by triangular shapes of color in chart and color key. Come up at 1 (**Fig. 5**); then split fabric thread to go down at 2.

Fig. 5

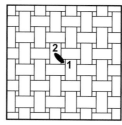

BACKSTITCH (B'ST)

For outline detail, Backstitch (shown in chart and color key by black or colored straight lines) should be worked after the design has been completed (**Fig. 6**).

Fig. 6

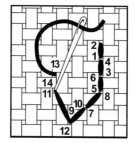

WORKING OVER 2 FABRIC THREADS

(**Note:** Using a hoop is optional.) Roll excess fabric from left to right until stitching area is in proper position. Use the "sewing" method, keeping stitching hand on right side of fabric and taking needle down and up with 1 stroke. To add support to stitches, place first Cross Stitch on fabric with stitch 1 - 2 beginning and ending where a vertical fabric thread crosses over a horizontal fabric thread (**Fig. 7**).

Fig. 7

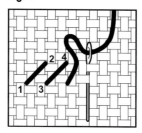

EMBROIDERY

RUNNING STITCH

Make a series of straight stitches with stitch length equal to the space between stitches (**Fig. 1**).

Fig. 1

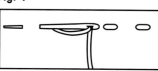

STEM STITCH

Referring to **Fig. 2**, bring needle up at 1; keeping thread below stitching line, go down at 2 and come up at 3. Go down at 4 and come up at 5.

Fig. 2

COUCHED STITCH

Referring to **Fig. 3**, bring needle up at 1 and go down at 2, following line to be couched. Work tiny stitches over thread to secure.

Fig. 3

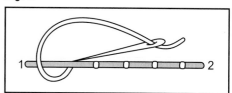

THREADED RUNNING STITCH

Referring to **Fig. 4**, work a line of running stitches. Using another length of same or contrasting thread, lace thread under running stitches, being careful not to catch fabric.

Fig. 4

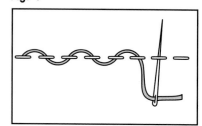

SATIN STITCH

Referring to **Fig. 5**, bring needle up at odd numbers and go down at even numbers with stitches touching but not overlapping.

Fig. 5

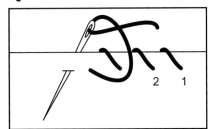

OVERCAST STITCH

Referring to **Fig. 6**, bring needle up at 1; take thread around edge of fabric and bring needle up at 2. Continue stitching along edge of fabric.

Fig. 6

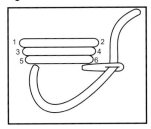

BLANKET STITCH

Referring to **Fig. 7**, bring needle up at 1; keeping thread below point of needle, go down at 2 and come up at 3. Continue working as shown in **Fig. 8**.

Fig. 7   **Fig. 8**

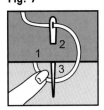

FEATHER STITCH

Bring needle up at 1; keeping thread below point of needle, go down at 2 and come up at 3 (**Fig. 9**). Go down at 4 and come up at 5 (**Fig. 10**). Continue working as shown in **Fig. 11**.

Fig. 9   **Fig. 10**

Fig. 11

HERRINGBONE STITCH

Bring needle up at 1; go down at 2 and come up at 3 (**Fig. 12**). Go down at 4 and come up at 5 (**Fig. 13**). Continue working as shown in **Fig. 14**.

Fig. 12   **Fig. 13**

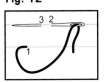 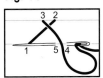

Fig. 14

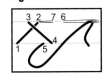

OPEN CRETAN STITCH

Bring needle up at 1; keeping thread below point of needle, go down at 2 and come up at 3 (**Fig. 15**). Go down at 4 and come up at 5 (**Fig. 16**). Continue working as shown in **Fig. 17**.

Fig. 15   **Fig. 16**   **Fig. 17**

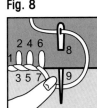

FRENCH KNOT

Bring needle up at 1. Wrap floss once around needle and insert needle at 2, holding end of floss with non-stitching fingers (**Fig. 18**). Tighten knot, then pull needle through fabric, holding floss until it must be released. For a larger knot, use more strands; wrap only once.

Fig. 18

QUILTING

Thread quilting needle with an 18" to 20" length of quilting thread; knot 1 end. Bring needle up through all layers of fabric and batting; when knot catches on back of quilt, give thread a short, quick pull to pop knot through backing fabric into batting (**Fig. 1**). To quilt, use a small Running Stitch (**Fig. 2**). At end of thread length, knot thread close to top fabric and take needle down through all layers of fabric and batting; when knot catches on top of quilt, pop knot through top fabric into batting. Clip thread close to backing.

Fig. 1

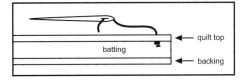

Fig. 2

CREDITS

We want to extend a warm *thank you* to the generous people who allowed us to photograph our projects in their homes.

- *Roly-Poly Pals:* Carl and Monte Brunck
- *Traditional Elegance:* Dr. Doyne and Margaret Dodd
- *Star of Wonder:* Linda Wardlaw
- *A Festival of Trees:* Carl and Monte Brunck, Frank and Carol Clawson, and Dr. Doyne and Margaret Dodd
- *Victorian Romance:* Dr. Dan and Sandra Cook
- *Handmade Holiday:* Frank and Carol Clawson
- *Peppermint Fun:* Carl and Monte Brunck
- *Jolly Old Gent:* Dr. and Mrs. Richard Calhoun
- *Big Top Christmas:* Mr. and Mrs. Shawn Fitz
- *Pines and Plaids:* Dr. Tony Johnson

To Magna IV Color Imaging of Little Rock, Arkansas, we say thank you for the superb color reproduction and excellent pre-press preparation.

We want to especially thank photographers Ken West, Larry Pennington, Mark Mathews, and Karen Shirey of Peerless Photography, Little Rock, Arkansas; and Jerry R. Davis of Jerry Davis Photography, Little Rock, Arkansas, for their time, patience, and excellent work.

To the talented people who helped in the creation of the following projects and recipes in this book, we extend a special word of thanks.

- *Roly-Poly Pals,* page 12: Susan Cousineau
- *Holy Family and Sheep,* page 22: Maryanne Moreck
- *Crocheted Heart Ornaments,* page 30: Shobha Govindan
- *Plastic Canvas Quilt-Block Ornaments,* page 33: Mary Billeaudeau
- *Nostalgic Santa Pillow and Afghan,* page 71: Needlework adaptation by Carol Emmer and Jane Chandler
- *Beary Elf Sweatshirt,* page 107: Lorri Birmingham
- *Pickled Yellow Squash,* page 117: Winnifred Latimer

We extend a sincere *thank you* to all the people who assisted in making and testing the projects in this book: Janet Akins, Judith Hassed, Dolores Lee, Ray Ellen Odle, Patricia O'Neil, and Karen Sisco.